QATAR

QATAR

Small State, Big Politics

With a New Preface

MEHRAN KAMRAVA

CORNELL UNIVERSITY PRESS
ITHACA AND LONDON

First published 2013 by Cornell University Press
First printing, Cornell Paperbacks, with a new preface, 2015

Printed in the United States of America

ISBN 978-0-8014-5677-0

The Library of Congress has catalogued the hardcover edition as follows:

Kamrava, Mehran, 1964– author.
    Qatar : small state, big politics / Mehran Kamrava.
       pages cm
    Includes bibliographical references and index.
    ISBN 978-0-8014-5209-3 (cloth : alk. paper)
    1. Qatar—Politics and government. 2. Qatar—Foreign relations.
I. Title.
    DS247.Q35K36 2013
    953.63—dc23   2013003359

Cornell University Press strives to use environmentally responsible
suppliers and materials to the fullest extent possible in the publishing
of its books. Such materials include vegetable-based, low-VOC inks
and acid-free papers that are recycled, totally chlorine-free, or partly
composed of nonwood fibers. For further information, visit our website
at www.cornellpress.cornell.edu.

Paperback printing   10 9 8 7 6 5 4 3 2 1

To Melisa, Dilara, and Kendra

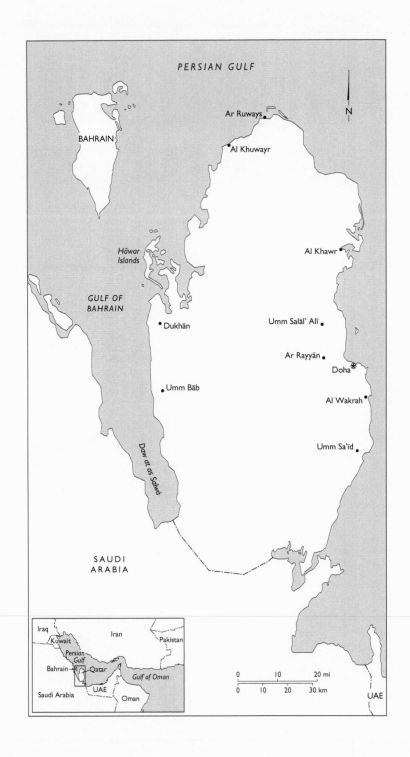

PERSIAN GULF

Ar Ruways

Al Khuwayr

BAHRAIN

Hāwar
Islands

Al Khawr

GULF OF
BAHRAIN

Dukhān

Umm Salāl' Alī

Ar Rayyān

Doha

Umm Bāb

Al Wakrah

Daw at as Salwá

Umm Sa'īd

N

SAUDI
ARABIA

Iraq

Iran

Kuwait

Pakistan

Persian
Gulf

Bahrain

Qatar

Gulf of Oman

Saudi Arabia

UAE

Oman

0   10   20 mi

0   10   20   30 km

UAE

Contents

Preface to the Paperback Edition

Much has changed in Qatar since this book was first released in the summer of 2013. As the book was making its way through the printing press, in June 2013, the country's ruler, Sheikh Hamad bin Khalifa Al Thani, surprised long-time observers of Qatar, myself included, by announcing his retirement from the position of emir and passing on power to his son and heir apparent, Sheikh Tamim bin Hamad. He was only sixty-one years old when the announcement was made, and Sheikh Hamad's voluntary departure from office was nothing less than revolutionary in a region where leaders of all kinds, including supposedly elected presidents, seldom relinquish power voluntarily and are often forced out of office through coups or mass uprisings. Across the Middle East, in what one scholar has called "a veritable kingdom of the old," Presidents-for-Life have historically competed with octogenarian kings and sultans in hanging on to power in their presidential palaces and royals compounds.[1] The timing of Hamad's retirement was particularly surprising given the continued unfolding of the consequences of the Arab Spring, and the ensuing multiple entanglements in the center of which Qatar had placed itself. In this preface, I will offer a few thoughts on the causes of some of the most consequential changes under way in Qatar since the book's original publication, the shapes and processes that these changes have taken, and their consequences.

Perhaps the biggest changes in Qatar since the book's initial publication have been in the areas of international relations and domestic politics. Political scientists and international relations experts have long called attention to the intimate nexus between domestic politics and foreign affairs and, as this book makes clear, at least in the contemporary Middle East, perhaps nowhere is this connection more pronounced than in Qatar.[2] Mindful of this mutually reinforcing relationship, in this brief update I focus on four interrelated, potential areas of change that I believe have been most consequential both for Qatar itself and for the larger Persian Gulf and Middle East regions. These areas include Qatar's domestic politics, its international relations, its economy, and the largely unintended consequences of its "branding" efforts in light of its successful bid to host the 2022 FIFA World Cup.

Domestic Politics

While the timing of the changeover came as a surprise, Sheikh Tamim's ascension to power had been expected for some time, especially as he had assumed an increasingly higher public profile as early as 2009–2010. Significantly, 2013 marked the first time in Qatar's history when there was a peaceful transition of power from one ruler to the next, a testament, as discussed in chapter 5, to the effective centralization and consolidation of power by Sheikh Hamad within his own household among the Al Thanis. Tamim's on-the-job training had culminated in commanding Qatari efforts in Libya in the lead-up to Moammar Qaddafi's overthrow, a task at which at the time he was generally thought to have been successful.[3] With Qaddafi's removal under his belt, Tamim in the position of emir initially steered Qatari efforts in Syria to replicate Qatar's apparent Libyan success in shaping the direction of the Arab Spring. But, as we shall see shortly, this was not to be, and Syria turned out to be far more complicated than anyone, especially the Qataris, seem to have calculated. Even the "Libyan success" proved ephemeral, and before long Libya too was plunged into a civil war of its own, albeit one less intense than the ones raging in Syria and Iraq.

Qatar's Libya and Syria policies raise the question of the degree to which the country's change of leaders has translated into changes in policy and direction both domestically and internationally. With less than two years in office as of this writing, larger, more sweeping changes in direction under Tamim have been difficult to discern. Insofar as domestic politics are concerned, the same patterns of decision-making and policy implementation that had emerged under Hamad appear to have so far remained in place. As chapter 5 outlines, political decision making in Qatar is a highly centralized process that involves no more than a handful of individuals. With the transfer of power from father to son, the personalities involved have changed. But the largely informal structures of rule remain mostly intact. The former emir's wife, Sheikha Moza, for example, though not technically retired from public life, has adopted a much lower public profile since 2013, and is less visibly active in the country's cultural arena, which was once perceived as her main area of concern. One of her daughters, Sheikha Mayassa, does however remain quite active and visible in cultural matters, heading the expansive Qatar Museums Authority. Also retired is Hamad bin Jassim Al Thani, the former emir's longtime prime minister and foreign minister and once perceived to be the country's second most powerful individual. Tamim has appointed two separate individuals to each of these posts, neither of whom shares Hamad bin Jassim's flare for the dramatic. In fact, with a decidedly different personality from his father's, Tamim is himself not expected to replicate the media spectaculars his father seemed to relish.[4]

These personality changes at the very top have not been accompanied by changes in the informal structures of high-level decision making. Nevertheless, Tamim has initiated institutional changes at other levels of the state bureaucracy. The new emir has brought with him new ministers—only a handful of his father's ministers had retained their posts a year after the transition—and he has also centralized many offices within the ministries. Most major state industries have been undergoing shakeups in personnel and finances, chief among them the Qatar Investment Authority, the Supreme Education Council, the Qatar Foundation, the Qatar Museums Authority, and the state petrochemical company Qatar Petroleum.

In order to carry out his ambitious reform programs with minimal disruptions to institutions resistant to change, Sheikh Hamad had set up several agencies parallel to the regular state bureaucracy and had tasked them with implementing his ambitious developmental agendas. While quite an effective means of fostering change without precipitous social and political unease, this was an inherently inefficient and economically costly strategy. Tamim and his inner circle are fiscal conservatives who want to streamline the state bureaucracy without abandoning the developmental vision that had guided their immediate predecessors. One of the means of doing so has been to dismantle some of the parallel institutions, as was the case with the Qatar National Food Security Program, which was folded into the Ministries of Economy and Agriculture. Most other institutions have experienced budget cuts and even layoffs, as has been the case with the Doha Film Institute, the Qatar Museums Authority, and the Qatar Foundation.[5] In his 2014 annual speech to the Shura Council, the emir's words of economic caution indicated the adoption of a more careful, deliberate policy on state spending:

> I stress that the waste, extravagance, mishandling of State funds, lack of respect for the budget, reliance on the availability of money to cover up mistakes are all behaviors that must be disposed of, whether oil prices are high or low. . . . Reasonable spending is an economic matter first and foremost, however, it is not only an economic matter but it is also a civilized issue related to the type of society that we want and the type of individual that we rear in the State of Qatar.[6]

Sheikh Tamim's steady changes to the personnel and structure of the bureaucracy have not necessarily been accompanied by a change in the state's overall ideological orientation. In fact, as chapters 4 and 5 demonstrate, the state that took shape under Sheikh Hamad was largely nonideological and was instead guided by the complementary logics of rapid economic development, high modernism, regime and state survival, and power and influence projection. So far, these same considerations have continued to inform the domestic and foreign policies of the Tamim administration. But what has differed since the 2011–2013 period is the larger regional and international contexts within which Qatari domestic and international policies are formulated, executed, and, importantly, perceived. In 2011, when the Arab Spring presented promises of a new era in the domestic and international politics of the Middle East, Qatar's international strategy of "hedging," discussed in chapter 3, placed it in an ideal position to ride the wave of change sweeping across the region and to deepen its ties with the ascendant Muslim Brotherhood and its sister organizations in places such as Egypt, Tunisia, Syria, and Palestine. But in Egypt, the elected Muslim Brotherhood president was overthrown in a military coup in July 2013 and the organization was banned; in Syria it was overshadowed by extremist and militantly violent groups as the country's civil war grew more intense and bloodier; and in Palestine the local incarnation of the Brotherhood, Hamas, suffered punishing losses in life and materiel in its devastating war with Israel in July–August 2014. In all these developments, Qatar's strategic relationship with the Muslim Brotherhood seemed to cast it on the wrong side of history. Qatar, it seemed, had suddenly taken a turn toward supporting regional Islamist movements near and far.

There is more to Qatar's relationship with the Muslim Brotherhood than mere instrumentalist, strategic reasons. For Qatar, the Brotherhood has long played an important, in fact critical, role in the state's carefully crafted process of nation-building. More specifically, for the last three to four decades, the brand of political Islam underlying the philosophy of the Brotherhood has been a useful source of religious cultural and national identity. For the Qatari state, the Islam of the Brotherhood has been an important distinguishing factor as compared to the Wahhabism of the Saudi state. In fact, well into the 1960s, clerics in Qatari mosques were predominantly Wahhabis from Saudi Arabia. Beginning in the 1960s, however, the Brotherhood's kind of political Islam enabled Qatar to fashion an Islamic identity of its own, independent of Saudi Arabia. This happened to be the same timeframe when one of the Brotherhood's most dynamic and popular intellectual figures, Yusuf Al-Qaradawi, left Egypt under political pressure and relocated to Qatar. Qaradawi quickly became a confidant and an advisor to the emir—and remained so despite successive palace coups— and his and the Brotherhood's influence continued to grow among both Qatar's religious establishment and the civil service. Some conservative Wahhabis remained influential in a number of government institutions, most notably in the ministries of justice and religious endowment. Nevertheless, the state's subtle efforts at de-Wahhabization continued apace. Throughout the 1980s to the 2000s, in an effort to reduce the influence of Wahhabism, the Qatari government promoted Sufi-minded professors at

Qatar University and, in preference over Saudi institutions, sent religious scholars to Al Azhar in Egypt to study as judges in Sharia courts.

This widespread adoption of Brotherhood-inspired political Islam has not been without consequences. The Qatari leadership, in fact, has identified the political Islam of the kind advocated by the Muslim Brotherhood as "the center of the spectrum" between the extremes of secularism on the one side and Salafi jihadism on the other. "Qatar marketed [its] policies as part of a wider effort to affect a new Arab renaissance—in media, education, the arts, the economy, and even in politics—with the emir packaged as a kind of Haroun al-Rashid of his time," Andrew Hammond suggests.[7] Today, political Islam continues to play a central role in the Qatari government's domestic and foreign policies, and the state remains invested in Islamist movements. The state has also used Qaradawi to moderate the impact of its own Wahhabi-leaning clerical base in both domestic and foreign policy endeavors.[8] Not surprisingly, Qatar happens to be the only Arab state of the Persian Gulf without an Islamist oppositional movement or even grouping. If the price for domestic political tranquility and a chronically docile population is occasional irritation by Saudi Arabia, so long as relations with the United States remain solid, for Qatari leaders the costs seem well worth the rewards.

This is not to imply, of course, that there are no manifestations of political unhappiness in Qatar whatsoever. In private *majlis*es, on social media, and even in a popular radio call-in program (*Good Morning, My Beloved Country*), robust conversations are commonplace on issues ranging from the erosion of Arabic culture and language and the overwhelming presence of American cultural content in the country to inflation and high property prices, alcohol consumption in hotels and on the national airline, and the difficulty of getting admitted into one of the American university branch campuses. A retired Qatar University professor named Ali Al Kuwari even went so far as to publish a tract in Beirut in 2012 outlining the need for urgent reforms in multiple areas. Although careful not to criticize the ruling family, the booklet, titled *The People Want Reform . . . In Qatar Too*, was nothing less than revolutionary.[9] According to Al Kuwari, Qatar suffers from "imbalances," in areas such as demography, absence of democracy and effective political participation, and overreliance on the United States for security. There are, he maintains, four obstacles to meaningful political reforms aimed at overcoming these imbalances. They are the concealment and unavailability of information related to public affairs, lack of transparency, absence of freedom of opinion and expression, and absence of clear boundaries between public and private interests.[10]

Al Kuwari argued that Qatari nationals "see their role in their own lives (which they regard as paramount) steadily declining, their societies shrinking into irrelevance, their oil wealth running dry and its available resources being squandered. They see all of this, and at the same time they are being prevented from deciding their own fate and safeguarding their future." Al Jazeera may be based in Qatar but is "neither particularly concerned with the country nor subject to its regulations and oversight of the public administration," and Education City, home of branches of six American universities, remains a "riddle" and out of reach for most Qataris. Women's role is also a victim of "repression and a narrow margin of freedom of expression and effective political participation." The state, meanwhile, has encouraged a steady decline in the percentage of national population as compared to nonnational residents as a means of political control, "turning them into an unproductive and vanishing minority in their own country."[11]

In the context of Qatar's largely closed, authoritarian political system, it is difficult to determine the resonance of Al Kuwari's demands for reform and change in the "imbalances" he identifies. But the general sense of frustration he conveys appears to have been largely confirmed in a 2013 public opinion survey that Qatar University conducted among Qatari citizens in which surprisingly large numbers complained about perceptions of preferential employment treatment accorded to Westerners (55 percent), their own economic standing as "weak" or "below" (36 percent), and the need for *wasta* connections in society to get things done.[12] This is all despite the continued robustness of the rentier political economy and the far-reaching entitlements the government bestows on its citizens. According to a 2014 government survey, on average 6 percent of the income Qataris earn comes in the form of various direct and indirect transfers from the state, as in periodic social assistance, government grants, pensions, and assistance for widows, divorced women, and the disabled. Conversely, reliance on employment wages decreased from 73 percent in 2001 to 57 percent in 2007.[13] Along similar lines, in 2014 the state-owned telecommunications company, Ooredoo, announced it will provide the country's residents with free access to the Internet.[14]

In sum, the overall nature and flavor of domestic Qatari politics appear not to have changed greatly under Tamim as compared to the last decade of his father's rule. A combination of relatively benign authoritarianism and careful state instrumentalization of political Islam, coupled with extensive social and economic entitlements bestowed on the citizenry, have resulted in a degree of political stability in Qatar that is the envy of states across the Persian Gulf and the whole of the Middle East. The state remains vigilant, of course, in ensuring that "chatter" about various frustrations does not manifest in various forms of collective action and remains only a means of venting on specific issues. According to documents released by WikiLeaks, for example, between 2010 and 2012 the Qatari government spent $877,000 on the purchase of computer software that would enable it to monitor email and other forms of online communication in the country.[15] A 2014 cybercriminal law criminalizes online expression that violates "social values" or insults the region's ruling families.[16] At the same time, based on opinion surveys carried out in 2011 and 2012, Qatari nationals continued to have high levels of confidence in various state institutions: on average 83 percent expressed confidence in the police, 82.5 percent in the army, 67 percent in the courts, 59.5 percent in the Shura Council, and 54 percent in the government.[17] There is no reason to believe this has changed over the last three years or so.

International Relations

Like those of its domestic politics, the overall parameters of Qatari foreign policy have not changed since the ascension of Sheikh Tamim to power. The central pillars of Qatari foreign policy that had emerged under Sheikh Hamad—namely continued reliance on the US security umbrella, hyperactive diplomacy and branding, and international investments—examined in chapter 3, all remain in place. In relation to the security relationship with the United States, in December 2013 Qatar and the United States signed a new, ten-year defense cooperation agreement that will see the US bases in the country operate until at least 2024.[18] In addition, in 2014 Qatar went on a buying spree from American and European weapons suppliers, in March buying $24 billion in tanks, helicopters, missiles, and artillery, and also considering the purchase of seventy-two new jet fighters. Included was an agreement signed with the United States in July 2014 worth $11 billion for the purchase of advanced weaponry, including Patriot and anti-tank missiles and Apache helicopters.[19]

Equally significant, Qatar's policy of hedging in international relations has continued under the new emir. According to the new foreign minister, Khalid bin Mohammed Al Attiyah, "we don't do enemies. . . . We talk to everyone. We cannot change geography—this is for sure—so whoever is in the vicinity of our geography has to be our close friend."[20] Hedging has been combined with a concerted branding campaign, which in addition to the Al Jazeera television network has included efforts at mediation and conflict resolution, thus presenting Qatar as a peacemaker in a region ravaged by continuous warfare. In line with this objective, in July 2014, as the devastating war between Israel and Hamas was raging, Qatar offered to mediate between the two parties and donated $500 million in humanitarian aid to the Palestinians.[21]

There has been, nevertheless, a pronounced shift in the regional context within which Qatari foreign policy has been formulated, and this contextual shift has had consequences for the country's international relations and even its once carefully crafted international image. As part of its branding efforts, during the course of the Arab Spring Qatar moved away from being a mediator to becoming a more active supporter of change in the Middle East region, deeply involving itself in what it assumed would be new eras first in Libya and then in Syria. Gradually realizing that perhaps it had overreached, it slowly adapted, and adopted a more pragmatic foreign policy. By 2014, some observers were arguing that Qatar had returned "to a policy of quiet backroom diplomacy."[22]

Conventional accounts maintain that in the wake of the Arab Spring Qatar has suffered "geopolitical defeat," resulting from and reflective of the fact that "Doha is unable to drive a regional diplomatic agenda."[23] In fact, by championing the Libyan and Syrian revolutions, Qatar attempted to divert and subvert them through its strategic relationship with and use of the Muslim Brotherhood, although it soon found itself giving aid also to some of the Salafi groups that were vying for control and dominance over the multiple opposition groups in Syria. Not surprisingly, most observers agree that "Qatar's Arab Spring interventions . . . greatly undermined the country's reputation for impartiality."[24] Throughout 2013 and especially in the aftermath of the coup in Egypt, Al Jazeera did in fact provide a forum for Muslim Brotherhood figures to criticize Egypt.[25] But the Egyptian military soon showed its violent intolerance of the Brotherhood, and "Syrian society proved far more complicated than Doha imagined . . . and the Brotherhood was for various reasons unable to deliver."[26]

Qatar's active and partisan involvement in regional trouble spots was not viewed with approval in most nearby capitals, especially in Riyadh, Abu Dhabi, Manama, and Cairo. Before long, the marriage of convenience that had drawn Qatar and Saudi Arabia temporarily together at the start of the uprisings gave way to bitter acrimony, largely because the Saudis viewed Qatar's active support for the Egyptian Brotherhood even after the 2013 coup as the crossing of an unacceptable red line. In an unprecedented move in the history of the Gulf Cooperation Council, Saudi Arabia, Bahrain, and the UAE withdrew their ambassadors from Doha in March 2013 as a measure by each state meant to "protect its security and security."[27]

Soon after the ambassador's withdrawal, a "murky anti-Qatar campaign," orchestrated by Saudi Arabia, the UAE, Israel, and Egypt, began to depict Qatar as "a godfather of terrorists everywhere."[28] According to the investigative journalist Glenn Greenwald, "this coordinated media attack on Qatar—using highly paid former U.S. officials and their media allies—is simply a weapon used by the Emirates, Israel, the Saudis and others to advance their agendas." Greenwald writes of "a new campaign in the west to demonize the Qataris as the key supporter of terrorism." Qatar was suddenly seen as "the dishonest broker," and Western journalists began wondering about solutions to "the Qatar problem."[29] Faced with skepticism and suspicion, even some of Qatar's humanitarian efforts were seen as cover for support for terrorist, or at best anti-Western, groups.[30] The allegations that Qatar supports terrorism became so widespread that Sheikh Tamim had to address the issue himself: "What is happening in Iraq and Syria is extremism, and those groupings are being partially funded from abroad, but Qatar has never and will never support terrorist organizations."[31]

Some of these allegations are not without justification. Anecdotal evidence, some presented by the sources cited here, suggests that private, nonstate funds have been funneled from Qatar, as well as from other Gulf states, to violent extremist groups operating in Syria, Iraq, and elsewhere. These fund transfers cannot possibly take place without some level of official knowledge and perhaps even complicity. According to the US State

Department, in fact, "despite a strong legal framework, judicial enforcement and effective implementation of Qatar's anti–money laundering/counterterrorist the financing of terrorism (AML/CFT) law are lacking," and there are "significant gaps" in Qatar's "enforcement activities to ensure terrorist financing-related transactions are not occurring."[32] In response to these reports, in September 2014, Qatar introduced regulations that would make it difficult for charities to send funds abroad.[33]

At least in symbolic ways, Qatar has also sought to distance itself from the Egyptian Muslim Brotherhood. In September 2014, in a move widely seen as a gesture to appease the Saudis, Qatar asked seven Muslim Brotherhood leaders to leave the country.[34] According to the activists themselves, they left voluntarily in order "to avoid causing any embarrassment for the State of Qatar," which was "a very welcoming and supportive host."[35] And in December 2014, Qatar endorsed a Gulf Cooperation Council (GCC) expression of "full support to Egypt" as well as the political program of the country's post-coup government under President Abdel Fattah el-Sisi.[36]

As of this writing, in early 2015, if the frequent declarations of fraternal ties coming out of the regional capitals are to be believed, it appears that Qatar's diplomatic spat with three of its GCC neighbors is over. Whether the UAE-funded and influenced media campaign against Qatar will also cease remains to be seen. For the foreseeable future, it does not appear that Doha has fundamentally changed course in its foreign policy pursuits. During the absence of the three ambassadors, for example, Qatar maintained its proactive diplomacy within and beyond the Persian Gulf region, ensuring that its relations with countries such as France, Oman, and Tunisia, and with the UN Secretary General Ban Ki-moon, were on solid ground.[37] Hyperactive diplomacy and hedging, albeit carried out with a different personal style, are likely to continue to mark Qatar's foreign policy.

The Economy

Perhaps what has changed the least since the coming to power of the new emir in 2013 is the continued growth of Qatar's economy. Over time, depending on exogenous conditions affecting the state's revenue streams and its budget, the rate of economic growth may change from year to year, but the economy itself continues to grow nonetheless. Although in 2013 state spending was up by 13 percent as compared to 2012 levels, that level of growth was the lowest in eleven years. In 2012, spending had been 10 percent higher than initially planned because of higher prices for oil and liquefied natural gas, fueling tremendous infrastructural growth in 2012 and 2013, much of which continued into 2014.[38] Nevertheless, despite a slowing of economic growth in 2014—from a high of 17.4 percent in 2011 to 6.1 percent in 2012, 5 percent in 2013, and 4.9 percent in 2014—the construction of mega-projects, linked both specifically to the 2022 World Cup and for purposes of general infrastructural development, is expected to continue unabated in the foreseeable future.[39] Some of these massive infrastructural projects include building the Doha Metro, expanding the newly opened Hamad International Airport, converting the city's once-ubiquitous roundabouts to four-way intersections, and constructing new sports stadiums in preparation for the World Cup. All this has been taking place at a time when Qatar is one of the most expensive places in the Middle East for construction.[40] Nevertheless, Qatar remains one of the top three markets for companies doing business with and in the Middle East. Between 2014 and 2019, a backlog of construction and infrastructural projects is expected to generate contracts worth $90 billion.[41] In 2013, fully 60 percent of Qatari companies went on a hiring spree.[42] And despite occasional slowdowns in rates of economic growth, Qatar continues to compete with Dubai as the top center for finance and banking in the Middle East and North Africa (MENA) region.[43]

Qatar's economy still relies heavily on revenues from the sale of oil and liquefied natural gas (LNG), though in recent years international investments by the country's sovereign wealth fund, the Qatar Investment Authority (QIA), have served as an additional and significant revenue stream for the state. Today oil and LNG account for approximately 60 percent of Qatar's gross domestic product (GDP) and 85 percent of its exports earnings.[44] The number of the country's LNG customers grew from 7 in 2010 to 21 in 2013, with Asia remaining as the center of Qatar's interest.[45] Not surprisingly, Qatar's GDP is expected to reach $230 billion by 2015 as the country's foreign currency reserves nearly doubled from an annual average of $730 billion in 2000–2009 to $1.374 trillion in 2013.[46] According to the IMF, the QIA could benefit from roughly $20 billion in cash inflows each year from hydrocarbon sales, for a total of $120 billion by 2019.[47] All this at a time when despite very high rates of population growth—10.7 percent between 2013 and 2014—the country's population numbers only 2.17 million.[48] Of these, the number of Qatari citizens is estimated at around 230,000, or slightly more than 10 percent of the total.[49] It was assumed that the rise in population would also spur non-oil growth in Qatar.[50]

For its part, the QIA remains "one of the world's most aggressive investors."[51] In 2014, QIA's assets were estimated at $175 billion.[52] Beginning in 2013, QIA launched "an aggressive expansion spree" in order to diversify its investments beyond Europe and into the Asian and North American markets.[53] This strategy is only likely to serve Qatar's global economic positioning and strengthen what in chapter 2 I describe as its subtle power:

> All in all, QIA's approach to allocating capital across international markets, which has positioned the fund as a capable dealmaker, built strong relationships to the commercial and political establishment of countries that carry substantial weight in the international economic arena. It has served Doha to build diversified networks across the entire spectrum of players in finance, economics, and politics. And though QIA's deals have had a strong financial rationale, they also have served a second bottom line, advancing Qatar's international standing.[54]

The Qatar Brand

One of the key pillars of Qatar's foreign policy has consisted of the country's efforts to project a carefully crafted image of itself as a modern, progressive nation with a rich Islamic culture and heritage. For more than a decade, this dynamic image rested on such innovations as Al Jazeera, mega-events and -projects, endless international conferences, and a world-class museum. These efforts culminated in the successful bid to FIFA to host the 2022 World Cup. But soon after the announcement of the World Cup bid, Qatar began attracting somewhat sustained, negative media attention from around the world regarding the conditions of the hundreds of thousands of migrant laborers working and living in the country. Coming especially from Europe and the United States, the criticism has focused on the country's labor regulations as well as the migrants' working and living conditions.[55] Similarly, persistent allegations and rumors began circulating in the Western press, especially in the United Kingdom, that both Qatar and

Russia had won the bidding for the World Cup only because of massive bribery and the pervasive corruption that is allegedly endemic to FIFA. In November 2014, FIFA's Ethics Committee cleared Russia and Qatar of any wrongdoing in their bids to host the games in 2018 and 2022 respectively, despite "certain indications of potentially problematic conduct."[56] By then, however, Qatar's reputation had already taken a severe beating because of both the bribery allegations and the country's labor practices.

Largely in response to these criticisms, the government started taking a series of measures aimed at improving conditions of laborers and the legal framework governing their entry, employment, and exit procedures. Among the more significant of such measures has been the establishment of the Supreme Committee for Delivery and Legacy, set up in order to, among other things, ensure the formulation and implementation of reforms to workers' conditions. Among the committee's works has been the drafting of a charter governing every aspect of labor conditions in Qatar, covering areas such as contracting, recruitment, safety conditions, housing and accommodation, and food standards.[57]

In 2014, the government also pledged to work on reforming the sponsorship (*kafala*) system in ways that would make it easier for workers to change employers and to leave the country without first having to secure their employer's permission. These proposed reforms are facing resistance from businessmen and entrepreneurs, however, for whom the *kafala* system can be a lucrative source of revenues.[58] Nevertheless, there appears to be a commitment at the highest levels of the state to improve labor conditions, and in the process to restore to Qatar its once positive international image. The emir, for example, has been quoted as saying that "there have been errors and problems, and we don't say we are an ideal state that makes no mistakes. . . . But I think the good news is that we have tackled a lot and have initiated many changes in relation to the situation of foreign workers and we are working seriously on improving the situation."[59] In his annual speech to the country's Advisory Council in November 2014, which acts as a consultative assembly of sorts in the absence of a parliament, the emir directed the prime minister to resolve "issues" regarding migrant workers, especially as it related to their housing. Only time will tell if these efforts, whether motivated purely for purposes of public relations or out of genuine concern for workers' conditions, will lead to improvements in both the lives of laborers working in Qatar and in the country's efforts at branding.

Conclusion

Sheikh Hamad's surprise retirement was, in hindsight, very much in line with the general tenor of his rule: dramatic, unexpected, a radical departure from the political history of both his country and its region. So far at least, Tamim has not shown a similar flair for the dramatic, preferring instead to work steadily on bureaucratic reorganization, administrative streamlining, and hammering fiscal discipline into state organs. On the diplomatic front, Tamim has already experienced what may well be one of the strongest tests of the GCC's resilience, and he appears to have emerged out of it with his resolve and his reputation and political capital intact. That he is different from his father is not in doubt; he has a different personality altogether. But the substance of his rule—the fundamentals on which Qatar's domestic politics and its international relations rely—is by no means different from that of the older Al Thani. Even if Tamim wanted to fundamentally alter course, some of the initiatives and innovations undertaken by his father, not the least of which include the massive Qatar Foundation and the 2022 World Cup, have now acquired lives of their own and cannot be easily dismantled or reversed. For now at least, the new emir has to contend with path dependent, structural dynamics that limit and shape the scope of his domestic and international decisions.

Since his ascension to power, Tamim has been mostly building on the dynamics initiated during his father's reign, sharpening them in the hope of giving the Al Thani rule and vision greater staying power. As one observer has commented, "ultimately the transition from Hamad to his son should be seen as a move calculated to ensure the continuation of the 1995 regime."[60] It is in fact the *regime* whose longevity is being perpetuated, changes in personality and administrative organization notwithstanding. At the same time, Qatar will likely continue to carve out for itself an independent and distinct political, economic, cultural, and religious identity that would distinguish it from its neighbors, especially Saudi Arabia. The country is therefore "likely to remain an unpredictable power."[61]

Acknowledgments

I am grateful to the many individuals who helped me navigate the science of Qatarology. In particular, Abbas Al-Tonsi, Talal Al-Emadi, Ali Al-Shawi, and Patrick Theros gave generously of their time and shared their insights into Qatari politics and society. Dirk Vandewalle was equally generous with information and sources on the extent and nature of Qatar's involvement in the Libyan civil war in 2011–2012. At different stages of work on the book, Reem Al Harmi, Dianna Manalastas, Melissa Mannis, and Kasia Rada provided invaluable research assistance, all too often digging up obscure sources and meeting unreasonable deadlines far ahead of schedule and in good cheers. Colleagues at the Center for International and Regional Studies (CIRS) at Georgetown University's School of Foreign Service in Qatar, where this book was conceived and completed, helped create a supportive intellectual environment for the book's writing. A semester's research leave, kindly provided by Georgetown University, allowed me to concentrate on completing the manuscript. Grateful acknowledgment goes to Carol Lancaster, Marcia Mintz, and James

O'Donnell for making the research leave possible, and for their friendship and their professional support over the years. A visiting professorship at the Institut d'Études Politiques at Sciences Po-Lyon provided an idyllic setting for writing the book's final chapters and for benefiting from the friendship and warm hospitality of Lahouari Addi and Vincent Michelot. Gary Wasserman and Robert Wirsing read all or parts of the manuscript and provided numerous invaluable comments and suggestions. Along with Roger Haydon and anonymous reviewers for Cornell University Press, they helped me refine, sharpen, and better articulate many of the book's arguments and saved me from a number of embarrassing mistakes. Closer to home, my wife Melisa and our daughters Dilara and Kendra, who have shared with me life in Qatar since 2007, put up with the ups and downs and the exhilarations and frustrations that come with writing a book. For putting up with me during the course of work on this book, and for all they do for me big and small, I dedicate this book to them.

QATAR

INTRODUCTION

The emergence of Qatar as an influential powerbroker in the Middle East and beyond over the past decade has puzzled students and observers of the region alike. How can a small state, with little previous history of diplomatic engagement regionally or globally, have emerged as such an influential and significant player in shaping unfolding events across the Middle East and elsewhere? This is the central question to which this book is devoted. Qatar is a young, small state, with a commensurately small population, sandwiched between giants Iran to the north and Saudi Arabia to the south. But, perhaps audaciously, the sheikhdom, which boasts the world's highest per capita income, has quickly become one of the most consequential and influential actors in the region. Domestically, Qatar has transformed itself into a global hub and a central pivot of globalization. Doha, the capital, changes by the day, featuring the latest and the best of everything in its streets and its gleaming skyscrapers. The country hosts world-class universities, a world-class museum, and a world-class airline. This much the next-door emirates of Dubai and Abu Dhabi also have.

But what sets Qatar apart are its foreign policy and its international relations. The country has pursued a high profile, proactive diplomacy. It has been an active, and mostly successful, mediator, having been instrumental in peace accords in Lebanon in 2008 and in the Sudan in 2011. Qatar played an important role in helping Libyan rebels put an end to Moammar Qaddafi's rule in 2011, and was similarly instrumental in helping isolate the Assad regime in Syria. Its support and influence is actively courted by powers big and small, near and far. By all accounts, as the events and trends of the past decade are proving, Qatar has undoubtedly emerged as an influential player.

But will it last? Is Qatar's influence only ephemeral or is it the product of a more lasting and more meaningful shift in power that is likely to mark regional politics in the Middle East for some time to come?

This volume argues that despite all limitations—diplomatic, political, infrastructural, and demographic—Qatar's powers are more than temporary. Qatar's influence is likely to continue for some time. In broad strokes, the book's arguments are as follows. A convergence of two trends, one regional the other global, has created conditions favorable to the rise of Qatar. Regionally, the Middle East has witnessed a precipitous decline in the powers of the some of its traditional heavyweights and a concomitant rise in the affluence and influence of the countries of the Arabian Peninsula. For a number of decades, the Middle East's centers of diplomatic, military, and ideological power lay in such capitals as Cairo, Damascus, Baghdad, and Tehran. By virtue of being the seat of "the custodian of Islam's holiest mosques," Riyadh was also a contender for regional power and supremacy. However, by the 1980s and 1990s, political rhetoric and appearances could no longer mask profound institutional and infrastructural weaknesses characterizing the Egyptian, Syrian, Iraqi, and Iranian polities. Youth bulges and burgeoning populations, economic underperformance and chronic inefficiency, broken infrastructures and reactive policies, all had the traditional powers of the Middle East fighting rearguard action, and, in the process, losing one political, economic, ideological, and diplomatic battle after another. This decline has continued into the 2000s and 2010s, its consequences made all the more dramatic by the outbreak of the Arab Spring of 2011.

At the very time as this steady decline has been occurring in parts of the Middle East, elsewhere in the region, along the southern shores of the

Persian Gulf, a group of dynamic, innovative upstarts have been busily filling the ensuing vacuums and making their own presence felt. In sharp contrast to the sluggish, even stalled and broken politics and economics of their fellow Middle Easterners, the countries of the Gulf Cooperation Council (GCC) have proven themselves to be adept at change, proactive, dynamic, and focused. That they are only a mere decades old, and that most would not have existed today had it not been for oil, only adds to their dynamism and their determination to succeed. Within the GCC, Qatar stands out, benefiting from a number of comparative advantages that the other states do not have, having transformed itself from a poor backwater and a practical vassal of Saudi Arabia a few decades ago into one of the region's richest, most recognizable, and highly influential states.

This steady shift has occurred within the context of a second, global trend, namely a qualitative change in the nature of international power. Power has traditionally been assumed to come from the barrel of a gun, or a tank, or, more recently, from the force of ideals and values. Both hard and soft powers do and will continue to remain highly consequential for the foreseeable future. But we cannot ignore the significance of a new form of power and influence, one less obvious and more discreet, rooted in a combination of contextual opportunities and calculated policies meant to augment one's influence over others. This "subtle power" is what Qatar has and what is likely to sustain its influence for some time to come.

States may appear powerful and influential internationally but be rotten—or at least weak—at their core. What is the Qatari state's core like, and what are the sources of its resilience or weakness? Can the archaic-looking system of personal rule, that relic of a bygone era in the post–Arab Spring Middle East, continue to survive and to thrive into the twenty-first century? Does power, even in its subtle variety, not require strength and stability within?

Here the argument becomes somewhat problematic since agency, that unpredictable variable of human actions and initiatives, becomes a far more consequential factor than the role of circumstances and institutions. There can be no doubt that in Qatar and elsewhere in the Arabian Peninsula monarchy as an institution—as an integral part of the social fabric—will continue to be on solid grounds for decades to come. Since the mid-1990s, one of the biggest distinguishing factors about the Qatari monarchy has been the acumen, determination, and savvy of the current monarch,

Sheikh Hamad bin Khalifa Al Thani. Driven and ambitious, Hamad has been a master-balancer, successfully striking multiple balances between domestic, regional, and international actors while steadily enhancing his own, and his country's, position. Whether the next monarch can have the same drive and determination, the same uncanny ability to position himself at the apex of an uncontested domestic power structure and the country as a regional leader and a global player is an open question. The heir apparent, Sheikh Tamim bin Hamad Al Thani, has so far remained largely in the shadow of his father. All indications are that the emir and the heir apparent see eye-to-eye on matters of policy and direction. But the son remains as yet untested. Nevertheless, in chapters 4 through 6 I make the case that Hamad has positioned both the institution of the monarchy and Qatar's international profile in such ways that even a less capable or ambitious heir cannot significantly lessen the country's international influence or slow the pace of its upward ascent.

A Snapshot of Qatar

At first glance, it is easy to dismiss Qatar and most of the other countries of the Arabian Peninsula. Many in the Arab world sarcastically dismiss the small states of the Arabian Peninsula as "oil well states" (*al-dawla al-bi'r*), pointing to their need to incorporate the word "state" into their formal name as an indication of their self-doubt as viable states.[1] Even scholars have long neglected Qatar, with only a few articles and an odd book here or there published on the country well into the 1990s.[2] Even today, despite the belated realization of the country's growing international significance, there are still no more than a handful of serious treatments on Qatar's domestic and international politics.[3] Of late a promising cadre of younger scholars have pointed to the growing strategic and commercial significance of the Persian Gulf. Still, Qatar itself remains largely below the scholarly radar, frequently overlooked by observers of the region in favor of its larger or more troubled neighbors—the United Arab Emirates, Saudi Arabia, or Bahrain.

Well into the twenty-first century, like the rest of the states of the GCC, Qatar continues to "struggle for self-definition and redefinition."[4] Part of the problem with visibility and recognition has been the country's small geographic and demographic size. With a landmass of only 4,416 square miles, Qatar is one of the smallest countries in the Middle East, second only to Bahrain with 274 square miles. The country also has the second smallest population base in the Middle East. According to the latest national census, in 2010 Qatar had a total population of 1.74 million.[5] Although the census does not distinguish between nationals and nonnationals, expatriates are estimated to make-up approximately 85 percent of all individuals living in the country. That means Qatari nationals number somewhere in the neighborhood of 250,000. Of these, some 10,000 to 15,000 are thought to be members of the extended ruling Al Thani family.

Despite claims by members of the ruling family that the country's origins date back to the Phoenicians, there is little archeological evidence to suggest that Doha was much more than a dusty and largely inhospitable fishing village well into the 1920s and 1930s. Chapter 4 discusses the state's efforts and inventing and reinventing Qatari tradition and heritage, and today's Doha, where three-quarters of the country's population lives, seems obsessed with its image as a modern city that remains mindful of its past. Writing on Dubai, Jeremy Jones has used the designation "the airport state" to describe a city that has all the accruements and the modern façade and conveniences of an airport, but is, also like airports the world over, characterless and without a soul of its own.[6] He might as well have been describing Doha. Though considerably less hyper—and hyped—than Dubai, Doha is also a city with little character or charm of its own. The city has a fascination with making and remaking itself, resulting in what is an incongruent collection of impressive but nonharmonious buildings and neighborhoods. Romanticized replicas of Venice form luxury areas and landmarks of the city, bearing names such as Aspire (sports complex), the Pearl (artificial island), and Villaggio (shopping mall). *Time* magazine called the country "the magic kingdom."[7] Some old forts, a few on the outskirts of the city, are being restored in an effort to buttress the state's invention—or reinvention—of a Qatari tradition. The heritage industry is doing brisk business in Qatar, seeking to reinvent tradition, so far with uneven success.

Doha may lack Dubai's obsession with bling, but it is still filled with a glitz that numbs the senses and distorts perceptions of reality. Many parts of the city resemble a surreal and incongruent mixture of Hong Kong, on the one hand, and Tucson, Arizona, on the other. It is not surprising that today's Doha is one massive construction site. No sooner are city maps printed that they become obsolete, as new roads and multilane highways replace old, snaky streets. Roundabouts, marvels of traffic engineering from a bygone era of few cars and manageable street flows, are being steadily replaced with four-corner junctions with timed traffic lights. Cranes and other heavy construction equipment are ubiquitous features of the urban landscape. Doha, it seems, is addicted to tearing up its asphalted streets as soon as they are ready for use. Entire neighborhoods made-up of older shops and large, single-family homes are razed with unsettling frequency and replaced by tall, glass-covered, gleaming buildings. Remembering directions to points of interest is often an exercise in futility. Taxi passengers frequently find themselves giving directions to their drivers, most of whom are recent arrivees from Bangladesh or Ethiopia.

Doha's roads and streets, meanwhile, are seldom without mangled cars strewn on the sides, a product of one of the world's highest and deadliest traffic accident rates.[8] The municipality's installation of speed cameras all across the city has done little to encourage a culture of driving safely.[9] Unsurprisingly, most Qataris prefer larger, presumably safer cars. The ubiquitous Toyota Land Cruiser, overwhelmingly in white, is the king of Doha roads, the preferred car of Qataris, and a significant status symbol. In recent years, more daring colors of black and gray can also be seen darting around town.

All the while, the city's armies of construction workers, in their tens of thousands, remain as inconspicuous and hidden from public view as possible. The state employs a discourse revolving around the protection of the family to bar "bachelors" from shopping malls and the *souq* on "family days" and from living in "family residential areas."[10] In this sense "bachelor" is code word for unskilled migrant workers from South Asia and "family" designates everyone else, married or not. The biggest interaction between unskilled migrant workers and the rest of the country's residents, save for household maids, occurs on Doha's congested streets, where, stuck in traffic, tired eyes peer through half-open windows of old American school buses or grungy ones made by Tata as the workers are driven from future high-rises to their distant labor camps.[11]

Why Qatar?

The study of Qatar is important in four significant respects. First, Qatar allows us to re-examine some of the basic premises of "rentier" theory, looking, specifically, at the mutually dependent nature of the relationships that develop between the state (i.e., the ruling family) and influential social actors as a result of rent-based political and economic arrangements. The nature of state capacity in Qatar has enabled the ruling family to abandon its repeated mentions of political liberalization and to instead push forward with ambitious agendas of economic and social change. Significantly, an expansion in the state's capacity has occurred at the same time as its deepening financial and institutional ties with social actors, thereby involving private capital more intimately in the country's march toward economic growth and modernization. The genesis of such ties trace back to rent-based clientelism, but today these ties have become so robust and multidimensional that even economic downturns are unlikely to turn social actors against the state and its expansive patronage network.

Historical patterns of state development across the Arabian Peninsula have long featured close alliances and interconnections between ruling families and other influential allies made-up of powerful clans, merchants, and foreign resident agents. With the introduction of oil economies and the growth of rentier arrangements, in recent decades these previously informal political alliances have assumed multilayered economic, commercial, and even political dimensions, therefore cementing the mutual links between ruling families, on the one side, and strategically located allies, on the other. Rentier theory has long seen merchants and the rentier classes as dependent on the state. In looking at Qatar, I maintain that the dependent relationship is a mutually reinforcing one, with the state often in need of support from dependent groups as much as is the case the other way.

A second feature of Qatar that makes it an interesting case study is the country's hyperactive diplomacy. Small states have traditionally assumed certain specific roles and profiles in the international arena, many of which—as a prototypical small state—also characterize Qatar's position in the international community. But Qatar has not been content with remaining in the shadows of regional superpowers like Saudi Arabia and Egypt or, for that matter, even global superpowers such as the United States. It has not shied away from irritating allies and foes alike through Al Jazeera; it has engaged in a number of successful mediation efforts across the Middle East and parts of Africa; it has taken on several high-profile showcase projects, most notably the 2022 FIFA World Cup, a world-class museum, and a global advertising campaign; and it has maintained close relations with such eclectic friends and allies as Iran, the United States, different Palestinian factions, and until 2008 even Israel.

There are several underlying causes for the nature of Qatar's hyperactive, seemingly maverick foreign policy. First is an aggressive pursuit of "hedging" as a foreign policy tool, meant to maintain friendly relations and open lines of communication with allies and potential adversaries alike. Second, Qatar has embarked on an equally aggressive "branding" campaign, meant to give international recognition to the small country as an international educational, sporting, and cultural hub and a good global citizen committed to mediation and conflict resolution. Third, Qatar has been able to employ its comparative advantage in relation to other GCC states with great effectiveness. As starkly evident by the events of February and March 2011, Qatar is one of the few GCC states that continues to enjoy remarkable political stability. This political stability is rooted in the country's comparative social cohesion (lack of sectarian tensions as in Bahrain and Saudi Arabia), its unitary polity and small size (compared to the United Arab Emirates and Oman), and a relatively apolitical, small national population (compared to Kuwait). These factors have combined to give the state relative latitude in pursuing foreign policy agendas it may not have otherwise been able to pursue. Finally, vast revenues derived from oil and natural gas have given the state the capacity and the financial resources to embark on projects and initiatives—such as Al Jazeera television or extensive mediation efforts—that have given it a relatively unique identity in the international arena.

A third significance in the study of Qatar lies in the broader lessons we can draw for international relations theory from the country's international profile and its diplomatic initiatives. As discussed in chapter 2, small states are generally assumed to be on the receiving end of power rather than its originators. But Qatar, a small state, has managed to become a consequential, and in many ways influential, player on the international stage. What does this say about the evolving nature of power relationship in the international arena? More specifically, what kind of power has

Qatar accumulated that accounts for its international behavior? Although Al Jazeera has enhanced the country's international stature, particularly in the wake of the Arab Spring, Qatar is too small and its cultural products too limited and narrow to have bestowed the country with meaningful levels of "soft" power. Nor can the country be said to have amassed "smart" power, which strategically combines soft and hard powers for specific purposes. Qatar has accumulated its power through a track record of high-profile mediations, generous spending and commercially strategic investments across the globe, doses of soft power (through Al Jazeera), and a hyperactive diplomacy. Clearly, Qatar's ability to do these things is significantly enhanced, if not made entirely possible, by the military protection afforded to it through the American security umbrella.

I posit that in Qatar's case this new form of international power may best be conceptualized as "subtle" power, which is contingent on a combination of interrelated elements. To begin with, *military security*, guaranteed by the US security umbrella, enables the state to devote its attention to issues that are not strictly security-related and to instead pursue goals and strategies that enhance its diplomatic stature and strengthen its political economy both at home and abroad. Equally important is the state's considerable *wealth*, which gives it enhanced domestic autonomy and leverage in co-opting domestic actors, on the one hand, and, on the other, the ability to pursue a wide array of international goals and strategies. For Qatar, many of these international goals and strategies have revolved around buying influence and using financial largesse to set or at least to influence agendas. A small state with little history, Qatar has sought to spend its way into a position of Arab leadership. But by itself money is not a sufficient ingredient of subtle power; how it is deployed is. Qatar's leaders have a clear vision of their ideal role in the Arab world, namely as one of its most visible leaders and agenda-setters, and to make that vision a reality they seem to be sparing no expenses. In doing so they have adopted an aggressive global *branding* campaign aimed at portraying the country as dynamic, progressive, stable, and investment friendly. The ensuing visibility and the pursuit of a positive international image is reinforced by an *active diplomacy* meant to further enhance the country's stature and influence. This active diplomatic profile, part of the state leaders' carefully crafted vision, has been aided by the persistently tumultuous politics of the Middle East, ranging from the near-chronic instability of Lebanese politics to the reverberations of the Arab Spring in North Africa and the Levant, thus presenting Qatar with repeated windows of opportunity to interject itself into the regional political scene.

Fourth, Qatar's very experimental nature as a country offers us insights into processes of state- and nation-building. Through the deployment of vast oil and gas revenues, the Qatari state is engaged in a frantic effort to construct an entirely new society. Although the emir's *National Vision 2030* promises to navigate social and economic change while ensuring continued anchor in tradition, the pace of change is breakneck and its nature awe-inspiring. Can material culture change so rapidly and fundamentally while political values remain static and traditional? Can the state continue to delay political development while fostering profound social change? Given the small population base, and the nationals' ever-increasing dependence on rent income despite state efforts to usher in a knowledge-based economy, is this model of development sustainable? How long can the Qatari varieties of high modernism and political antiquity coexist side-by-side?

In exploring these questions, I have adopted an integrated approach to the study of Qatar's domestic and international politics, taking into account the importance of leadership and choices, the role of institutions, and the importance of context. As the arguments throughout this book make clear, agency and structure are both important. Neither institutions nor individuals alone have been responsible for making Qatar what it is today. Agency, contingency, and institutions have all gone hand-in-hand in the making of contemporary Qatar into a force to be reckoned with.

The Book's Plan

I make three main, interrelated arguments in this book. First, I argue, there has been a steady shift in the regional balance of power in the Middle East away from the region's traditional heavyweights and in the direction of the states of the Gulf Cooperation Council. Not that long ago, the political, military, and diplomatic centers of gravity in the Middle East rested in Cairo, Damascus, Baghdad, and Tehran. In their own ways, Algiers and Tripoli also sought to overcome their geographical remoteness from the region's heartland and tried to shape the Middle East's, or at least the Arab world's, destiny as much as possible. Each might had its moment in history, but that moment is now over, at least for the time being, eclipsed by the combined effects of crumbling domestic infrastructures, mounting economic difficulties, and, perhaps most detrimentally, stale and increasingly reactive leaderships.

Not all states of the GCC have been immune to the maladies plaguing the larger Middle East, and, as the events of the Arab Spring have shown, the less wealthy states of the Persian Gulf—namely Bahrain, Oman, and even Saudi Arabia—have largely staved off its repercussions. Overall, it is the GCC states that are exhibiting a new economic dynamism and a new vibrancy that is turning them into the Middle East's new center of gravity. Within the GCC, a series of comparative advantages have given Qatar a significant edge over the other states, not the least of which is the country's huge hydrocarbon resources and its wealth in relation to its population, its comparative social cohesion and lack of sectarian and other political tensions, and, perhaps most important, its visionary and determined leadership. Agency is as important as the institutional constraints and opportunities within which states find themselves.

Mention must be made here of Iran and its position within the Persian Gulf region and in the larger Middle East. In recent years Iran may have achieved a number of successes insofar as its relations with the Lebanese Hezbollah and with Hamas, or its ties with certain Shia groups in Iraq are concerned. But the larger context within which the Iranians have been able to project power has steadily narrowed, increasingly constricting their ability to influence outcomes and to achieve their desired objectives. The Islamic Republic's stewards, in fact, have repeatedly scored own goals when it comes to Iranian interests.[12] Tehran's denials to the contrary, the United States has indeed succeeded in significantly limiting the circle of Iran's friends across the Middle East and especially in the Arab world, Bashar Assad's Syria left as the Islamic Republic's only meaningful Arab ally. Iran's relations with Qatar, discussed in chapter 3, is a prime example of a relationship characterized by diplomatic niceties but void of in-depth substance and cooperation. And Qatar tends to be friendlier to Iran than almost any of the other GCC states save for Oman.

A second, related argument has to do with the changing nature of power in the international arena in general and its utilization by Qatar in particular. In the twenty-first century, we can no longer conceive of power only in its traditional "hard" or "soft" varieties. Just as important as hard power projection or the allure of values is the power that comes with the combination of agility, dynamism, influence, financial resources, and the ability to capitalize on emerging opportunities. Neither hard nor soft power are obsolete, and, both separately and in tandem, they continue to constitute compelling forces in the international arena. But neither adequately captures the essence of the kind of power that Qatar is beginning to amass and exercise. To be certain, Qatar benefits from two key ingredients of hard power, namely military protection, provided by the United States, and money, and thus massive international investments, with which comes influence. But when agency is added into the mix, in the form of a leadership determined to carve out a place of influence for itself diplomatically and regionally, then we are no longer looking at a form of power that is strictly "hard." In Qatar's case, the country's leaders try to maximize its powers by carving out for it a highly visible position of centrality in relation to regional peace and stability. This they have accomplished through aggressive branding and diplomatic hedging. I have labeled the new form of power that Qatar has carved out as "subtle" power.

The book's third main argument revolves around the developmental capacity of the Qatari state. Underwritten by inordinate financial wealth, the state has enormous capacity in relation to its society. The particular way in which the state has employed its wealth has enhanced the depth and breadth of its relationship with social actors by making them beholden to its own developmental success. In the Qatari context this developmental success has meant undertaking rapid infrastructural growth and development—an ambitious, nationwide building project rivaled only by Dubai and Abu Dhabi—in which the state has brought in social actors as employees and shareholders in its lucrative enterprises.

The ensuing developmental state, although fundamentally authoritarian, exhibits remarkable stability due to the depth and apparent strength of its ties with actors across the social spectrum. Having thus incorporated large swathes of the population into its developmental projects, even in times of economic difficulty, were they to ever come, the state is unlikely to face serious challenges for the population. As the 2008 economic meltdown in Dubai showed, in the wealthy rentier states of the Persian Gulf, in times of economic difficulty social actors tend to continue to rely on the state to bail them out rather than to oppose and undermine it. In these polities, the state has long been a source of safety and comfort, a political and especially economic patron par excellence. Undermining it in times of crisis is self-defeating at best.

Chapter 1 traces the emergence of the countries of the Arabian Peninsula—and more specifically the states of the GCC—as regional and global powerhouses. The chapter begins with a survey of the international relations of the Middle East, examining the emergence of the GCC as a new center of gravity in light of the mounting economic and political problems faced by the Middle East's traditional powers (e.g., Egypt, Syria, Iraq, and Iran). The chapter concludes with an examination of the comparative advantages of Qatar in relation to the other GCC states, looking at the combination of political dynamics and economic resources that have facilitated Qatar's rise in recent years.

Chapter 2 provides an in-depth examination of the concept of power, critically analyzing realist and neorealist assumptions about hard power as well as Joseph Nye's concepts of "soft" and "smart" powers. None of these notions, the chapter argues, have lost their relevance in contemporary world politics. But it cannot be denied that countries such as Qatar exercise a form of power and influence that is not adequately described by any of these categories. Qatar's influence may be more accurately attributed to "subtle" power, rooted in its effective mobilization of circumstances and developing opportunities to its advantage, its enormous financial wealth, and its strategic use of the country's sovereign wealth fund, as well as its carefully calibrated foreign policy of hedging.

Chapter 3, on foreign policy and power projection, examines "balance of power," "bandwagoning," and "hedging" as foreign policy alternatives, at times pursued in overlapping fashion, and looks at Qatar's adoption of hedging as a deliberate, carefully crafted option. Hedging involves taking a big bet one way, as with security and military alliance for example, and smaller ones another way, as with friends who can be dispensed with if need be. For Qatar this has meant seeking shelter under the US security umbrella while at the same time maintaining cordial relations with Iran and Hamas. Qatar's relationships with the United States and Iran in particular, and also with Hamas and Israel, are emblematic of its hedging. Its employment of Al Jazeera for foreign policy purposes, subtle and indirect as it may be, its mediation efforts, and its spearheading of several world-renowned showcase projects all combine to enable the country to project a power that is incommensurate with its small size and is far beyond traditional practices in the Middle East region, or, for that matter, expectations within the theoretical literature.

The storms unleashed by the Arab awakening of 2011 did not reach Qatar. Chapter 4 examines the root causes for the stability of Qatar's benign autocracy. The Qatari political system remains sultanistic and personalist, with a handful of individuals making all of the major policy decisions. State consolidation occurred in the context of weak organizational mobility on the part of potential contenders for political space, such as merchants or religious classes, thus enabling the Al Thanis to monopolize politics and emergent state institutions early on, buttressed in time with oil revenues, used to buy off any potential opposition. The chapter chronicles attempts by Sheikhs Ali (r. 1949–1960), Ahmad (r. 1960–1972), and Khalifa (r. 1972–1995) to consolidate their own personal power as the country's rulers and within their own large and bitterly fractious family. Success was often elusive, and for much of their reigns they had to contend with plotting brothers, sons, or cousins. Shaikh Hamad's reign, however, has been remarkably transformative in finally putting an end to the bitter rivalries within the Al Thanis and for achieving an unprecedented level of political consolidation resulting from the centralization of power within his own household. In the process, benefitting from seemingly endless oil revenues, he has reignited a frantic process of state-building that had remained sclerotic under his predecessors. Part of the process of transformation in Qatar, and reinforcing it, has been a recrafting and reigniting of state-centered politics, with the emir and his new—and now uniformly loyal—inner-circle of coteries as its central core.

The system remains remarkably stable not so much because of its inherent authoritarianism but because of its popular legitimacy among an overwhelming majority of Qatari nationals. The regime remains intolerant of any signs of dissent. But at the same time it enjoys considerable legitimacy rooted in a deep nexus between society and the state, or, more accurately, between society and the ruling family. By all standards, "Qatari society" remains small and thus relatively easily governable. This has enabled the state to provide for the welfare of the national population with extensive, cradle-to-grave social benefits. The stability of benign authoritarianism in Qatar is rooted in a highly robust rentier political economy and in the state's deepening roots in society.

These deepening roots are the subject of chapter 5, which looks specifically at the state's attempts at enhancing its developmental capacity, on the one hand, and its efforts at implementing projects of "high modernism," on the other. These two endeavors have reinforced and strengthened one another. Thanks to massive financing by the state and its publicly funded corporations, Doha continues to expand and to grow, vertically into the air and horizontally into the sea. Massive profits are made in the process, even if through frequent state intervention, thus solidifying private capital's continued dependence on the state. High modernism, meant to catapult the county into the modern age, is inadvertently serving to maintain in power a political system that is a relic of the past.

The concluding chapter comes back to the question posed in this introduction, namely the riddle of Qatar's power and permanence. One of the questions asked frequently by academics and policymakers alike is whether or not the Qatari model is viable? Equally important is the question of the state's ability—or lack thereof—to effectively manage the unintended consequences of several of the dynamics that it has currently set in motion. Diplomatically, is Qatar taking on more than it can handle? Domestically, what will the state do about the growing chasm between its rhetorical support for democracy and its authoritarian underpinnings? How will it handle the social consequences of the profound changes it has triggered in Qatari society, the most notable of which is the invitation of Western universities whose graduates are now entering into the workforce and the social mainstream?

I do not claim to have the answers to these and other similarly important questions. But these are indeed the questions on which the future of Qatar rides. As the volume makes clear, Qatar's present—its foreign and domestic politics, its social and cultural rhythm, and its economic development—has been deeply and profoundly shaped by the force and personality of its current leader, Hamad bin Khalifa Al Thani. Hamad has created new institutions, and has injected vigor and discipline to some and dispensed with others. But he has been the driving force behind the changes, institutional and otherwise, that Qatar has witnessed in the past decade and a half. Even after he departs from the scene, there is no reason to believe that the force of personalities—agency—will play any less of a determining role in Qatar's foreseeable future.

1

Setting the Stage

The strategic map of the Persian Gulf has been undergoing a steady change over the past three decades. This shift has been punctuated with major, tectonic shifts that have fundamentally altered the balance of power in the strategic waterway every time they have occurred. First, beginning in 1978–1979, Iran's Islamic revolution removed from power the self-ascribed "gendarme of the region" and an unquestionable ally of the Western powers. In the 1980s, with Tehran's Ayatollahs accused by the West of having turned Iran into a global pariah and an exporter of revolutionary radicalism, it was Iraq that emerged as the Persian Gulf's dominant power. At the time Iraq was underwritten by Saudi and Kuwaiti funds in its war against Iran, Western technical advice and material support, and moral as well as financial cheerleading by the Persian Gulf's various Arab states weary of Iran's Islamic revolutionary impulses. All of this changed when Iraq invaded Kuwait in October 1991, with Saddam Hussein now universally portrayed as "the butcher of Baghdad" and a threat to regional stability and peace. Throughout the 1990s Iraq was seen by virtually all states of the region as a dangerous bully, its injuries from war and sanctions making it unpredictable and prone to extraterritorial acts of violence.

The September 11 attacks once again changed the equation, leading the United States to lump Iran and Iraq into an "Axis of Evil" along with North Korea, giving America's crusading president an excuse to invade and occupy Iraq, maintain unrelenting financial and diplomatic pressure on Iran, and, as much as possible, courting the other Arab states of the region to join Washington's "war on terror" and to endorse its unilateralism and hegemonic approach to the larger Middle East.

After the US invasion of Iraq in March 2003, the Persian Gulf and the Middle East became subjected to a full-blown Pax Americana. But beneath this larger umbrella, one shaped and defined by US military presence across the region, the regional balance of power was far from certain. Iraq, once feared and begrudgingly admired by its Arab brethren for having stood up to Iran, was in tatters and slipped in and out of civil war for at least the first five years of its occupation by the Americans. Iran was squeezed and isolated, headed, from 2005 to 2013, by a populist president determined to revive the revolutionary slogans of thirty years earlier, even if it cost the country whatever international gains it had painstakingly made earlier among its leery neighbors. I argue later that despite seeming gains in Iraq and to a lesser extent in Afghanistan, from 2005 on the strategic position of Iran in the Persian Gulf has declined steadily through a combination of domestic, regional, and international factors, most of which revolve around Mahmoud Ahmadinejad's ill-fated presidency.[1] Saudi Arabia, the Persian Gulf's other power, meanwhile, is in no position to project its influence across the region, confronted with its own brewing problems with fundamentalists, Sunni-Shia sectarian tensions, and a string of octogenarian kings and heir apparents with ill health and uncertain tenures in office. Apart from the United States, an extraneous power, after 2003 the Persian Gulf has not had any regional superpowers that can cast a definitive shadow over the region.

Providing the larger regional context within which Qatar's ascendance has been made possible, I argue that there has been a steady shift in the center of economic and diplomatic power in the Middle East away from the region's traditional powerhouses and in the direction of heretofore marginal players, namely the comparatively smaller sheikhdoms of the Persian Gulf. For one reason or another, the "big and powerful" regional actors that once dictated the course of events in the Middle East—Iran, Iraq, Egypt, Syria, and, if we stretch the analysis a bit, Libya—all witnessed steady declines in their relative power and influence in the region. At the same time, new players, with Qatar and the United Arab Emirates (UAE) chief among them, began making their presence increasingly felt. In Qatar's case, it was more than merely a question of having the small sheikhdom be seen and heard. Qatar sought, and is seeking, to project power far beyond its small borders. Within a relatively short period, Qatar has emerged as one of the region's most consequential players.

I begin with a quick survey of the international relations of the Middle East and the strategic role that the Persian Gulf has played in regional politics. Historically, the Persian Gulf has been an area of intense attention by regional and global powers, with the United States having long maintained a presence there both indirectly, through proxies, and directly through its own military forces. The chapter then zeroes in on the Persian Gulf itself, and particularly on the states of the Arabian Peninsula, examining the dynamics that have facilitated their increasing emergence, especially after the second oil boom of the early 2000s, as regional powerhouses both across the Middle East and beyond. I focus specifically on the role and attention of the United States toward the region in military and security terms at a time when the Persian Gulf has found itself increasingly closer to Pacific Asia in areas of trade and investments.

Ascendance is not without its risks, and many deep-seated structural limitations impede, or altogether threaten, the meteoric rise of the Middle East's newest heavyweights. I argue that in many ways Qatar is immune to many of these risks and limitations, and, insofar as its international profile and power-projection abilities are concerned, it has therefore been able to stand above the rest of the pack so far. This unique rise of Qatar is facilitated by a combination of factors that are both structural and contextual, in relation to its neighbors, and agency related—that is, its own resources and its employment of those resources and its agendas for purposes of power projection. The chapter ends with an examination of the context within which the rise of Qatar has been facilitated.

This is not to imply that the "Qatar model," if there is one, is not without its problems. By virtue of being a personalist system with a narrow ruling circle, Qatar faces significant uncertainties in its long-term political trajectory. These uncertainties in the domestic arena, discussed in chapter 5, are bound to have consequences for Qatar's international relations and power-projection abilities in the long run. For now, however, the stewards of the Qatari state have successfully managed to keep the surfacing of structural shortfalls and contradictions in check. How long and to what extent they can keep doing so remains an open question.

The Persian Gulf in World Politics

An inescapable feature of the international system is the rise in the powers of newly emerging nations and a concomitant loss of ground by the great powers. By nature, both the preponderant regional hierarchies and the global hierarchy are dynamic and changeable.[2] Such power transitions within the international system, whether on a regional scale or bigger, are often accompanied by a fair amount of friction and, potentially, conflict.[3] The international system is comprised of a series of hierarchies in which subordinate states relegate certain components of their sovereignty— usually defense and security—to more powerful, dominant states.[4] Along with balance of power, international law, various diplomatic mechanisms, and war, hierarchies are part of what Hedley Bull called "the managerial system of the great powers" in maintaining international order.[5] Sovereignty, as David Lake claims, is divisible, "and has been divided between authorities at different levels, including between states."[6] Within hierarchies, a nation may achieve parity with another, coming close to possessing the resources of the dominant power, or it might overtake it, by surpassing the resources of the previously dominant state.[7]

International hierarchies change not only through wars and other coercive means but also through steady changes in access to power resources in general and to economic power in particular. According to this perspective, "differences in rates of economic change among national resource potentials" are the most important drivers of shifts in global hierarchies. International economic relationships are inextricably tied to power relationships.[8]

While not all challenges are successful, those that are bring with them "a major transference of power and privilege from the dominant nation and its supporting coalition to the challenger and its supporters."[9] More often, subordinate states resort to under-compliance or over-reaching, thus exposing themselves to the risks of discipline and punishment by the dominant power. Today's international hierarchies tend to be "more constrained or attenuated" as compared to the past because of the dynamic, evolving relationships that characterize them. This is not to imply that hierarchies are always resented or resisted by those in the lower rungs. In fact, through the provision of incentives and benefits on which subordinate states come to depend, dominant states often ensure that hierarchies become more robust and more legitimate.[10]

Within the international system, particular kinds of hierarchies are noticeable. The most visible tend to be security hierarchies, signified by military alliances and cooperation between a subordinate and dominant state, and economic hierarchies, the best indicators of which are levels of monetary policy autonomy and trade dependence.[11] The United States tends to control multiple, and multidimensional, international hierarchies built on security and economic pillars.[12] Two of these overlapping and reinforcing hierarchies have been in the Middle East, one for the larger region and another in specific relation to the Persian Gulf. Making matters more complicated have been shifting hierarchies within the Middle East, transferring regional centers of gravity from Cairo steadily eastward, ending up, most recently, in the Arabian Peninsula. The core of this center of gravity currently resides in Qatar.

From the earliest days of its formation in the 1950s, the modern Middle East state system has been in a state of near-constant flux and transition. A number of factors have combined to result in this dynamic impermanence of the regional power structure, one of the most important of which is the limited power and autonomy that Middle Eastern states have historically been able to exercise within the international system. According to Tareq Ismael, "as relative newcomers to an old international game, the states of the Middle East are forced to operate under rules and within parameters not of their own making."[13] On the whole, Middle East states have been weak hegemons and poor balancers due to the absence of a strong and durable hierarchy, the presence of entrenched and powerful identities, and the pervasiveness of external influences.[14] The international relations of the Middle East are constantly reshaped by often overlapping and reinforcing, local, regional, transnational, and international pressures. It is not surprising that a number of Middle Eastern states have vied for regional leadership at one time or another, eclipsing the others with shouts and promises of spearheading a liberation around the corner, proclaiming a milestone of epic proportions here, another one there. None, however, has been able to construct a regional order of its liking, limited by a combination of its own regional isolation, external dependence, and domestic structural shortcomings.[15]

Looking at the region through unabashedly constructive lenses, Michael Barnett saw changes in the international relations of the Arab world as "conversations" and "moments of normative contestation," of which, he argued in the early 1990s, there have been five: from 1920, when the Ottoman Empire collapsed, to 1945, the year the Arab League was established; from 1945 to the founding of the Baghdad Pact in 1955; from the 1956 Suez Canal War to the 1967 Arab-Israeli war; from 1967 to the 1990 Persian Gulf War; and from 1990 on.[16] The political landscape of the Arab world, and also that of the larger Middle East, continues to be hotly contested by divisive debates and competing narratives.[17] If Barnett were to update his timeline, he would surely add distinct periods in inter-Arab politics before and after the 11 September 2001 watershed or the 2003 US invasion of Iraq. In either case, the Middle East has changed dramatically in its contemporary history, and there is no reason to believe that such dynamics will subside anytime soon.

For a brief period in the early 1970s, an informal "Arab Triangle" of the largest Arab state (Egypt), the richest (Saudi Arabia), and the most Pan-Arab (Syria) emerged and sought to forge an Arab consensus around issues of war and peace.[18] But soon the effort fell victim to distrust among the leaders involved and their increasingly divergent priorities. The ensuing paralysis lasted well into the 1990s with a paralyzed Arab League not meeting even once between 1990 and 1996.[19] The narrow leverage that some regional states had been able to carve out diminished once the Cold War ended, narrowing their autonomy even more and facilitating unchecked US hegemony.[20] The result, expectedly, has been the steady erosion of the bargaining power of the Arab states in the international system. "The Arab core," one observer went so far as to say, has been dissolved, making references to "an Arab world" seemingly "obsolete" and meaningless.[21]

The early 2000s were no kinder to the vanishing Arab core. Egypt, the self-proclaimed "spiritual and political leader of the Arab world" as far back as the 1950s,[22] had by the 1980s degenerated into a "stalled society" thanks to the immovable kleptocracy sitting atop its political system.[23] Bids for the leadership of the Arab world notwithstanding,[24] the next couple of decades did not necessarily see a noticeable rise in Egypt's fortunes domestically or internationally. President Hosni Mubarak, like his equally unsavory Tunisian cohort Zine El Abidine Ben Ali, might have masked his own age thanks to hair dye, but he could not mask the ailments of his aging regime. Egypt tried once again to emerge as the Middle East's undisputed leader, but there was little it could do to reverse or to at least slow the increasing penetration of the United States into the region and the spreading of American military "footprints" from Afghanistan to Morocco. For its part Iran sought to play a leadership role across the Middle East and the Muslim world, and for a few brief years former president Mohammad Khatami's pleasant demeanor and smiles made some inroads among the chronically suspicious political elites in the Arabian Peninsula. But before long Khatami's successor, Mahmoud Ahmadinejad, managed to erode what appeal and soft power Iran had acquired. The country did manage to collect a series of strategic allies to countenance some of the combined pressures on it by Israel and the United States—Hamas, Hezbollah, Syria, Iraqi Shia leaders—but alliance-making with actors of dubious durability does not a powerbroker make. Iran's desperate forging of alliances should not be mistaken for a sign of power and confidence. By the end of the 2000s, the region's leader remained as elusive as ever.

But soon the states of the Middle East had bigger problems on their hands than not having a regional leadership core. In 2011, the Egyptian kleptocracy's death was hastened by throngs of Cairians who, inspired by the Jasmine Revolution in Tunisia, gathered in the iconic Tahrir Square and refused to leave until the dictatorship was gone. By the time Tahrir's temperature was on the rise Ben Ali had already left for exile, in Saudi Arabia, so hurried in his departure that stashes of cash worth millions of dollars were left in one of his palaces. The contagion soon spread. Yemen erupted next, followed by Bahrain, Libya, and Syria. An Arab Spring got underway, reaching as far from its epicenter as the Eastern Province of Saudi Arabia and prompting its panicked reaction and calls for a counterrevolution aimed at reversing the tide.[25]

Colonel Moammar Qaddafi's fall in Libya was perhaps the most emblematic of the tide sweeping across the region. When the Libyan uprising was first gathering steam, Qaddafi dismissed the protestors as "rats" and vowed to eradicate them with unmatched fury. Six months later, dirty and on the run, he was found by Libyan fighters hiding in a sewer pipe near the city of Sirte, begging his captors not to shoot him. They did not oblige. Tellingly, in a sign of broader trends across the region, on the day that Qaddafi's palace in Tripoli fell to the rebels, the flag that was hoisted atop the building was that of Qatar, a sign, no doubt, of the tiny sheikhdom's surprising reach and power. Qatar's flag was soon replaced by Libya's own new flag. But the symbolic importance of seeing the Qatari flag over Qaddafi's one-time headquarters was hard to miss. A new regional power had risen.

This had been the result of the convergence of a number of factors. As Vali Nasr observes, it is "economics [that] has more to do with determining the pecking order in the Middle East than the region's miasmic tumult of feuds, wars, and saber rattling would lead one to believe."[26] At the same time, throughout contemporary times, international regimes and institutions in the Middle East, such as those constructed by the Arab League and the Gulf Cooperation Council (GCC), have tended to be weak due to low levels of mutual trust among their constituent members, strong preference across the region for bilateral treaty arrangements over multilateral arrangements, low levels of economic interdependence and trade, and low levels of functional cooperation.[27] This has in turn opened up space for the smaller and more affluent states to make their presence felt in regional politics.

Further, the critical role played by globalization cannot be denied. With the forces of globalization proving themselves difficult to stop even for the most insular of states, some states have found themselves better situated in the core-periphery structure to profit from interaction with and integration within the new global political economy.[28] Globalization has its winners and losers; some, like Iran, are excluded from it by a combination of US policies and their leaders' fears of the forces it might unleash, while others, like the UAE and Qatar, are positioned not just to embrace it but to ride its crest on their own terms and to their own advantage.

Slowly but surely the balance of power is shifting toward the Persian Gulf monarchies, whose wealthy, sophisticated private sector is leading the charge to integrate into the various currents of globalization. The GCC states are emerging as a "strategic and commercial pivot" around which tectonic shifts in the global balance of power are taking place.[29] Although in many parts of the Middle East globalization is seen as a threat and an opportunity by the forces of the West for further exploitation of national resources,[30] in the oil monarchies its financial and economic benefits are embraced and welcomed. The world is indeed witnessing the "multifaceted and dynamic participation of the GCC states within the processes of global change."[31] In the political economy of the twenty-first century, as Luciani rightly observes, it is these public and private actors who have a much better chance of success as compared to the rest of the region.[32] One of the critical factors that sets GCC economies apart from those of the rest of the Middle East is the region's increasing financialization, rooted in the precipitous growth of its financial capacity as a result of investments during the second oil boom.[33] There is broad consensus that the states of the Arabian Peninsula are emerging as "new regional muscles" in the multipolar world economy and are not shying away from flexing their economic muscles.[34]

Today, the Persian Gulf is emerging as the new center of gravity of the Middle East because of its energy reserves and its financial resources.[35] The region's non-oil states have yet to come to terms with the new realities of regional politics and the ascendance of those they once so readily dismissed as irrelevant and marginal. "Simply put," maintains Luciani, "the 'historical' Arab states have been unable to accept that the basis of power in the contemporary world has changed: not only are oil barrels more important than guns, but also money is more important than population size."[36] Luciani's astute analysis was written before the Arab Spring erupted in 2011, following which the GCC's relative immunity to the uprisings, with the exception of Bahrain, only further strengthened its comparative advantage over those Middle Eastern states racked by popular uprisings, the instability they endured, and their resulting preoccupation with reconstituting political order rather than furthering economic progress.

Luciani talks of the Arab states' resentment toward the rise of the newcomers, but he might as well have included Iran also. By virtue of its size and geographic position—a 2,400-kilometer coastline along the northern shores of the Persian Gulf, a number of deep-sea ports, and vast deposits of oil and natural gas—the size and apparent capabilities of its armed forces, and its comparative strategic depth, Iran assumes that it indeed is the dominant power in the Persian Gulf. And, insofar as brute force is concerned it may indeed be.[37] Iran is, after all, "the most important country in the region in terms of the future of Persian Gulf security and

stability."[38] But, as argued earlier, in today's world hard power is a
sufficient or even adequate instrument of furthering national in[
Along with the likes of Egypt, Iraq, and Syria, Iran's troubled relationship with the global economy, and its inability to come to terms with the
dynamic currents of economic change and transformation swirling around
it, are bound to drag it behind its neighbors to the south. Iran may be strategically important to the Persian Gulf, but it is rapidly running the risk
of becoming an obsolete dinosaur amid a group of dynamic transformers.

Significantly, the ascendance of the GCC states in the global financial
arena appears to be part of a broader realignment of global power away
from the West and in the direction of the East. According to Joseph Nye,
power in the world is distributed in a pattern that resembles a three-
dimensional chess game. On top there is the unipolar military power of the
United States, followed in the middle by multipolar economic powers such
as those of the US, Europe, Japan, and China, capped at the bottom by a
complex web of transnational relations that include both state and nonstate
actors.[39] But Nye would be the first one to agree that his pyramidal conceptualization of the world is far from static and that its configuration is
bound to change soon, or perhaps is already changing. In fact, the states of
the Arabian Peninsula appear to be "enmeshed in a transformative rebalancing of the global balance of geo-economic power from west to east."[40]
As the West has been going through a period of profound financial distress
and economic crisis since the late 2000s, the GCC states have been using
their enhanced financial powers to buy up high-profile and iconic global
brands (Harrods, Ferrari, and Porsche), recapitalize otherwise depleted
Western financial institutions (Merrill Lynch, Citigroup, and Barclays
Bank), and carve out distinctive niches for themselves in global interest
areas (mediation and renewable energy).[41]

How did we get to where we are today? The international relations of
the Persian Gulf have always revolved around controlling its strategic resources, be they safe passage, pearling, or oil. The region has thus received
sustained attention from outside military and political powers dating back
to the early 1500s, when the Portuguese first arrived on the scene.[42] From
the earliest times, there has been a dynamic interplay between internal and
external factors across the Persian Gulf, helping shape the region's state
system.[43] The twentieth century brought with it the discovery of oil, and,
soon thereafter, the seemingly inescapable British. Oil helped shape the

consolidation of the emerging fragile states and ensured their otherwise doubtful survival into the twenty-first century.[44] Oil gave the region its strategic significance, but it also increased the likelihood of conflict. On rare occasions, it also facilitated cooperation among the regional actors.[45] More frequently, however, it has drawn to the region the kind of attention it did not need.

When the British withdrew from the region, between 1961 and 1971, many of the fledgling states that dotted up and down the Persian Gulf were unsure of their survivability, and worried about the expansionist threats of Iraq, Iran, and Saudi Arabia. But, as fortune would have it, they survived, and, in fact, thanks to a boom in oil prices, thrived. Throughout the 1970s, amid a collective sense of unease and apprehension, state-building processes were set into motion across the Arab Peninsula.[46] By the 1980s, their resilience proven, these small states were ready for a bigger stage.

State behavior is conditioned by the opportunities and challenges it faces, both internally and from the outside. Middle East states, especially the GCC oil monarchies, resort to omnibalancing in their efforts to maintain and enhance their legitimacy by simultaneously responding to pressures from below and from the outside.[47] Gregory Gause maintains that the states of the Persian Gulf are prompted to action not so much by concerns over the distribution of power in the region but by perceived threats to their own domestic stability. The biggest of these threats, Gause argues, are the salient transnational identities that can be used by regional actors to mobilize support across national boundaries. In the hands of ambitious leaders, these identities can be a potent force for political mobilization and quite possibly instability, particularly for vulnerable states with questionable legitimacies. Earlier, the Iranian Revolution had ended the tacit agreement that had emerged among regional states not to interfere in each other's domestic politics. A collective panic had set in that the revolution's fury would reach the largely tranquil shores of the Arabian Peninsula. "It is," after all, "at the intersection of ideational and material factors that we will find the explanations of the war and alliances we see in the Gulf."[48] It was these fears that in 1981 prompted the six oil monarchies of the Arabian Peninsula to set up a buffer against Iraq and Iran in the form of the GCC.

From its very inception, the GCC suffered from lingering suspicions among some of its members, principally Qatar and later also the UAE, that it was a forum meant to legitimize and institutionalize Saudi Arabia's hegemony over the smaller sheikhdoms.[49] Lack of mutual trust has meant the continued preference of the GCC states for bilateralism over multi-lateralism, thus undermining the emergence of internal consensus among its member states and weakening its collective decision-making frame-work.[50] According to Joseph Kostiner, "GCC strategic planning is an ex-ercise in disparate security, displaying similar perceptions but particular priorities."[51] Qatar in particular revels in its pursuit of an independent, at times seemingly maverick, diplomacy of its own. In recent years, the United Arab Emirates, in an effort to highlight its diplomatic autonomy in relation to Saudi Arabia, is also trying to have a more dynamic, indepen-dent, and innovative foreign policy of its own.[52] The GCC state's continued preference for the preservation of the status quo has had the ironic effect of spurring them into action in times of acute regional crisis—as was the case during the Arab Spring—to prevent the crisis from deepening.

Uncoordinated and underdeveloped as it has been, the GCC security ar-chitecture has two pillars—the United States and the six member states.[53] The Persian Gulf is often seen as "a cauldron of insecurity" in which the United States has sought to play the role of an "active balancer."[54] This bal-ancing has more often been directed against prevailing threats rather than against a predominant power.[55] This is despite the fact that most regional actors, in line with other small states, have shown a marked preference for diplomacy over armed action as a means of conflict resolution.[56] Ul-timately, it has been American-led balancing, most recently against Iran, that has shaped the Persian Gulf's intra-regional politics. Up until the 2003 US invasion of Iraq, the Persian Gulf was a tripolar regional system with Iran, Iraq, and Saudi Arabia as the region's three major players, with the US playing an active, increasingly direct role in balancing against threats to its interests and its regional allies.[57] The US invasion removed Iraq from the equation and left Iran and Saudi Arabia as the two dominant regional powers, along with the ever-present United States. As Ulrichsen points out, this balancing system, in place since the early 1970s, has been anything but successful; it has led to three bloody wars, and has done precious little to lessen the region's chronic tensions.[58] However, there are no signs that it will be transformed or dismantled anytime soon.

The steady rise in influence of countries such as Saudi Arabia, Qatar, and the United Arab Emirates, is "affecting regional politics in ways that do not always meet with the interests of the major regional actors,"[59] most notably those of Egypt, Syria, and Iran.[60] The shift between "leadership" and "strategic follower" roles has created tensions between Egypt, on the one side, and Qatar and Saudi Arabia, on the other, and also between Qatar and Saudi Arabia.[61] But intraregional relations have not all been rosy either, with intense competition, and at times quite serious friction, particularly between Saudi Arabia, the self-ascribed leader of the Arabian Peninsula, and the new kid on the block, Qatar. Realists often categorize states into major, middle, and small powers, ascribing to each different goals and interests based on their capabilities rather than the institutions to which they belong or the ideas they espouse. Unlike major powers, which have the broadest range of interests spanning the length of the international system, small powers "often remain on the sidelines . . . or succumb to the power of the larger states."[62] A number of other scholars have added to the top of the pyramid a "dominant power," which manages the international (or regional) system "under rules that benefit its allies and satisfy their national aspirations."[63] According to this schema, states at the bottom of the hierarchy tend to have the most grievances and seek deliberately to change the rules and norms that underlie the international system, especially if they are located in the vicinity of a much more powerful and bigger state. In such cases, a relationship of "confrontational competition" is likely to characterize the relationship between the two unequal states.[64] As will be discussed in the chapters that follow, confrontational competition generally sums up Qatar's relationship with Saudi Arabia, a relationship that is sometimes more and sometimes less confrontational, but is always competitive. When a challenger nation is unsatisfied with the regional or international status quo and seeks parity with a dominant power, the likelihood of conflict is greater.[65] As the two cases of Qatar and Saudi Arabia and Qatar and the UAE demonstrate, parity and overtaking both have brought the small sheikhdom into frequent competition and rivalry with its two bigger neighbors.

No matter what might have happened in the lower rungs of the Persian Gulf's power hierarchy, the United States has placed itself at its top since the British withdrawal in 1971, ensuring that the waterway remains an "American lake" regardless of what happens to and among the regional states. The United States has consistently considered the Persian Gulf to be of strategic significance since World War II.[66] The US Navy, in fact, first started using naval facilities in Bahrain in 1948.[67] The "Americanization" of the Persian Gulf initially started out slowly. But it picked up pace with a vengeance in the 1990s, when American footprints began appearing across the Persian Gulf region in unprecedented numbers. Still, for much of the twentieth century US policy in the Persian Gulf was one of "reactive engagement"; bereft of a grand strategy and with occasional inconsistencies and contradictions, the United States frequently found itself simply reacting to regional developments and challenges as they arose.[68]

In 1979, two major crises led to a fundamental reassessment of US strategy toward the Persian Gulf—the Iranian Revolution and the Soviet invasion of Afghanistan—both of which brought with them a direct military role for the United States in the Persian Gulf.[69] Ironically, although at the time tensions between the United States and Iran were at an all-time high due to the storming of the US embassy in Tehran and the holding of American diplomats hostage by the Iranian revolutionaries, the United States began worrying about a Soviet attack on Iran in order to gain access to the Persian Gulf. In his 1980 State of the Union address to the US Congress, in what was meant as a warning against such a possibility, President Carter outlined elements of what came to be known as the Carter Doctrine:

> Let our position be absolutely clear: any attempt by any outside force to gain control of the Persian Gulf region will be regarded as an assault on the vital interests of the United States of America, and such an assault will be repelled by any means necessary, including military force.[70]

The Soviets never did invade Iran. Neither did the Americans see any reason to leave the Persian Gulf. From the American perspective after all, as one former US ambassador put it, "the United States will have no choice but to remain a deeply engaged power in the region."[71] As US-Iranian tensions deepened throughout the 1980s and the 1990s, and as the collapse of the Soviet Union freed America's hands militarily, the United States steadily expanded its presence in the Persian Gulf. In 1987, the United States began reflagging Kuwaiti tankers passing through the Persian Gulf to protect them from the spillover effects of the Iran-Iraq war. Soon after the United States led the campaign to eject Iraqi occupation forces out of Kuwait in 1991, the American military presence in and around the Persian Gulf became increasingly expansive and semi-permanent. Throughout the 1990s, that presence deepened and assumed multiple dimensions.

By the late 1990s and early 2000s, three developments converged to bring to an end the US policy of balancing in the Persian Gulf. They included the rise of the United States as the world's only superpower following the end of the Cold War, the rise of transnational terrorism, and the ascent within Washington's policymaking circles of ideological neoconservatives who were determined to reshape global politics.[72] In fact, spurred on by the 9/11 attacks on New York and Washington, DC, America's neo-conservative policymakers substituted their strategic objective of stability in the Persian Gulf through balancing for an ambitious effort to redraw the region's international relations.[73] That the Iraqi campaign turned into a bloody and disastrous quagmire seemed to matter little to Washington's ideological crusaders. Soon, they began floating ideas of regime change in Iran also. The appearance of a kinder, gentler US foreign policy under President Barak Obama, conveyed through the new president's Muslim-friendly rhetoric, hardly masked the continuity in America's hawkish foreign and security policies toward the Middle East and the Persian Gulf. As one observer put it, the "smothering embrace" of the United States continued unabated.[74]

This smothering embrace is welcomed by the GCC states, which continue to be the biggest purchasers of US military hardware. According to a 2012 US Congressional report, from 2007 to 2010, the GCC states spent over $26.7 billion on American arms purchases, more than any other region in the world, and in 2011 alone, the United States agreed to sell Saudi Arabia $29.4 billion in fighter aircrafts, in what is to date "the single largest arms sale in the history of the [country]."[75] As the report concluded, despite phenomenal investments in their militaries, "most Gulf states are not yet fully capable of independently sustaining significant tactical support to the United States in times of crisis,"[76] a limitation of which especially the smaller sheikhdoms are keenly aware. The United States, therefore, is most likely to "remain a central part of the Gulf security framework" in the near future,[77] with the full and eager consent of the GCC states.

Paradoxically, although "Washington is a direct, day-to-day player in Gulf politics now"—or perhaps because of it—"the new disposition does not appear to be stable at all."[78] The Persian Gulf is more volatile today than at any other time in the past, on the brink of a catastrophic eruption as each of its claimants to power—Iran, Saudi Arabia, the United States—looks at the other warily and threatens to unleash its wrath if push comes to shove. One of the primary beneficiaries of these tensions, ironically, has been Qatar (for more on this, see chapter 3). In light of the increasingly ideological and unilateralist foreign policy during the George W. Bush Administration, tensions grew between the United States and its close ally Saudi Arabia, and questions were raised about how the kingdom could continue to fit into the US security architecture.[79] This opened up space for Qatar to deepen the niche it was carving out for itself as a critically important player and a reliably dependable ally located in the heart of the Persian Gulf.

Another important dimension of the international politics of the Persian Gulf is its increasing trade and investment ties with Pacific Asia. Strong and comprehensive trade ties between the two regions—involving especially the GCC and China, Japan, and South Korea—have transformed what was only a few years ago a mere "marriage of convenience" into a "comprehensive, long term mutual commitment" binding the two sides along multiple axes involving trade and investments. China and Japan have the second and third highest oil consumption needs in the world, behind the United States, and South Korea is also among the world's top ten energy consumers. Despite their overt dependence on hydrocarbon imports from the Persian Gulf, Pacific Asian countries make little efforts to conceal or alleviate their dependence and are, instead, expanding their trade and investment ties with the Persian Gulf on several additional fronts. Japan remains the Persian Gulf's single most important exporter. China's nonhydrocarbon trade with the Persian Gulf is also growing at a precipitous rate.[80]

The ensuing commercial ties between the two sides run deep, with Japanese overseas development assistance to the Persian Gulf growing significantly in the 1970s.[81] In the 1980s, Saudi Arabia, at the time the dominant diplomatic power in the Arabian Peninsula, consented to the GCC states establishing trade and diplomatic relations with China.[82] It did not take long for trade between the two sides to mushroom. Between 1981 and 2004, GCC imports from the United States decreased by 15 percent while imports from China and the rest of the non-Western world increased by the same percentage.[83] Across the Persian Gulf, Pacific Asian companies are being awarded major contracts, further deepening the growing economic interdependence between the two regions. The 2008 credit crunch introduced some wrinkles into the Persian Gulf–Pacific Asia economic relationship, but it did not significantly affect the depth and upward direction of the growing trade and investment between the two regions.[84] By 2010, imports from Pacific Asia to the Persian Gulf monarchies amounted to some $63 billion a year, most of it in the form of manufactured goods and services.[85] This was a product of the GCC's "look East" policy of the early 2000s, viewing the expansion of trade and investment ties with East Asia as "logical" because it "carries no political agenda."[86]

Today, the GCC's eastward look has resulted in the expansion of trade and economic ties between the two regions along manifold lines, except for defense and security, which remains an American preserve. India has signed defense cooperation agreements with Qatar and Oman, but the agreements are superficial at best and cover areas such as maritime security, the sharing of data, and common threat perceptions.[87] It is, instead, in trade and investments, flowing in both directions, in which the real interface between the GCC and Pacific Asia lies. Almost all of Qatar's oil sales go to China, for example, and China has signaled its commitment to long-term energy trade with Qatar.[88] Despite concerted efforts at diversification, China's gas imports are likely to grow in the future, principally from the Persian Gulf.[89] Japan and South Korea are both also heavily dependent on gas and oil imports from the Persian Gulf, with Japan importing fully 96 percent of its gas from the region and South Korea 93 percent.[90] Equally important is the role of migrant labor, with approximately 70 percent of the GCC's labor force coming from Asia, and sending home some $40 billion in remittances annually.[91]

A New Center of Gravity

By all accounts, the GCC has emerged as a global economic powerhouse. In fact, along with the other so-called mega-emergers, comprised of the BRIC countries (Brazil, Russia, India, and China) and Mexico, the economies of the Arabian Peninsula are expected to grow until 2020–2030, before convergence with OECD levels of per capita gross domestic product is expected to dampen their growth potential.[92] GCC policymakers have developed a consensus on three themes, namely asset market liberalization, privatization through initial public offerings, and increased investment in infrastructure, each of which have enhanced the attractiveness of the region as a source for increased foreign direct investment.[93] Both individually and in combination with one another, these developments have turned the GCC into an important economic force.[94]

This economic rise has been facilitated through a confluence of three primary developments. First, there continues to be sustained high global energy demands, whose prices have been consistently high due to market speculation and chronic tensions in the Persian Gulf region, most notably between the United States and Iran. Global energy demands, which have been growing at 1.85 percent over the past decade, are expected to grow at a robust annual rate of 2.9 percent to 2020, before gradually retreating to 2.1 percent per annum through the 2030s and to stabilize around 1 percent per annum thereafter.[95] Energy demands on the parts of the BRICs, with whom the GCC maintains close and expanding commercial relations, are projected to grow around 5.3 percent annually into the mid-2010s before declining to 2 percent in the 2020s and 1.3 percent thereafter.[96] The Persian Gulf remains central to the global energy industry. In 2010, the Persian Gulf states, including Iraq, were estimated to hold more than 54 percent of the world's oil reserves and more than 40 percent of its natural gas.[97]

In the coming decades, the GCC is expected to continue to capitalize on its energy resources to supply the bulk of global demand. It is estimated that between 2005 and 2030, approximately 38 percent of the projected increase in the global oil supply will come from the GCC, whose production will grow by 72 percent.[98] In specific relation to Qatar, the sheikhdom is expected to lead the GCC's natural gas production in the coming decades, which is expected to grow by 200 percent between 2005 and 2030.[99] This will not be inexpensive. The International Energy Agency estimates that the total capital expenditure needed by the GCC states to sustain a steady 2.2 percent increase in crude oil production and a 5.6 percent increase in natural gas production will be approximately $650 billion over the next twenty-five years (at 2006 prices).[100] If current dynamics and trends continue, there is no reason to believe that the GCC states will not be able to come up with the needed resources, either on their own or through FDI flows, to continue investing in their oil industries.

A second development facilitating the GCC's economic rise has been the increasing ability of local actors to make the best use of oil windfall revenues.[101] This has been facilitated by the development of absorptive financial and infrastructural capacity on the part of the GCC states, which has enabled them to retain much of the windfalls from the second oil boom (2002–2008) within the region instead of recycling it through Western financial institutions as they did in the 1970s.[102] The establishment of a number of additional investment vehicles, the most notable of which are sovereign wealth funds and government investment corporations, in addition of course to Central Banks, is a case in point.[103] Between 2001 and 2006, GCC-based bank assets doubled to $500 billion.[104] Although GCC sovereign wealth funds (SWFs) took heavy hits during the 2008 financial crisis, they were used effectively to shore up and stabilize domestic economies.[105] Martin Hvidt maintains that even at a modest 5 percent interest earning on current investments, GCC states will earn an additional $77 billion on annual income.[106] The combined global wealth managed by the SWFs is expected to grow at 15 percent per annum until 2015, reaching $10 trillion. For many countries, especially those in the Arabian Peninsula, this means that they will become increasingly asset-based rather than commodity-based economies as their revenues from foreign assets will exceed their commodity revenues.[107] There are also massive sums of private revenues that are being invested by the so-called high net worth individuals.[108] According to one estimate, private individuals who actively invest in global financial markets hold at least 40 percent of the foreign wealth purchased with petrodollars.[109]

The ensuing financial influence has brought the GCC states active membership and influence in international financial organizations such as the World Trade Organization. Along with the BRICs, in fact, Saudi Arabia has sought to reshape the architecture of international financial institutions.[110] The GCC states have also begun taking "proactive steps in reshaping the institutional design of global frameworks of governance."[111] According to one observer, membership in such international forums enables the GCC to "benchmark domestic governance to international standards, while participation in an international rules-based system introduces a new dynamic to domestic reform processes. It also enhances regional familiarity with global values and helps to embed them in local discourses while situating Gulf states' views of global governance within a broader non-Western paradigm shared by many developing countries, including India and China."[112] This is one of those areas where the rubber of globalization hits the road, and in so doing, makes the GCC states beneficiaries of their expansive engagement with the global economy.

Further enhancing the GCC's nexus with the global economy has been the establishment of world-class airlines that are playing critical roles in facilitated linkages between industrial and financial hubs in the East and the West. Etihad, Emirates, and Qatar Airways have all emerged as "super-connectors" capable of connecting any two parts of the world with one stopover in the Persian Gulf, therefore bringing about a "fundamental reshaping of the map of global aviation power."[113] As high-profile national symbols, these airlines also serve important branding purposes, flying thousands of passengers from one destination to another through GCC-based national flag carriers. By 2015, Emirates is expected to become the world's largest operator of wide-body jets.[114]

Related to this has been a third development, namely savvy investment decisions on the part of the GCC, resulting in flows of ever-increasing amounts of FDI into the region from both the East and the West. FDI flowing into the GCC shot up from $392 million in 2000 to approximately $63 billion in 2008, an increase of 160 times.[115] Although following the 2008 global financial crisis the flow of FDI into the larger Middle East declined significantly, FDI flow into the UAE (Abu Dhabi and Dubai), Saudi Arabia, and Qatar have continued to grow after 2009.[116] These investments reflect decisions meant to minimize the effects of sharp oil price movements and other exogenous shocks, such as an eruption of hostilities involving Iran, to which the region remains vulnerable.[117]

Two features of the current GCC investments are particularly noteworthy. First, insofar as their domestic investments are concerned, in addition to enhancing infrastructure and attracting further FDIs, revenues from the second oil boom are being used to invest substantial sums in human development, most notably tertiary education, health care, and the fostering of knowledge-based economies in preparation for the post-oil period.[118] Perhaps the most dramatic example of this type of investment has been in the establishment of new universities, or the attraction of branch campuses, which resulted in the growth of universities in the GCC from 1 in the 1950s (in Saudi Arabia) to 13 in the 1970s, 29 in the 1980s, 40 in the 1990s, and 117 in the 2000s, an increase of over 290 percent in a decade (Figure 2.1). Similarly significant investments have been made at the primary and secondary school levels, as well as in public health, skills enhancement and job creation schemes, and other areas of human development.

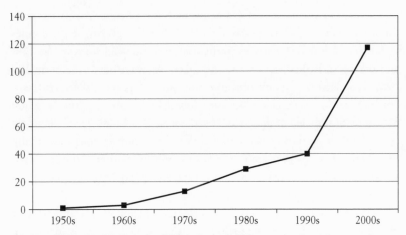

Figure 1.1. Number of universities in the Gulf Cooperation Council states
Note: Data collected by author.

Second, in addition to investing domestically, GCC states have decided to invest regionally, within the Middle East, specifically in North Africa and the Levant. These investment decisions, which have helped perpetuate the uneven relationship between the GCC and other parts of the Arab world, are driven by several factors. These investments are seen as one way to help ensure economic stability in a region from which many Gulf-based migrant laborers come.[119] Equally helpful have been major economic reform programs launched in the Mashreq beginning in the mid-1990s, such as the one initiated in Egypt in July 2004, meant to offer regional investors attractive investment environments. There have been other indirect benefits, such as increased remittances from GCC-based laborers back to their home countries, and expanding exports and tourism revenues, especially before the 2011 uprisings.[120] To help stem the tide of the Arab Spring from engulfing other regional monarchies, Saudi Arabia, Kuwait, the UAE, and Qatar each pledged $1.25 billion worth of developmental assistance to Jordan, though by late 2012 none of the aid had yet materialized.[121] Most countries of the Middle East are clamoring for Persian Gulf investments, having made the attraction of private sovereign capital from those they once frowned on as one of the cornerstones of their national development strategies, with the small sheikhdoms "dominating development throughout the region."[122] For example, by one account approximately 50 and 75 percent of stocks in the Egyptian and Jordanian stock exchanges, respectively, are owned by Persian Gulf Arabs.[123]

There has been another critical issue that has facilitated the phenomenal economic growth of the GCC states, namely inexpensive and compliant labor. A proper treatment of this important topic is beyond the scope of the task at hand here.[124] But brief mention must be made of the significant comparative advantage that politically pliant labor has given the GCC. Demographic limitations and labor shortages have long prompted the countries of the Arabian Peninsula to rely on imported labor for their economies. In the 1950s and 1960s, most migrant workers to the Persian Gulf were Egyptians, Palestinians, and Yemenis, many of whom had strong revolutionary and often antimonarchical sentiments and therefore became sources of political tension within their host societies. In the ensuing decades, culminating in the aftermath of Iraq's ejection from Kuwait in 1990, across the Arabian Peninsula Arab migrant workers were steadily replaced by imported labor from South Asia, who came with no ideological baggage and who were far more easily segregated from the rest of the population. Since then labor migration has been used for purposes of both rapid economic development—through relying on relatively cheap and pliant labor—as well as political consolidation.[125] Although there are still significant communities of migrant workers from the rest of the Arab world in the GCC states, many belong to the ranks of professionals, most are nonideological, and are more interested in commercial pursuits, and all depend on highly restrictive residency permits that make the risks of political activism outweigh any potential benefits.

Altogether, a combination of structural changes rooted in global economic currents, savvy domestic and regional investments, and careful planning have combined to result in the transformation of the GCC states into highly consequential—indeed in most cases powerful—global economic players. The continuing windfalls of the 2002–2008 oil boom, coupled with systemic flaws in the Western-led Washington Consensus of economic development, have facilitated the enhanced positions of the Arab Peninsula states, resulting in "Gulf policymakers' increasing confidence in the international arena and greater awareness of their pivotal position within the global rebalancing of economic and political power."[126] More important, if present trends continue, and there appears no reason to believe they would not, the disparities between the wealthy, increasingly more powerful states of the Persian Gulf and the rest of the region are likely to grow.[127]

This largely positive analysis of the GCC states in general and their economies in particular is not to imply that there are no potential and actual signs of trouble in paradise. In fact, the GCC states face multiple challenges in areas of security, politics, and even economic development. Although Qatar is by no means immune to these challenges, I maintain that it is better positioned, both through the policies pursued by its leaders and though structural conditions with which they have had little to do, to deal with these challenges. Before elaborating on Qatar's comparative advantages, I outline some of the more serious existing or potential security, political, and economic challenges with which the other GCC states have to contend.

Insofar as security challenges are concerned, Fred Lawson has identified four nearly intractable security dilemmas faced by the Persian Gulf states. The first is what he labels as "the classic security dilemma" in which states must choose whether or not to enhance their security in relation to another state. The second is "the alliance dilemma" in which states have to manage relations with allies and adversaries simultaneously. Third is the trade-off between relying on an outside power for protection and maintaining domestic political stability. Fourth is the "paradoxical choice between forging strategic partnerships with external patrons and keeping the region insulated from global rivalries and disputes."[128]

Kristian Ulrichsen somberly asserts that "difficult challenges lie ahead for the oil monarchies of the Gulf."[129] He calls for attention to "non-military sources of potential insecurity"[130]—ranging from environmental depletion to food and resource scarcity—which run the risk of upsetting internal social cohesion and are likely to "inject potent new sources of tension and sites of contestation into the intra- and international relations of the Gulf States."[131] The flood of expatriate workers, both skilled and unskilled, deepens "long-felt existential fears."[132] Given the rapid and profound processes of change underway across the Arabian Peninsula, there are often troubling questions about the perceived erosion of national identity and the pace and direction of the changes altering social norms and mores.[133] These and other security challenges are likely to be more stark and more pressing in the era of globalization and especially in the post-oil era, and they are far more likely to revolve around issues of human security rather than on the state.[134] For example, the increasing connections between two previously distinct regional security complexes, namely those of the Persian Gulf and the Horn of Africa, are likely to draw the GCC states closer to the ripple effects of chronic instability in Yemen and Somalia.[135] In particular, if Yemen were to become a failed state, it could "expose the GCC to the multiple sources of human insecurity emanating from the Horn of Africa-Yemen nexus."[136]

Perhaps no other development is as threatening to all of the states of the Persian Gulf as the very real possibility of running out of oil. Although the ruling elites have demonstrated remarkable adaptability and survivability, their ability to navigate the post-oil era without fundamental and far-reaching reforms is questionable. While the GCC states have shown a capacity to evolve and to survive, they have also demonstrated a persistent hesitation to implement much-needed reforms that might result in any loosening of political and economic control.[137] The younger generation is unable to relate to the pre-oil era, or to comprehend the post-oil era. But the need for reformulating the current social contract is inescapable in the post-oil era. It is doubtful that the current cradle-to-grave welfare states of the GCC can survive into the post-oil era. Already, oil reserves in Bahrain and Oman are projected to run out by 2025.[138] How the Omani and Bahraini polities react to such a development when it does occur is an open question.

Even in stable economic times, the phenomenal ascendance of the GCC is not without its problems or its unintended negative consequences. Uneven distribution of energy resources and therefore wealth across the Arabian Peninsula has led to the creation of "pockets of energy poverty" throughout the region.[139] To the Omani and Bahraini question marks posed above one may add the resource-poor emirates of the UAE—especially Ajman, Fujairah, Ras al-Khaimah, Sharjah, and Umm al-Quwain—and their coping mechanisms, or lack thereof, with the increasingly glaring discrepancies in their levels of wealth compared to Abu Dhabi, Qatar, Kuwait, and perhaps even Dubai.

Similarly, it is not clear who will live and work in the thousands of properties that are being built across the GCC at breakneck speed.[140] From oil wells have sprung up gleaming cities, touching the skies with their high-rise towers and protruding into the seas with their artificial islands. Deserts have been transformed into green cities with millions of trees already planted and millions more planned for the future.[141] But there simply are not enough nationals demographically to occupy the apartments in all the high-rises being built, with which, incidentally, their traditional housing preferences have little in common. There are also only so many wealthy Western expatriate professionals, and low-skilled migrant workers cannot afford luxury accommodations even if they were allowed to occupy them. After the Dubai real estate bubble burst in 2008, many construction projects across the GCC were scaled back in order to avoid a similar fate in the construction and the real estate sectors.[142] But in almost all of the region's major cities occupancy rates continue to remain low, while new high-rises continue to go up.[143] Whether there is merit in the philosophy of "build it, and they will come" is another open question.

Politics is notoriously unpredictable, and Middle East politics is especially notorious. But the broader trends that I have outlined are hard to ignore. The Middle East's center of gravity has shifted. The traditional power centers of the region—Cairo, Baghdad, Tehran, and Damascus—are being overshadowed by their much younger, smaller, and far more agile counterparts of Abu Dhabi, Doha, Dubai, and Riyadh. At a time when Egypt continues to be gripped with the aftereffects of its historic revolution, when Syria teeters on the verge of a civil war, when Iran preoccupies itself with picking fights with a West only too keen to bully it around, and when Iraq tries to finds its way after the hasty departure of its American occupiers, the countries of the GCC build new infrastructures and deepen existing ones, invite expertise from around the world to help them innovate and develop, plan incessantly for their futures, and concentrate on securing the health, wealth, and development of future generations. That much cannot be denied. Nor can it be denied that they face real obstacles and challenges in making their lofty goals a reality, and even, closer to home, at times holding the present course steady as occasional opponents pop up. In Bahrain's case we saw beginning in February and March of 2011, and before that from 1994 to 1999, the state's opponents rise up more than occasionally. Qatar is not by any means immune to the prospects of these challenges or the many potential insecurities that Ulrichsen outlines. But it does benefit from certain comparative advantages that enable it to better meet and deal with emerging challenges and to more effectively project its power.

Qatar's Comparative Advantage

Qatar's comparative advantage in relation to its neighbors across the Arabian Peninsula can be traced to four distinct yet interrelated factors. The first has to do with the structure of regional politics and Qatar's role and position within it. Kenneth Waltz's caution some years ago that an international system should not be reduced to its constituent units applies very much to the rise of Qatar and its regional role and international profile.[144] Surely Qatar's ascent regionally and globally is not Qatar's doing alone and is as much a product of systemwide changes as it is a direct result of the policies pursued by the Emiri Diwan. Earlier allusion was made to the preoccupation of the Middle East's traditional powers with more existential issues—as is the case with Egypt, Iraq, Syria, and Iran, for example—and the decline of their regional and international influence relative to more agile and focused actors. The regional system has thus opened the space and the opportunity for Qatar to make its presence felt and to push forward its regional and international agendas.

Reinforcing this was the exponential growth in Qatar's strategic importance for the United States following 9/11, the US military's subsequent departure from Saudi Arabia and its relocation in Qatar, and the US invasions of Afghanistan and Iraq, during which Qatar became home to the US military's Central Command and its largest forward operations base. As Robert Hunter points out, "Qatar—a country less subject to religious fervor than Saudi Arabia and also concerned about possible ambitions and intentions both of that large Arab neighbor and of Iran—became the primary locus for U.S. forces deployed on the ground in the region."[145] This did not mean that Qatar would automatically become a vassal or protectorate of the United States, or even bandwagon with it, but instead it embarked on a carefully calibrated policy of hedging whereby it ensured that it maintained open lines of communication with as many parties and actors as possible, even if they happened to be adversaries to one another. Raymond Hinnebusch correctly points out that there is a direct correlation between economic resources and security, on the one hand, and the ability and willingness of state leaders to "challenge or adjust the impact of external forces on the state," on the other.[146] This precisely explains Qatar's ability to take risks that others cannot afford.

The reference to Waltz should not be taken as an exclusive endorsement of realist explanations of Qatar's regional and international rise. Michael Barnett, the constructivist quoted earlier, sees, with some justification, inter-Arab politics as a constant struggle over determining "the norms of Arabism." The primary motivator in Arab international politics, he claims, has not been balance of power but rather the competition to see who can "more deftly deploy the symbols of Arabism."[147] Power emanates not from the barrels of guns and tanks—the effective use of which Middle Eastern leaders have excelled at only against their own peoples and not the enemy afar—but from the ability to define and control the symbols that give meaning to surrounding realities. Leaders have sought to control their rivals "through strategic framing and symbolic exchanges."[148] This appears to be exactly what Qatar is trying to do—to define and to lead, both symbolically and factually, what Arabism means in the twenty-first century.

Purposive leadership and attempts at agenda setting bespeak of the importance of agency. This has to do with a second factor that has facilitated Qatar's emergence as a tiny giant, namely the institutional autonomy and the policy agendas of the Qatari political leadership. Unlike the Kuwaiti system, whose proactive parliament at times brings the country's entire policymaking process to the brink of paralysis, or the factional politics of the Saudi royal family, or the besieged and largely unpopular Bahraini royals, Qatar's leadership is focused, unencumbered by the hassles of parliamentary politics, and, made-up as it is of a handful of individuals, is driven and determined in its pursuit of domestic, regional, and global ambitions. The emir of Qatar has articulated an ambitious vision of the country as a leader in Arab diplomacy, arts and culture, scientific innovation, and development. How realistic or substantive these goals and ambitions are is ultimately less important than the ability to pursue them—whether through purchase and wholesale importation or through mobilizing domestic resources, or both—and the perceptions that come with such pursuits. Justifiably or not, Qatar is generally perceived to be a leader, or to have substantive claims to leadership, in the Arab world. Perceptions often shape and become reality, regardless of whether or not they are accurate.

A third factor facilitating Qatar's rise to regional prominence, this one structural, has to do with domestic dynamics, namely lack of domestic fissures and fragmentations. Compared to most of its regional cohorts, Qatar enjoys remarkable social cohesion. Given their over-reliance on hydrocarbon exports, most GCC states have been quite vulnerable to cycles of boom and bust.[149] The one thing certain about oil is the uncertainty of its prices.[150] States with a fragile resource base in particular—most notably Bahrain, Yemen, and Saudi Arabia—can face serious challenges in times of economic downturns. The existence of numerous "fault-lines" and "fissures," along sectarian lines for example, can "heighten regime vulnerability to future politicization and contestation if resource scarcities develop and persist."[151] This is not the case in Qatar, where the sectarian tensions of Bahrain between the Sunni and the Shia, the confederation divisions of the UAE, and the sectarian and geographic disparities marking Saudi society are all conspicuously absent. Qatar's estimated 10 to 20 percent Shia minority is comparatively well integrated into the economic mainstream and even, to the extent possible, into the political establishment. Within the Arabian Peninsula, Qatar stands out uniquely for its absence of social frictions arising from societal divisions.

A fourth and final factor that ties the other three together and underlies the whole Qatari phenomenon is the abundance of financial resources at the disposal of the state. Qatar is an inordinately wealthy country, with a very small population. As table 1.1 indicates, Qatar has the highest growth rate in its real gross domestic product compared to any other country in the GCC or the larger Middle East. This has enabled the ruling elites to ensure socio-economic security for their citizenry, and mitigated potential political dissatisfaction.

Much of this wealth comes from Qatar having strategically positioned itself as the world's largest supplier of liquefied natural gas (LNG).[152] As it happens, Qatar and Iran share the world's largest gas field,

TABLE 1.1. Real GDP growth in MENA, GCC, and Qatar (annual change and percentage)

	Average 2000–2005	2006	2007	2008	2009	2010	Projection 2011	Projection 2012
MENA	5.2	6	6.7	4.6	2.6	4.4	4	3.6
MENA Oil Importers	4.1	6.4	6.1	6.4	4.9	4.5	1.4	2.6
GCC	5.5	6.5	5	6.4	0.3	5.4	7.2	4
Qatar	8.7	26.2	18	17.7	12	16.6	18.7	6

Source: IMF. Regional Economic Outlook, Middle East and Central Asia, October 2011. (Washington, DC: IMF, 2011), pp. 31, 82.

covering an area of 9,700 square kilometers, of which 3,700 square kilometers is in Iranian territorial waters (called South Pars by the Iranians) and 6,000 square kilometers is in Qatari territorial waters (called the North Field or North Dome by the Qataris). Hampered by protracted delays and international sanctions, Iran has hardly been able to capitalize on its gas resources, extracting only 35,000 billion barrels per day from the gas field as compared to Qatar's 450,000 barrels per day.[153] Although Qatar first began LNG production from the North Field in 1991 and started its LNG exports only in 1997, by 2006 it had become the world's largest LNG exporter. Aided by massive investments by international oil companies, most notably ExxonMobil and Shell, and also by the state-owned Qatar Petroleum, the country's LNG production went from 23.7 billion cubic meters (bcm) in 2000 to 116.7 bcm in 2010.[154] The resulting financial windfalls, especially for such a small country, have been nothing short of phenomenal.

Chapter 5 discusses Qatar's pursuit of what James C. Scott calls "high modernism" and, in Qatar's case, the creation of a new country and a new society almost from scratch.[155] The bulk of the next two chapters are devoted to examining the means through which Qatar uses its wealth to further its geostrategic interests. Here I mention only a couple of examples to illustrate how Qatari resources are used to enhanced the country's regional position in relation to its immediate neighbors: the Dolphin project, through which LNG is supplied to the UAE and Oman, is meant to "strengthen political ties" and to enhance Qatar's position within the GCC as a supplier of energy to other energy-rich countries. Gas sales to the West and to Pacific Asia are used for similar purposes. Finally, talks of opening up the local economy to Bahraini labor will add a dimension of economic dependence to Bahrain's relationship with Qatar.[156] Qatar's wealth, and its strategic use of that wealth, have everything to do with what the country has turned into today.

Given this chapter's focus on the international relations of the Persian Gulf, it seems befitting to end it with a note on Qatar's regional role. A central question here has been whether Qatar, through its foreign policy pursuits and resulting international conduct, is influencing, at least on the margins, or perhaps even giving shape to an emerging international regime in which it plays a highly consequential, even central, role. International regimes "authorize certain types of bargaining for certain purposes" and "facilitate negotiations leading to mutually beneficial agreements among governments."[157] As "rational egotists," states monitor each other's behavior, develop self-enforcing norms and principles, slowly adjust their own behavior accordingly, and give rise to "rule of thumb" for international behavior.[158] Whether or not Qatar is actively trying to carve out an international regime—or is even in a position to do so—is far from clear.[159] What is obvious is that within the larger US-dominated international regime over much of the Persian Gulf and the Middle East, Qatar is making changes around the margins, pursuing its own interests whenever and as much as possible regardless of who else's interests they might be in variance to, and in the process is making a huge splash internationally and ruffling feathers both far and near.

2

THE SUBTLE POWERS OF A SMALL STATE

Conceptions of international relations have traditionally revolved around the importance of the great powers. The story of international relations has been one of great powers and of their rivalries and power machinations.[1] Scholars of international politics have long seen power as the preserve of the big. Size, when it comes to the conduct of interstate relations, matters. Kenneth Waltz has been one of the most notable proponents of this line of thinking. "The theory, like the story, of international politics," he writes, "is written in terms of the great powers of an era."[2] Interactions among the major states are far more likely to be consequential for the larger international system than among the minor ones. In fact, he maintains, "a general theory of international politics is necessarily based on the great powers."[3]

As already discussed, at least insofar as the distribution of power in the Middle East and North African subsystem is concerned, there has been a steady shift in the direction of the Persian Gulf in general and the position and powers of Qatar in particular. With the broader regional context thus examined, we now turn our attention to the specific case of Qatar and the dynamics that underlie its regional and global positions of strength and power. This chapter examines the broad parameters of Qatar's position in the international system, looking specifically at its sources of what may be called "subtle power."

I begin with a discussion of the typical roles, profile, and position of small states in the international system. For the most part correctly, international relations scholars have situated small states on the receiving end of power rather than as influencers and, much less, as sources of power. Qatar, a small state by any definition, bucks the trend.

I argue that traditional conceptions of power no longer adequately describe emerging trends shaping the international system. Realist and neorealist thinkers have viewed power in terms of access to and control over tangible resources, especially manpower and military strength. More recently, notions of first soft power and then smart power have sought to rectify seemingly narrow and increasingly unfeasible focus of realists on force and military hardware. None of these conceptions adequately describe the underlying dynamics that account for the position that Qatar—an otherwise small state on the margins of global power politics—has been able to carve out for itself. That Qatar has been able to create a distinct niche for itself on the global arena, that it plays on a stage significantly bigger than its stature and size would warrant, that it has emerged as a consequential player not just in the Persian Gulf and the Arabian Peninsula but indeed across the Middle East and beyond, all bespeak of its possession of a certain type and amount of power. By definition, it cannot be hard or soft power, or their combination of smart power. It is a type of power that may be best viewed as "subtle power."

Small States in World Politics

International relations literature has generally treated small states as peripheral actors in international politics, seeing them often in need of protection from more powerful patrons and forced to adopt various accommodative strategies toward both stronger neighbors and international actors.[4] Thus relegated to the shadows of greater powers, small states are generally assumed to be at best of secondary importance in international power politics and lacking the necessary means and resources that affect the circumstances in which they find themselves.[5] More recently, attention has focused on not just the small states' vulnerability, which is a structural condition, but also on their resilience, which is a product of agency and strategy.[6] Given the right circumstances, however, small states can actually go beyond simple resilience—that is dealing with adversities and the limitations that size and demography impose on them. In fact, they can become highly influential both regionally and in the larger global arena, to the point of exerting significant amounts of power and influence in their immediate neighborhood and beyond.

This is indeed the case with Qatar, which has emerged as a major player in the Persian Gulf and Middle East subregions, despite a preponderance there of much larger and more powerful actors. In Qatar's case, several factors have combined to facilitate this emergence as an influential regional and international player. They include a highly calibrated and carefully maintained policy of hedging; an equally aggressive global campaign of branding; significant capacity on the part of the state; and prudent use of the country's comparative advantage in relation to neighbors near and far.

When it comes to regional and international diplomacy, Qatar's foreign policy appears to be at best an incongruent reflection of the idiosyncrasies of its chief architects—namely the country's emir and the prime minister—and at worst inconsistent and maverick. On the surface, Qatar also appears to consistently "punch above its weight."[7] Especially for a small state located in one of the world's toughest neighborhoods, Qatar's foreign policy appears woefully out of step with the size of the country, the preponderance of "great" and "secondary" powers vying for regional influence and position—most notably the United States and Iran—and the conventional power capabilities at its disposal.[8] Nevertheless, on closer examination Qatar's foreign policy pursuits are actually quite logical, a product of the country's successful, and in some ways fortuitous, positioning of itself as a small but highly influential actor in fostering regional peace and stability in a neighborhood that is justifiably renowned for its instability.

I posit two central theses here. First, I maintain that small states can indeed become influential players in the international arena, and, although they may be in need of military protection from others, they can use foreign policy strategies such as hedging to greatly strengthen their leverage vis-à-vis potential foes and friends alike. Although constrained by a number of structural weaknesses and vulnerabilities, small states can use their "individual actor-ness" not only to overcome vulnerabilities and demonstrate resilience, but, in fact, to become regionally and internationally important players.[9]

Next, my argument points to the need to rethink and refine existing conceptions of power, with traditional assumptions about power as rooted in military strength or cultural values—that is, hard and soft power—no longer adequately describing the emerging nature of Qatar's position in the Persian Gulf and in the larger Middle East. Qatar's influence and power are neither military nor cultural—nor a combination of the two, the so-called smart power[10]—but are derived from a carefully combined mixture of diplomacy, marketing, domestic politics, regional diplomacy, and, through strategic use of its sovereign wealth fund, increasing access to and ownership over prized commercial resources. This bespeaks of a new form of power and influence, one that is more subtle in its manifestations and is less blunt and blatant, one that may more aptly be dubbed subtle power.

The discussion begins with a brief examination of the role and position of small states in world politics, and the policy options they tend to adopt in order to adjust to international circumstance and to protect and further their interests in the international arena.[11] Despite serious disadvantages in military and diplomatic power, small states resort to one or more of three options—alliances, norm entrepreneurship, and hedging—in order to enhance their position and leverage in the international arena.

Small states do indeed face a number of both political as well as economic disadvantages in the international arena. Economically, they have to contend with a number of inherent vulnerabilities and deficiencies, such as inadequate or insufficient resources, limited opportunities for diversification, trade dependence, limited institutional capacity in the public and private sectors, comparatively high costs for services and transportation, and exposure to environmental and other exogenous shocks.[12] The political and diplomatic disadvantages that small states face in the international arena tend to be just as restrictive. The position and role of small states in the international arena are often at best reactive, vulnerable to outside events, and naturally contingent on the priorities and postures of the great powers, on whom the small and the weak rely for security and protection.[13]

All of this is not to imply that small states are hapless recipients of power and influence by the stronger actors in the international arena. In fact, small states have been able to enhance their leverage and influence both within the community of greater powers and between them using one or more of three options, namely through forging alliances, mustering up issue-specific power, and a delicate balancing act commonly referred to as "hedging."

One of the more prevalent, as well as effective, ways in which small states compensate for their lack of power and influence in the international arena is through entering formal or informal alliances with more powerful patrons. According to Walt, states join alliances in response to threats and not necessarily out of ideological affinity or because of "bribery" (aid, development assistance, etc.), the latter two tending to strengthen existing alliances rather than creating them.[14] For small states, alliances with a greater power may be informal or may take the form of signing of a formal treaty of protection from outside threats.[15] Besides providing protection, alliances serve as enabling mechanisms for small states in a number of important ways.

Small states that bandwagon or enter into formal alliances often do so through a delicate series of bargains that enhance their leverage vis-à-vis the great power protector. These bargains may entail one or more combinations of formal negotiations, bargains with separable elements of the great power, and influencing domestic opinion and private interest groups through lobbying efforts.[16] Moreover, alliances enable small states "not only to enhance their military security but also to obtain a variety of non-military benefits, such as increased trade or support for domestic political regimes."[17] Equally important are the benefits of membership in multistate alliances and institutions, the most notable being the European Union (and the European Commission in particular) and the Association of Southeast Asian Nations, whose decision- and policymaking structures tend to be biased in favor of small states and in which small states tend to be overrepresented.[18] In the United Nations, small states often "intervene to provide a basis for compromise on divisive issues."[19]

Alliances, of course, do not come without costs, inhering potentially glaring contradictions between influence, on the one hand, and autonomy, on the other.[20] Small states especially risk losing policy autonomy or flexibility in the face of international crises involving the more powerful patron.[21] "In their more benign forms," according to one observer, the trade-offs between sovereignty and protection are "negotiated and transparent."[22] They can, however, take the form of "less opaque infringements on sovereignty." There are also the risks of "entrapment" and "abandonment" for small states that enter into alliance with a larger power, with the former arising when a strong dependence on the alliance locks the small state's policy options to those of the stronger ally even if they are harmful to the small state's interests, and the latter becoming a possibility when alliance ties are too loose and the pluses of breaking them outweigh the costs of maintaining them.[23]

Apart from using alliance politics and other systemic factors to their advantage—for example the structure of the international system (hierarchical, hegemonic, or balance of power), or the state of the international system (in terms of degree of tension)—small powers may also resort to international norms, as well as their own agency and actions, in order to enhance their influence in international politics.[24] In particular, through persistent activism in and unrelenting attention to specific issues, some small states have been able to emerge as important norm entrepreneurs on the international stage. According to Kingdon, when it comes to agenda-setting, a policy entrepreneur is more likely to be taken seriously if recognized as an expert on the policy issue in question.[25] Unsurprisingly, a number of small (European) states have developed reputations as "forerunners" and "role models" on certain norms and issues, thus exerting disproportionate influence in the relevant policy areas: Sweden on environmental issues; Sweden, Denmark, and the Netherlands on issues related to gender; and Belgium and the Netherlands on monetary and economic union.[26] Needless to say, for small states aspiring to become policy entrepreneurs, the likelihood of success is enhanced if they are seen as impartial and honest brokers interested in the greater good.[27] Having sufficient financial and human resources to support a particular initiative can only be a plus. Undoubtedly, there are a number of states that are small and weak. There are also states that are small and influential, of which Israel, the Nordic countries, and Singapore are prime examples.[28] Qatar belongs in the latter category.

In addition to alliances and issue specialization, small states tend to rely on hedging as a strategy to enhance their position in the international system. Hedging may be defined as "a behavior in which a country seeks to offset risks by pursuing multiple policy options that are intended to produce mutually counteracting effects, under the situation of high-uncertainties and high-stakes."[29] Hedging stresses engagement and integration mechanisms, on the one hand, and realist-style balancing and external security cooperation, on the other.[30] An insurance policy of sorts, hedging can be seen as "a set of strategies aimed at avoiding (or planning for contingencies in) a situation in which states cannot decide on more straightforward alternatives such as balancing, bandwagoning, or neutrality."[31] As such, hedging is "a luxury of the weak only" and prompts weaker states to adopt a middle line of engagement and indirect balancing. This is not to imply that hedging means lack of a clear commitment as to where one's security and interests lie. It is a carefully calibrated policy in which the state takes big bets one way—for example, in Qatar's case opting for the US security umbrella—while it also takes smaller bets the other way, as in maintaining friendly ties with Iran and regional Islamists.

Generally, if a state faces an unequivocal threat from an actor, it is likely to pursue a balancing strategy in relation to that actor. Alternatively, if the state views an actor as a principal source of profit, then it is likely to bandwagon with it.[32] More often, however, smaller states face risks that are "multifaceted and uncertain."[33] At the same time, small states often find that their relations with the major powers need to be deliberate and studied. Too close of an alliance could mean losing their independence and inviting unwanted interference, whereas too distant of a relationship can put them "in an unfavorable position if the Great Power gains pre-eminence in the future."[34] Small states, therefore, are likely to engage in hedging by pursuing simultaneous strategies of return-maximizing and risk contingency. In order to maximize their returns vis-à-vis a great power, they pursue economic pragmatism, limited bandwagoning, and binding engagements (in the form of formal treaties), all the meanwhile careful, through dominance-denial and limited balancing, to reduce their risk exposure if things go awry.[35] All too often, dominance-denial and limited balancing take the form of maintaining relations with the great power's adversaries and competitors, at times as perfunctorily as simply keeping lines of communication open, and at other times in the form of warm and cordial ties. Whatever form these endeavors may take, their ultimate outcome is a deliberately crafted, highly active diplomatic profile on the part of the small state which, on the surface at least, may seem incongruent with its position in the international system.

Varieties of Power

Power is an essentially contested concept.[36] One of the most enduring definitions of power was offered by Robert Dahl, who defined power as the ability to control the behavior of others, or, more specifically, to get others to do what they would not otherwise do on their own.[37] Power does not necessarily mean control, but does bring with it greater autonomy, permits a wider range of actions, "a wider margin of safety in dealing with the less powerful," and a bigger stake in the system and "the ability to act for its sake."[38] Power and persuasion have a close, interconnected relationship. If we take *power* to mean the ability to get others to do what they would not do otherwise, *influence* is to do so through persuasion.[39] A similar definition is offered by Michael Barnett and Raymond Duval, though for them power is the capacity to determine one's own existence. They maintain that power is "the production, in and through social relations, of effects that shape the capacities of actors to determine their circumstances and fate."[40]

Whether it presents itself through coercion or persuasion, or directed at controlling others or at asserting the self, for realist thinkers power revolves around material capabilities rather than influence or outcome. For Waltz, state power is derived from a combination of tangible resources: "the size of population and territory, resource endowment, economic capability, military strength, political stability and competence."[41] Others have similarly defined power in terms of population, economic productivity, and relative political capacity.[42] Writing at the turn of the twenty-first century, a group of scholars saw population as the key ingredient of power. "Population is the sine qua non for greater power status," they wrote. "The size of populations ultimately determines the power potential of nations. Population is the element that determines in the long run which nations will remain major powers."[43]

John Mearsheimer, another realist theorist, similarly sees power as the product of two main resources—namely a sizeable population and high levels of wealth—both of which enable a country to construct a formidable military. States with small populations cannot be great powers. Power represents "nothing more than specific assets or material resources that are available to a state." For Mearsheimer, as for most other realists, power is the very essence of international politics, the very prize over which states compete with one another. States, he maintains, seek power not just to maintain the international status quo, but for the purposes of dominating other states. Accordingly, states focus on each other's capabilities rather than on intentions. Wealth is important, but only insofar as it enables states to maintain an effective military force. Wealth underpins military power, and wealth by itself is a good indicator of latent power. There are two kinds of power: latent power and military power. Latent power "refers to the socio-economic ingredients that go into building military power; it is largely based on a state's wealth and the overall size of its population." In international politics, a state's effective power is ultimately a function of its military forces and how they compare with the military forces of rivals. More specifically, it is the size of land forces that matter. According to Mearsheimer, power needs to be defined "largely in military terms because . . . force is the *ultima ratio* of international politics."[44]

Along similar lines, Paul Kennedy points to the importance of resources as the basis of national power. Economics is an important ingredient of power, Kennedy maintains. But it is one of its ingredients, others being factors such as geography, military organization, national morale, the alliance system that affect a state's powers relative to others.[45] He argues that there is "a significant correlation *over the longer* term between productive and revenue-raising capacities on the one hand and military strength on the other." Robust productivity and military strength combine to result in power. Technological and economic changes, which are inescapable features of human history, bring about shifts in levels of national and international power. Major shifts in military power balances have been followed by alterations in the productive balances, as confirmed by outcomes of major wars between the great powers. States need to maintain three essential tasks—provide for military security, meet economic needs and demands, and ensure sustained growth. To achieve great power status, they have to strike a rough balance among the three competing demands of defense, consumption, and investment. Power necessitates balanced focus on both the economic as well as military facets of power. Excessive focus on military strength and security runs the risk of neglecting and burdening economic strength, thus leading to decline. Spending on unproductive armaments takes away from productive investments, leading over time to an erosion of power.

Robert Keohane similarly links wealth and power. He defines power in terms of control over such key resources as raw materials, markets, and sources of capital, as well as competitive advantage in the production of highly valued goods. Access to crucial raw materials, control over major sources of capital, maintaining a large market for imports, and holding competitive advantage in goods with high value added that yield relatively high wages and profits are all key elements of power. For Keohane, exclusive access to these resources adds up to the making of a "hegemonic power."[46] But in the real world such access is hardly exclusive, enjoyed by many—but by no means all—resource-rich countries that have positioned themselves appropriately in the international system.

Joseph Nye's concept of "soft power," which he initially introduced in 1990, altered our understanding of power in a number of respects. Whereas the resources associated with hard power are tangible (e.g., force and money), the resources of soft power are intangible (e.g., institutions, ideas, values, culture, and perceived legitimacy of culture).[47] Soft power shapes the preferences of others. It involves "getting others to want the outcome that you want" and "co-opts people rather than coerces them."[48] Soft power is more than just influence or persuasion; it is also the power of attraction—"an intangible attraction that persuades us to go along with others' purposes without any explicit threat or exchange taking place." Power does not always have to be deliberate in nature and in its exercise. There is also a "structural" aspect to power, which is to get the desired outcome without resorting to bribes or threats. In international politics, soft power is produced from three primary sources: values expressed in a nation's culture, examples set by internal practices and policies, and the way a nation handles its relations with others.[49]

Nye argues that power should not be seen so much in terms of resources but instead should be viewed in terms of influencing and getting desired outcomes. States endowed with resources that are traditionally seen as sources of power do not always get their desired outcomes.[50] Transforming resources into sources of power requires well-designed strategies and skillful leadership. What is important is how resources are turned into outcomes based on strategies and context. "Power conversion" is the capacity to transform potential power into actual power.[51] Some countries are far more effective at converting potential power into actual power.[52]

Power resources are not static and differ based on different historical contexts.[53] Over the past five hundred years, each century has featured a different source of power, often held by a different country. In the eighteenth century, conceptions of power revolved around population size and control over minerals and metals, all of which provided favorable conditions for the Industrial Revolution.[54] In today's world, the main indices of economic power are information and professional and technical services. In the twenty-first century, new notions of security are coming to the fore, revolving not just around survival but also economic welfare, group autonomy, and political status.[55] In today's information age, "it may be the state (or nonstate) with the best story that wins."[56] New circumstances call for new power resources, such as the capacity for effective communication and for developing and using multilateral institutions. Although force remains a viable and necessary form of power in the anarchic, self-help international system, new instruments of power such as communications, organizational and institutional skills, and "manipulation of interdependence" are just as critical and important.[57] Therefore, any attempt to devise a single index of power is doomed to fail.[58]

More important, Nye argued, an important source of power is agenda-setting and determining the framework in which preferences and decisions are formulated.[59] There are three aspects or faces of power: commanding change, controlling agendas, and establishing preferences.[60] Power may be indirect and co-optive, resting "on the attraction of one's ideas or on the ability to set the political agenda in a way that shapes the preferences that others express."[61] International institutions set agendas and define issue areas, thus setting rules of conduct in interdependent relationships among states. States try to use these international institutions to shape the overall agenda and set the norms of interstate conduct in relation to specific issues.[62]

The transformation of the nature of power is taking place alongside with its diffusion. By nature soft power is diffuse and has an impact on the general goals of a country and is not focused and targeted in nature, and depends also on the receiver and interpreter.[63] At the same time, this diffusion is being reinforced by the development of broader trends, including economic interdependence, transnational actors, nationalism in weak states, and changing political issues.[64] The spread of information technology is making power even more diffuse. Through making information more accessible and affordable, revolutions in information technology are changing the nature of power and increasing its diffusion.[65]

Nye argues that in today's world it is becoming increasingly less feasible to use military power because of the impracticality of nuclear weapons, rise of communications technology and nationalism, and the growing concern of postindustrial democracies with welfare rather than military glory.[66] Nevertheless, despite the increasing costs of military conflict, and the dangers of nuclear escalation, military power is likely to continue to play an important role in international politics.[67] The spread and importance of soft power does not mean a complete obsolescence of force and military power in international politics.

A few years after introducing the notion of soft power Nye introduced the concept of "smart power," which he maintained is "the combination of the hard power of coercion and payment with the soft power of persuasion and attraction."[68] In simplest terms, smart power is the ability to combine soft and hard power resources into effective strategies.[69] A smart power strategy provides answers to several key questions: What goals or outcomes are preferred? What resources are available and in which contexts? What are the positions and preferences of the targets of influence attempts? Which forms of power behavior are most likely to succeed? What is the probability of success?[70] Small states, Nye maintains—especially Singapore, Switzerland, Norway, and Qatar—are often particularly adept at employing smart power strategies.[71]

One of most important elements in "the toolbox of smart power policies" is the effective employment of economic power in a world that is becoming increasingly interconnected and interdependent. Because it is based on tangible resources, economic power constitutes hard power "in its most direct manifestation" as it can be used to coerce or bribe nations into doing what they would not otherwise do.[72] At the same time, economic power can also be used as soft power through foreign aid, charity, and investments that endear the donor to the recipients.[73] More important, economic power can be used as leverage in what Nye calls "asymmetries of vulnerability."[74] In interdependent relationships, if one party is less dependent than the other one, it has power over the more dependent actor. "Manipulating the asymmetries of interdependence is an important dimension of economic power." Economic power is produced through balance of asymmetries; it is highly contingent on the particular context of the market. States, therefore, try to capitalize on asymmetries of interdependence by manipulating economic interactions in areas where they are strong and avoiding those areas in which they are weak.[75]

Nye's concept of smart power finds close parallels in what Giulio Gallarotti calls "cosmopolitan power." According to Gallarotti, similar to smart power, cosmopolitan power involves the optimization of national influence through a combination of hard and soft power. Cosmopolitan power has three "signature processes"—soft empowerment (rising influence through increased use of soft power), hard disempowerment (avoiding the self-defeating pitfalls of overreliance on hard power), and combining soft and hard power. Anarchy continues to be a pervasive feature of the international system, Gallarotti writes, despite the fact that norms and cooperation can and do function as important instruments of national power. The optimization of both absolute and relative power is a legitimate exercise of statecraft, and nations do what they can to optimize their security. This power optimization and security can occur only through a combination of soft and hard power.[76]

Based on the survey just presented, several important threads about the study of power stand out. Given its polymorphous character, we need multiple conceptions of power and a conceptual framework that pays attention to power in its different forms.[77] Whatever the type of power, the context for its use is quite important.[78] What is becoming increasingly more important in the contemporary world is "contextual intelligence," which may be defined as "the ability to understand an evolving environment that capitalizes on trends."[79] Due to changes in information technology and the entry of new, often nonconventional actors—such as Al Jazeera, Al Qaeda, and Wikileaks—international politics has become more complex, more volatile, and less contained within national boundaries.[80] Power has become less coercive and also less tangible. Power resources are becoming less fungible, increasing the importance of context and the actual amount of power that can be derived from various power resources. A capacity for a timely response to new information is an important source of power, as is effective organization skills and flexibility.[81]

But do the different sources and manifestations of power so far analyzed adequately describe the conditions, position, and international profile of a country like Qatar? Any casual observer would be hard pressed to ascribe to the country the kinds of power that are described by realists as hard power, in terms of military prowess and population resources, or those alternatively described by more recent theorists as soft or smart power. Flush with inordinate wealth, it would be easy to think of Qatar as endowed with economic power, and that surely the country has. But there is more to Qatar's international standing and its place and significance within the world community than simple economic power. Whatever economic power may be, Qatar's global profile goes far beyond whatever wealth might accord it. At least insofar as Qatar is concerned—and perhaps for other comparable countries with similar sizes, resources, and global profiles, such as Switzerland and Singapore—a different conceptualization of power may be more apt. Along with a handful of other comparable countries, Qatar may be said to have acquired for itself subtle power.

Before examining the key components and the manifestations of subtle power, some of the overall features of power in general bear keeping in mind. First, following insights by Nye and others, power should not be viewed in terms of resources only. Although without resources the exercise of power would be difficult or altogether impossible, power should be seen in terms of the ability to affect outcomes and reach desired objectives. Resources are a necessary but in themselves insufficient component of power. Resources provide *the potential*, not *the manifestations* of power itself. What is important is how resources are marshaled and employed— in Nye's terms "converted" or transformed[82]—in a manner that facilitates reaching objectives.

Transforming resources into power involves more than institutional and structural dynamics; it also involves agency. State behavior is strongly conditioned and constrained by the international environment. As Keohane points out, the international behavior of states is the product of a confluence of several factors that are both internal and exogenous to the state. They include the international distribution of power, distribution of wealth, international regimes, and individual diplomatic initiatives.[83] Equally important in the construction of state behavior, and in determining the nature and tenor of a state's diplomatic initiatives, is the role of agency.[84] Agency may manifest itself in a variety of ways, including self-esteem and notions of identity and self-perception.[85] More specifically, Richard Ned Lebow points to reason, appetite, and what he calls "spirit" as the driving forces of state behavior, with honor and standing as important motivators.[86] "With standing comes influence, which to some degree is fungible and can be used to enhance security or material well-being."[87] The international system, Lebow claims, is a site of contestation in which both state and nonstate actors claim standing on the basis of diverse criteria. "States invest considerable resources in publicizing and justifying their claims and in making efforts to impress others."[88]

Another feature of power is that it may be as indirect and diffuse as it may be direct and targeted. Barnett and Duval distinguish between four different kinds of power—compulsory, institutional, structural, and productive—and argue that whereas compulsory and structural varieties of power often manifest themselves in the form of direct control, institutional and productive powers tend to be indirect and diffuse and are mediated through rules, procedures, and outcomes.[89] The powers of agenda-setting, shaping preferences, and greatly influencing or altogether determining frameworks cannot be underemphasized.[90] We should not think of power *over* others but rather power in terms of goals accomplished *with* others.[91] The ability to get others to do what they would not do otherwise may come through compulsion and force, or bribes and sanctions. But it is just as likely to result from persuasion, commanding respect, manipulating circumstances, or pulling strings from behind the scenes.

Finally, at the risk of stating the obvious, it is worth remembering that different varieties of power often coexist side by side, and may, in fact, reinforce one another. The lines between compulsion and persuasion are often blurred by a multitude of complexities. A country's vote on a particular issue at the United Nations, for example, may be a product of many complex calculations having to do with the vote's repercussions for its diplomacy, military alliances, and investment potentials and portfolio.[92] Countries are persuaded to bandwagon—enter into alliances with a potential adversary—because of the other party's hard power and the potential threat it would pose if the alliance did not exist. Mixed appropriately, hard and soft power result in smart power. Power, in sum, is far from a one-dimensional phenomenon. It can manifest itself in multiple forms simultaneously or at different times.

Insofar as subtle power in specific is concerned, it may best be defined as the ability to exert influence from behind the scenes. It revolves around the ability to influence outcomes to one's advantage through a combination of bringing resources to bear, enjoying international prestige derived from and commensurate with norm-entrepreneurship, and being positioned in such a way as to manipulate circumstances and the weaknesses of others to one's advantage.[93]

There are four key components to subtle power (table 2.1). The first involves safety and security as guaranteed through physical and military protection. This first component does not necessarily involve force projection and the imposition of a country's will on another through coercion or bribe. This sense of security may not even be internally generated and could come in the form of military and physical protection provided by a powerful patron—say, the United States. It simply arises from a country's own sense of safety and security. As such, it frees up political leaders to expend available resources on other, potentially equally or more costly, endeavors aimed at building up international prestige and buying influence. Political leaders can never take the safety of their own position or of their country for granted. Waltz's sobering claim that all too frequently the state "conducts its affairs in the brooding shadow of violence" may be an exaggeration of an international system that is, nonetheless, governed by self-help and anarchy.[94] But only when a state can reasonably rest assured that its security is not under constant threat by domestic opponents or by international enemies and adversaries, can it then devote its attention to enhancing its external powers and influence. A state preoccupied with setting its domestic house in order, or paranoid about plots hatched by domestic and international conspirators bent on undermining it, has a significantly more difficult time trying to enhance its regional and global positions than a state with a certain level of comfort about its domestic stability. The two contrasting cases of Iran, whose intransigent regime is under the chronic threat of attack from Israel or the United States, and that of Qatar, which is confident of US military protection but aggressively pursues a policy of hedging, are quite telling.

A second element of subtle power is the prestige that derives from brand recognition and developing a positive reputation. Countries acquire

TABLE 2.1. Key elements of subtle power

Sources		Manifestation
Physical and military protection	→	Safety and security
Marketing and branding efforts	→	Prestige, brand recognition, and reputation
Diplomacy and international relations	→	Proactive presence as global good citizen
Purchases and global investments	→	Influence

a certain image as a result of the behaviors of their leaders domestically and on the world stage, the reliability of the products they manufacture, their foreign policies, their responses to natural disasters or political crises, the scientific and cultural products they export, and the deliberate marketing and branding efforts they undertake. These may be derived from such diverse sources as a political leader's speeches to home crowds or at the United Nations, the consumer products that are affiliated with a country (especially automobiles and household appliances), movies or other artistic products that are exported abroad, or commonplace portrayals of a country and its leaders in the international media. When the overall image that a country thus acquires is on the whole positive—when, in Nye's formulation, it has soft power—then it can better position itself to capitalize on international developments to its advantage. By the same token, soft power enables a country to ameliorate some of the negative consequences of its missteps and policy failures.[95]

Sometimes a positive image builds up over time. Global perception of South Korea and its products is a case in point. Despite initial reservations by consumers when they first broke into American and European markets in the 1980s, today Korean manufactured goods enjoy generally positive reputations in the United States and Europe.[96] At other times, as in the cases of Dubai, Abu Dhabi, and Qatar, political leaders try to build up an image and develop a positive reputation overnight. They hire public relations firms, take out glitzy advertisements in billboards and glossy magazines around the world, buy world-famous sports teams and stadiums, and sponsor major sporting events that draw world-renowned athletes and audiences from across the world. They spare no expenses in putting together national airlines that consistently rank at or near the top, spend millions of dollars on international conferences that draw to their shores world leaders and global opinion-makers, and build entire cities and showcase buildings that are meant to rival the world's most magnificent landmarks.

By themselves, prestige and reputation are of little utility in international affairs. But properly crafted and employed, they can help a country carve out strategic niches for itself in targeted areas. Prestige can enhance overall effectiveness in agenda-setting and in influencing frameworks and preferences. Through focused expenditures on and apparent specializations in specific fields—such as sports, aviation, heritage conservation, interfaith dialogue, or international conflict resolution—a country can acquire expertise and aspire to norm entrepreneurship in that particular field. In international forums and even within regional and international organizations, such as the Gulf Cooperation Council or the European Union, it can develop a positive reputation and even influence in that field.

This positive reputation is in turn reinforced by a third element of subtle power, that is proactive presence on the global stage. International branding and marketing efforts may be done by state-owned or even private enterprises with indirect support by the state. But they are complemented by a deliberately crafted diplomatic posture aimed at projecting an image of the country as a global good citizen. This is also part of a branding effort, but it takes the form of diplomacy rather than deliberate marketing and global media advertising. In Qatar's case, this diplomatic hyperactivism is part of a hedging strategy, as compared to bandwagoning or balancing, that has enabled the country to maintain open lines of communication, if not altogether friendly relations, with multiple international actors that are often antagonistic to one another (such as Iran and the United States). What on the surface may appear as paradoxical, perhaps even mercurial, foreign policy pursuits, is actually part of a broader, carefully nuanced strategy to maintain as many friendly relationships around the world as possible.

Qatar has sought to carve out a diplomatic niche for itself in a field meant to enhance its reputation as a global good citizen, namely mediation and conflict resolution.[97] In a region known for its intra- and international crises and conflicts, Qatar has, so far largely successfully, projected an image for itself as an active mediator, a mature voice of reason calming tensions and fostering peace. The same imperative of appearing as a global good citizen were at work in Qatar's landmark decision to join NATO's military campaign in Libya against Colonel Qaddafi in March 2011. Speculation abounds as to the exact reasons that prompted Qatar to join that campaign.[98] Clearly, as with its mediation efforts, Qatar's actions in Libya were motivated by a hefty dose of realist considerations and calculations of possible benefits and power maximization.[99] But the value of perpetuating a positive image through "doing the right thing," at a time when the collapse of the Qaddafi regime seemed only a matter of time, appears to trump other considerations. The remarks of a well-placed official and a member of the ruling family are telling. "We believe in democracy," he said, referring to Qatar's involvement in Libya. "We believe in freedom, we believe in dialogue, and we believe in that for the entire region . . . I am sure the people of the Middle East and other countries will see us as a model, and they can follow us if they think it is useful."[100]

The final and perhaps most important element of subtle power is wealth, a classic hard power asset. Money provides influence within and control and ownership over valuable economic assets spread around the world. This ingredient of subtle power is the influence and control that is accrued through persistent and often sizeable international investments. As such, this aspect of subtle power is a much more refined and less crude version of "dollar diplomacy," through which the regional rich seek to buy off the loyalty and fealty of the less well-endowed. Although by and large commercially driven, these investments are valued more for their long-term strategic dividends than for their short-term yields. So as not to arouse suspicion or backlash, these investments are seldom aggressive. At times, they are often framed in the form of rescue packages that are offered to long-standing international companies with well-known brand names facing financial distress. Carried through the state's primary investment arm the sovereign wealth fund (SWF), international investments were initially meant to diversify revenue sources and minimize risk from heavy reliance on energy prices. The purported wealth and secrecy of SWFs has turned them into a source of alarm and mystique for Western politicians and has ignited the imagination of bankers and academics alike.[101]

By itself, a SWF or other forms of international investment do not yield influence and power.[102] But wealth does give the state controlling the SWF the confidence it would not otherwise have had in its domestic and foreign policy pursuits. In international politics, wealth by itself does not garner power and influence. But it does foster and deepen self-confidence among the political leaders of wealthy countries. Wealth enables state leaders to aggressively brand their country, if they choose to do so. It also gives them the confidence and the resources to be diplomatically proactive and to engage in hedging. Wealth facilitates access, provides opportunities and space for being heard, and enables leaders to be better positioned to devise a "grand strategy" for their country. In Nye's words,

> A state's "grand strategy" is its leaders' theory and story about how to provide for its security, welfare, and identity, . . . and that strategy has to be adjusted for changes in context. Too rigid an approach to strategy can be

counterproductive. Strategy is not some symmetrical possession at the top of the government. It can be applied at all levels. A country must have a general game plan, but it must also remain flexible in the face of events.[103]

Clearly, agency is an important component of subtle power. More specifically, subtle power emerges not so much as a result of a confluence of institutional and structural forces, but is instead a product of deliberate decisions and carefully calculated choices made by policymakers. There are a number of wealthy countries in the Persian Gulf and elsewhere, some of which even employ proactive diplomacy as a favored foreign policy option. In Southeast Asia, for example, Malaysia and Singapore's foreign policies in response to a rising China give meaning to the very essence of hedging.[104] Others with similar predicaments may also be engaged in aggressive branding and marketing campaigns. The emirates of Abu Dhabi and Dubai, for example, often compete with one another and with Qatar in their global branding efforts.[105] But subtle power requires coordinating synergies between all four of its ingredients—military protection and security, global branding, hedging and proactive diplomacy, and international investments—and such a coordination does not occur on its own. It requires purposive choices and carefully calibrated policies. Uniquely, the Qatari leadership has been able to combine all four elements, resulting in a foreign policy that on the surface may appear "maverick" or "paradoxical," and the cause of much speculation, and fulltime employment, for Western journalists and diplomats.[106] In reality, it is a foreign policy aimed at deepening, and at the same time regenerating, the country's subtle power.

Qatar and the Pursuit of Subtle Power

Realists famously see the international arena as one existing in a state of anarchy, which fosters self-help on the part of individual states, whereby states cannot help but to look after their own interests. Doing so requires relying "on the means they can generate and the arrangements they can make for themselves."[107] It appears that this is precisely what Qatar is doing. Despite structural constraints imposed by its small size and its unenviable geographic location, sandwiched as it is between Saudi Arabia to the south and Iran to the north, the dependent variables outlined here—hedging, branding, state autonomy, and comparative economic advantage—have combined to propel Qatar into a position of prominence and influence. Undoubtedly, size does matter.[108] But it necessarily need not be a constraint. In fact, as we have seen Qatar has gone beyond ensuring its survivability and resilience and has managed to emerge as a regional powerhouse of sorts commercially and diplomatically.

Qatar's emergence as a significant player in regional and international politics is facilitated through a combination of several factors, chief among which are a very cohesive and focused vision of the country's foreign policy objectives and its desired international position and profile among the ruling elite, equally streamlined and agile decision-making processes, immense financial resources at the hands of the state, and the state's autonomy in the international arena to pursue foreign policy objectives. Reinforcing all this has been a tremendous amount of self-confidence on the part of the state elites in foreign policymaking. This self-confidence has resulted in the country beginning to play a regional role far beyond its size and youth would otherwise accord it. Qatar may be a young and small state, but the chief architects of its foreign policy, namely the emir and the prime minister, and, increasingly, the Heir Apparent Sheikh Tamim, perceive their country as a regional agenda-setter and a central player in regional politics and diplomacy.

Before delving into the details of how Qatar goes about constructing its new regional and international profile, it is important to see what, if any, generalizable conclusions can be drawn based on the Qatari example concerning the study of power and also small states. Insofar as power is concerned, the Qatari case demonstrates that traditional conceptions of power, while far from having become altogether obsolete, need to be complemented with considerations arising from new and evolving global realities. For a few years now, observers have been speculating about the steady shift of power and influence away from the West—its traditional home for the past five hundred years—to the East. In Fareed Zakaria's words, the "post-American world" may already be upon us.[109] Whatever this emerging world order will look like, it is obvious that the consequential actions of a focused and driven wealthy upstart like Qatar cannot be easily dismissed. Even if the resulting changes are limited merely to the identity of Qatar rather than to what it can actually do, which they are not, they are still consequential far beyond the small sheikhdom's borders.

Change in the identity of actors—in how they perceive themselves and are perceived by others—can lead to changes in the international system.[110] Qatar may not yet have redrawn the geostrategic map of the Middle East, and whether that is indeed what it seeks to do is open to question. But its emergence as a critical player in regional and global politics, and its seeming continued ascent, are theoretically as important as they are empirically observable.

One of the key lessons to be drawn here is that small states cannot always be relegated to the margins of power politics. With traditional conceptions of power—whether revolving around population size and military strength, or having to do with the appeal of cultural values and products—no longer adequately describing the forces that influence international politics, we cannot assume that small state are invariably on the receiving end of power and influence. Power and influence may manifest themselves in ways that are not always readily observable and apparent. They may be exercised from behind the scenes, arise from a combination of resources and opportunities, and accrue over time as a result of calculated or ad hoc moves that capitalize on preferential positioning in the worlds of global finance and diplomacy. As such, the central resources for the exercise of this type of power become a clear vision of how to achieve preferred positions in institutions that are consequential on a global scale, or at regional levels, or within the domestic arenas of countries; the drive, determination, and situational opportunities of achieving such positions; and the wherewithal and the financial resources necessary to do so. For achieving these objectives, a country's small size is of little or no hindrance at all. What matter are vision, drive, and financial means.

Neither, it seems, is democracy a prerequisite for achieving a status of power. Nye correctly asserts that how a country conducts its affairs domestically becomes part and parcel of its overall attraction and appeal to those looking at it from the outside.[111] That may indeed be the case for the exercise and appeal of soft power. And, assuming that democracy is a universally sought-after value, democratic countries are on the whole more likely to have greater soft power than nondemocratic ones. But insofar as subtle power is concerned, streamlined decision-making processes and more centralized leadership are likely to give political leaders greater agility and responsiveness to emerging circumstances and opportunities as they develop regionally and globally. Particularly in a country with a largely depoliticized population as Qatar, where domestic pressures on the state for political accountability and representation are conspicuous in their absence, lack of democracy has actually served as an asset in the exercise of subtle power rather than a hindrance.

The flip side of the coin is equally valid. Just because a state may be small and nimble, undemocratic, and wealthy, it does not inevitably emerge as a powerful actor in global affairs, or, for that matter, a necessarily consequential actor in international and regional politics. Singapore and Hong Kong both fit the bill, as do, to a lesser extent, Taiwan, which is a quasi-democracy, and Kuwait, whose designation as democratic would be a disservice to the notion.[112] These countries may have the resources and the potential for the exercise of subtle power in international affairs. But the missing ingredient in each case is the purposive drive by state leaders to transform potential into actual power. Size may not matter, but agency does.

In this sense, in Qatar's determined drive to capitalize on its comparative advantage in terms of its resources, its location, and even its size, the sheikhdom stands apart from comparable countries in the Persian Gulf region as well as in the rest of the Middle East. That Qatar is purposefully trying to redraw the geostrategic map of the Persian Gulf and the Middle East through resort to subtle power is not in doubt. What remains unanswered is the extent to which the Qatari drive is sustainable in the long run, especially in light of its domestic social makeup, with some 85 percent of the country's residents being noncitizens, and a state structure that resembles a family-run business. The country's location in an ever-changing and notoriously unpredictable region also introduces several imponderable variables. For example, will there once again be a militarily powerful Iraq capable of force-projection within the Persian Gulf region and beyond? What does the future hold for Iran in terms of its chronically fluid domestic politics and its role and position both in its own neighborhood and beyond? Closer to home, will Bahrain's aborted Arab Spring reignite again, and if so will there be consequences for others in proximity of the divided kingdom? These and countless similar questions cast shadows over the long-term prospects of Qatar's continued ascent as an emerging regional and global power. For now, however, it seems that the small sheikhdom is indeed succeeding in playing a leading and influential role in both the Persian Gulf and the Middle East.

3

FOREIGN POLICY AND POWER PROJECTION

Competing with Bahrain and the United Arab Emirates (UAE) as the Persian Gulf's most attractive business destination and entrepôt, Qatar has managed to carve out an impressive niche for itself in global finance and trade. More important, Qatari leaders have assumed an extraordinarily active diplomatic profile that more than anything else is designed to enhance the country's stature and diplomatic standing. While Qatar's "maverick" diplomacy is a product of its hedging, its diplomatic hyperactivism is meant to enhance its branding and soft power. Whereas hedging may have given Qatar self-confidence insofar as its survivability and resilience are concerned, branding and soft power have brought the country visibility in the commercial and diplomatic arenas. In doing so, state elites have enjoyed considerable policymaking leeway and autonomy from potential constraints inside and outside of the country.

This autonomy is rooted in two distinct yet complementary sources: massive revenues accrued from hydrocarbon exports, specifically from liquefied natural gas; and elite institutional cohesion, thus streamlining policymaking decisions and ensuring political and diplomatic agility. This agility is further reinforced by Qatar's comparative advantage in relation to its neighbors, compared to whom it has an upper hand in one or more key areas: more politically stable compared to Bahrain; more cohesive compared to the UAE; more aggressively self-assured compared to Oman; and far more effective at branding compared to Egypt, Saudi Arabia, or Iran. Providing the larger background and context to all this is the Al Jazeera news channel and its extraordinary influence across the Arab world, bestowing on Qatar a unique source of soft power against which most other competitors have proven far less effective.

Compared to the other regional actors in the Persian Gulf, Qatari diplomacy is characterized by an unusual level of hyperactivism. This is partly due to the built-in agility of the state and the comparative efficiency of its foreign policymaking process. In addition to the structural dynamics that enable greater state responsiveness to emerging opportunities, there are also the goals and priorities of policymakers that distinguish Qatar from the rest of the pack. For one reason or another, none of Qatar's regional counterparts engage in quite the same level of diplomatic activism.

A detailed treatment of the foreign policies of other states of the Gulf Cooperation Council (GCC)—particularly the smaller states of Oman, the UAE, Bahrain, and Kuwait—is beyond the scope of this chapter. At the broadest level, however, none engage in hedging, at least not nearly to the same extent that Qatar does as a regular feature of its foreign policy. Insofar as the UAE is concerned, the country's primary focus has been *economic* rather than *political* development, with policymakers across the Emirates placing much greater priority on economics rather than politics or diplomacy.[1] Within the context of a highly pragmatic diplomacy conducive to entrepreneurial pursuits, the country has long identified Iran as a primary threat to its security, a perception Emirati leaders shared about Iraq prior to 2003.[2] As such hedging has not been perceived as a viable option, at least between Iran and the US camp, and the UAE has therefore placed itself squarely within the American security orbit.[3]

Similar concerns have shaped the foreign policies of Bahrain and Kuwait, for both of whom the United States and Saudi Arabia have been seen as primary protectors. Comparatively resource-poor, Sunni minority-ruled Bahrain's solid security alliance with Saudi Arabia and the United States can be explained on structural grounds.[4] Conversely, Kuwait is not resource-poor—by 2010 having foreign assets in excess of $277 billion.[5] Yet its leaders have opted for close alliance with Saudi Arabia and the United States instead of hedging. This is as much a product of policy preferences by Kuwaiti leaders as it is derived from the country's geographic proximity to primary sources of perceived threats, namely Iran and Iraq. Of the group, Oman has pursued a much more nuanced, finely calibrated, independent foreign policy in which close security cooperation with the West and the GCC is balanced with continuously cordial relations with Iran.[6] This is a reflection of the preferences of Oman's ruler, Sultan Qaboos, and the regional and global roles he has envisioned for his country since assuming power in 1970.[7]

By way of comparison, it is important to note that Qatar's foreign policy in the contemporary era has been informed by four general sets of dynamics. The first set has had to do with the history of the country's relationship with Saudi Arabia going back to the preindependence era and into the 1970s and 1980s, during which the former emir, Shaikh Khalifa bin Hamad Al Thani (r. 1972–1995), sought to guarantee his country's safety by seeking shelter in the Saudi security umbrella. In return, the emir frequently paid homage to his Saudi protectors, thus alienating younger Al Thanis who resented their country's treatment as a perceived feudal vassal by the Saudis.[8] In the meanwhile, the first Gulf War exposed the Saudis' inability to protect themselves and their allies from regional threats, driving home the need to more firmly anchor Qatar's security within the US protective shield. Hence a second dynamic came to influence Qatari foreign policy, namely an increasingly in-depth reliance on the United States since the early 1990s to provide military protection against external threats. The imperative of US-provided military security directly touched on a third concern of Qatar's foreign policy, namely the nature of the country's relationship with a revolutionary—and often threatened and thus unpredictable—Iran. At the same time as it sought to balance its relations with Iran and the United States, Qatar decided to put its massive wealth to use to break out of the Saudi shadow. It aimed to compete with other regional upstarts such as the UAE, Bahrain, and Kuwait, and—through initiatives such as Al Jazeera television and conflict resolution efforts—to make its presence felt regionally and globally. The last aspect of Qatari foreign policy—its financially fueled diplomatic activism—has enabled it to behave quite unlike most other states of its size and stature. As a small state in a rough neighborhood, Qatari leaders have crafted foreign policy with the country's physical and political security paramount in their minds. In the process, they have transformed survival strategies into sources of influence and perhaps even power.

Qatari foreign policy behavior offers a textbook example of hedging. In fact, Qatar's successful employment of hedging, buttressed by an efficient and streamlined foreign policymaking process and considerable self-confidence, has resulted in the state emerging as one of the most influential players in the Persian Gulf region.

Qatari Foreign Policy Hedging

Located at the mouth of the Straits of Hormuz, at the heart of the Persian Gulf waterway, Qatar has found itself between two belligerent powerhouses—Iran and the United States—not shy of frequent bellicosity. Although military tensions between the two powers declined markedly after the end of President Bush's tenure in office, the possibility of an open eruption of hostilities between the United States and the Islamic Republic remains ever-present, especially as the animosity and the resulting mutual threats of military action between Iran and Israel show no signs of abating. The fact that tens of thousands of American troops are in the immediate vicinity of Iran, and that Qatar houses one of the largest US airbases in the world, keeps tensions between Iran and the United States high and perpetuates Qatar's perilous position in the eye of the storm should one erupt.[9] The warnings implicit in Iran's repeated assurances that its response to any American or Israeli attacks will be decisive and far-reaching has not been lost on regional leaders, especially those whose countries house US troops and equipment.[10]

Qatari leaders perceive another potential threat to their rule, this time from transnational identities in general and Shi'ism in particular. In this sense the ruling Al Thani family is not that different from the Persian Gulf's other ruling families in its perception of the primary threat to regime stability—the salience of transnational identities that transcend relatively recent, and largely arbitrary, national borders. Gregory Gause has identified these transnational identities—Arab, Muslim, Shi'a, Sunni, tribal, etc.—as "the most important and distinctive factor in the Gulf regional security complex" because they are "seen as threats by leaders to their own regimes' stability."[11] The Iranian Revolution heightened Shi'a self-awareness and identity across the Persian Gulf and the Arabian Peninsula, from Iraq in the north to Yemen in the south. Correspondingly, the revolution magnified the sense of concern and fear that each of the region's Sunni-ruled states felt toward its own Shi'a population. No sooner had fears of a spillover of Iranian revolutionary fervor subsided then the political rise of Shi'a politicians and parties in the chaotic politics of post-Saddam Iraq renewed regional fears of another supposed Shi'a revival. Soon after the fall of Baghdad, scholars and policymakers the world over began wondering whether "the Shi'a revival in Iraq may well lead to other regime changes in the region."[12] The ensuing state reactions ranged from one of watchful neglect to outright and violent repression, in Oman and in Bahrain, and Saudi Arabia, respectively. Along with the UAE, Oman, and Kuwait, Qatar represented one of the few Gulf Arab states that chose to monitor and scrutinize but not repress its Shi'a population.[13]

In Qatar, the relationship between the ruling family and the country's Shi'a minority has generally been a positive one. In fact, unlike most other parts of the Arab world, the Shi'a are comparatively well integrated into Qatari society, have never been among the rulers' opponents, and, as the career of the long-time Finance and Economy minister Yousef Kamal (1998–) exemplifies, they often participate in the various institutions of the state at the highest levels.[14] Qatari Shi'as represent some of the country's wealthiest families, with the Al-Fardans and their empire of luxury car dealerships, real estate holdings, and multiple other commercial ventures being a prime example.[15]

The Al-Fardans and most of the other Shi'a immigrated to Qatar from the Iranian side of the Persian Gulf either at the end of the Qajar era in the late 1800s or around the 1960s and 1970s. Most Qatari Shi'a either trace their ancestry back to Iran, or they are popularly seen—at times mistakenly—as having Iranian roots.[16] Tellingly, until its renovation for the 2006 Asian Games, Doha's main bazaar was known as the Iranian Souq. Despite their integration into Qatari society, the state appears reluctant to test the loyalty of its Shi'a population if the need arises. Interestingly, the Shi'a presence in the country, unofficially estimated at around 15 to 20 percent of the total population,[17] is not captured in any of the state's official statistical publications.[18] In fact, insofar as Doha's Shi'a mosques are concerned, the state keeps a distant, respectful, but nonetheless watchful eye on them. Although Qatari Shi'a are not popularly perceived of as an Iranian fifth column—as they sometimes are in Dubai, for example—they do figure into state calculations concerning domestic policies and international relations. The state's inability to predict the voting preferences of the Shi'a, for example, is often cited as one of the reasons for indefinite delay so far in holding elections and convening a parliament as stipulated in the 2004 constitution.[19] In foreign policy, the Shi'a factor figures prominently with regard to the country's relations with Iran.

Qatar, then, needs to craft its foreign policy with deliberate care and caution, with an eye toward the Iranian behemoth in the north, the Saudi giant in the south, and the American empire that is omnipresent. A small state with no meaningful armed forces or other military force projection abilities of its own, Qatar finds itself between a rock and a hard place. Its leaders firmly committed to remaining within the Western economic and diplomatic orbits while doggedly unwilling to abandon those causes or entities—such as the Hamas or Ahmadinejad's Iran—to whom the West strenuously objects.[20] The three other smaller sheikhdoms of the Persian Gulf also find themselves facing a similar predicament. But each of these three has given more weight to the security alliance with the United States on these and other contentious issues rather than to try to proactively balance out countervailing forces and agendas.[21] Conversely, Qatar has chosen to pursue a carefully calibrated policy of hedging—taking big bets one way and smaller one another—particularly when it comes to the two archenemies of Iran and the United States. Where its safety is concerned, Qatar has placed itself firmly at the mercy of the United States. At the same time, it actively maintains cordial relations with actors with interests inimical to those of the United States, chief among which are Iran and the region's various shades of Islamists. The US government, or at least its diplomats in Doha, are aware of this, predicting in 2010 that Qatar will continue to support what they perceive as "problematic players" such as Hamas, Hezbollah, and Syria, while at the same time maintaining close ties with both the US and the GCC.[22] "Qatar will continue to pragmatically pursue relations with Iran," claimed a US embassy cable in 2010, "pleasing as many players as possible."[23]

Precisely why Qatar has chosen hedging whereas others have not is a product of policy preferences by state leaders, on the one hand, and the structural opportunities and circumstances that have enabled them to articulate and pursue those preferences, on the other. As the country's Heir Apparent Tamim bin Hamad Al Thani once told the US ambassador to Qatar, the country cannot afford not to pursue a pragmatic policy. In its relations with Iran, for example, he remarked that "Qatar's boycotting Iran will not hurt Iran but will hurt Qatar—including our shared gas supply."[24] Compared to its neighbors, the Qatari state also benefits from a number of comparative advantages that have bestowed on it high levels of autonomy vis-à-vis Qatari society, some of the most notable of which include high rent revenues accrued from LNG, a small and relatively homogenous population, ruling elite cohesion, and policymaking agility. These comparative advantages have enabled the Qatari elite to choose from a wider menu of foreign policy options. In other words, Qatar's hedging has been made possible through a confluence of structural constraints and opportunities and state elite choices and agency.

One of the unconventional tools that Qatar uses in its foreign policy hedging is the Al Jazeera satellite television network. Had it not been for Al Jazeera, there would be much greater ignorance of Qatar around the world than is currently the case. Notwithstanding the network's own vocal protestations to the contrary, the links between Al Jazeera and Qatari foreign policy—whether they actually exist or are generally perceived around the world to exist[25]—cannot be denied or overlooked. Wikileaks cables show what at times appear to be close coordination between the Qatari government and the television channel. In 2005, for example, when Lynne Cheney, wife of the former US vice president, complained to the Qatari ambassador in Washington about "a particularly virulent essay on [Al Jazeera]'s website," the Qatari prime minister saw to it that the essay was removed.[26] In the same meeting, the Qatari prime minister offered to arrange for a softer Al Jazeera interview for Karen Hughes, at the time the US undersecretary for Public Diplomacy and Public Affairs. In an earlier interview with the channel, the PM maintained, Hughes has been "asked the wrong questions." "It is important that we know what she wants," he told the US ambassador, "so we can have the right result."[27] A few days later, the channel's managing director Wadah Khanfar met with the embassy's public affairs officer and mentioned that the contents of the objectionable essay had been "toned down" and that soon it would be removed from the website altogether.[28]

The network has pursued a similarly nuanced approach toward Saudi Arabia, a neighbor with whom Qatar has not always had cordial relations. Tensions between the two countries date back to border clashes in 1992, followed by alleged Saudi support for a countercoup in 1996 designed to oust Sheikh Hamad and to restore Sheikh Khalifa back to power. In 2000, Saudi crown prince Abdullah boycotted a summit of Islamic states held in Doha because of Qatar's hosting of an Israeli trade office, and in 2002 Riyadh recalled its ambassador from Qatar due to controversial remarks on Al Jazeera by a Saudi dissident. Things got personal when in the mid-2000s, Saudi-funded newspapers and senior Al Thanis, including the emir's wife Sheikha Moza, traded insults and accusations, a dispute eventually settled, in favor of the Qataris, in a London courtroom.[29] In February 2004, Al Jazeera reported that Saudi authorities had banned it from covering the annual hajj pilgrimage to Mecca by millions of Muslims from across the world.[30] Throughout this time, Al Jazeera's coverage of Saudi Arabia was hard-hitting and, similar to its overall reportage, often critical of the Saudi establishment.[31] But by late 2007, when relations between the two countries began to improve, Al Jazeera's tone toward Saudi Arabia began to soften. According to one Al Jazeera newsroom employee, "orders were given not to tackle any Saudi issues without referring to the higher management. . . . All dissident voices disappeared from our screens."[32] Later on, in 2011–2012, following the mass protests that swept across the Arab world and therefore brought Saudi and Qatari leaders closer together in their efforts to save the threatened Bahraini monarchy and to assert their own leadership over the Arab world, almost all critical reports on Saudi—and Bahraini—affairs disappeared from the network. As Bahrain dove deeper into turmoil, for a few critical months it appeared as if for the network's news editors and programmers it simply did not exist.

Perhaps the most critical test of Al Jazeera's political independence occurred during the 2011 Arab Spring, when, according to most observers, it aligned its coverage of the Arab revolts, sometimes more subtly than others, with Qatari foreign policy. Although the network provided extensive coverage of the rebellions in Tunisia and Egypt, describing the events there as "revolutions" early on, and later of Libya, Yemen, and Syria, it failed to give similar airtime to Bahrain. This prompted one observer to comment that, similar to the Saudi-owned and -funded Al Arabia channel, Al Jazeera is "tongue-tied by the Saudi military intervention" in Bahrain in March 2011.[33] As the *International Herald Tribune* observed,

The threat posed by Bahrain's protests was closer to home. Their success would have set a precedent for broader public participation in a region ruled by Sunni dynasties. More alarming for those dynasties, it would have given more power to Bahrain's majority Shi'ites, distrusted by Sunni rulers who fear the influence of regional Shi'ite power Iran.[34]

According to another observer, "There has been fantastic pressure from Saudi Arabia on Qatar to join in (the Gulf military operation) in Bahrain, and to at least rein in Al Jazeera."[35] This prompted yet another observer to claim that "Bahrain doesn't exist as far as Al Jazeera is concerned, and they have avoided inviting Bahraini or Omani or Saudi critics of those regimes" to comment on camera.[36] One of the station's Beirut-based reporters allegedly resigned over the network's lack of coverage of events in Bahrain.[37] After much criticism for its uneven coverage of regional uprisings, the network aired what was regarded as a "powerful" documentary on Bahrain, but showed it only on its English channel, in limited airings, and did not run it on its more widely watched and more popular Arabic channel.[38] Media observers were not impressed. In the words of one,

> The bias on the English channel may be more subtle than on the Arabic channel but can be plainly seen on its YouTube pages. Take, for example, the report on the human rights violations that occurred during the uprising in Bahrain. Al-Jazeera English disabled comments on all five videos uploaded on Bahrain yet no such restriction was placed on the videos about Syria, Yemen and Egypt uploaded on the same day. Let's not forget that Qatar, the home of Al-Jazeera, also sent troops to Bahrain to restore "order and security."[39]

The reporter went on to suggest that "Al-Jazeera English might consider changing one of its slogans from the ambitious 'all sides, all views, always' to the more realistic 'all sides, all views, sometimes'."[40] There have been similar criticisms of the network's uncritical—and at times even sensationalist—coverage of opposition rebels fighting the Syrian state in 2011–2012 and the election of the Muslim Brotherhood's Mohamed Morsi in May 2012 to the Egyptian presidency.[41]

This is not to imply that Al Jazeera's editorial choices are simply dictated by the foreign policy agendas and preferences of the country that houses it. That there is an overall, at times tenuous, coordination between the two, sometimes more pointedly than others, and sometimes more pronounced in the Arabic than the English channels, cannot be denied. Nevertheless, the channel's own internal dynamics, particularly insofar as path dependence is concerned, cannot be overlooked. The Qatari state established Al Jazeera for branding purposes and it did not mind if the station's broadcasts furthered its regional and global interests. But before long the station, as a complex institution and an important change agent, developed its own internal dynamics and preferences. Editorial choices were made based on the preferences of the station's editorial directors, many of whom had their own political and ideological backgrounds to promote. Wadah Khanfar, for example, who resigned as the network's director in 2011 after eight years of service, was often seen as anti-American by the US authorities.[42] The pan-Arabist leanings of other network decision makers often crept through their coverage of events as they transpired. In a candid article on Al Jazeera's programming and overall posture during the Arab Spring, the channel's program director admitted to the station's staff that reporters could not help but be influenced by the gravity of the events occurring around them, often in their own mother countries. "The Arabic speaking Al-Jazeera station was simply closer to the hearts of many Arabs because the latter related to its employees as one of them," he wrote. "This was the case, for in Al-Jazeera's newsroom one can find reporters and producers from every Arab country—with a fair distribution and representation—who are all impassioned about Arab and Islamic issues. They use the term umma (nation) a lot."[43]

Al Jazeera is only one—albeit important and highly visible—element in Qatar's delicate hedging between multiple actors. Equally important are Qatar's relations with many of the region's Islamist groups and actors, particularly those associated with the Muslim Brotherhood. Qatar's relationship with the movement is one of the "smaller bets" in its larger hedging strategy. There are several aspects to this seemingly inexplicable friendship, both domestically and internationally. Domestically, Emir Hamad is a masterful balancer of countervailing political trends and tendencies at home. As such, the Qatari state has long given refuge to the Egyptian-born cleric Yusuf al-Qaradawi (b. 1926) who for much of his life has been one of spiritual fathers of the Muslim Brotherhood. By providing patronage and giving a platform to one of the most outspoken and controversial clerics in the contemporary Muslim world, the Qatari state has been able to effectively place itself above religious criticism and to largely stem the possibility of the emergence of a home-grown Islamist movement.[44]

Reinforcing this shielding from Islamist criticism has been Qatar's support—at times more overt than others—for Muslim Brotherhood activists throughout the countries in which the Arab Spring has unfolded, from Tunisia and Libya to Egypt and Syria.[45] The precise reasons for Qatar's support for the movement's sympathizers in the Arab Spring have been subject to much speculation and controversy.[46] Two primary considerations appear to underlie this development. First, when the Arab Spring broke out, Qatari leaders appear to have calculated relatively early on that political incumbents were spent forces whose days were numbered. Thus former friends (e.g., Bashar Assad) were quickly jettisoned and instead military and diplomatic support was given to the groups opposing them. Second, given the destruction of organized opposition by these regimes, their opponents were bound to be Islamists, among whom Qatar found more affinity with the comparatively moderate Muslim Brotherhood activists and sympathizers. The Brotherhood's relatively radical counterparts, who are often lumped together under the general label of Salafists, are closer in sensibility to Saudi Arabia's more austere brand of Wahhabism. Once again, Qatari diplomacy, this time in relation to a re-emergent Muslim Brotherhood, is part of a carefully calibrated policy of hedging bets in multiple directions, and, in this case, choosing between what Doha considers as the lesser of two evils. That support for the Brotherhood addressed both a foreign concern and further blunted the potential for a similar domestic development was an added bonus. Both before and throughout the civil wars that wracked Libya and Syria in 2011 and 2012, Sheikh Qaradawi's Friday sermons often closely paralleled the positions taken by Qatar both in relation to these conflicts in specific and in the international arena in general.[47] So did, incidentally, Al Jazeera's coverage: detailed and often sympathetic coverage of the ongoing anti-Assad rebellion in Syria and the Egyptian Muslim Brotherhood's Mohamed Morsi's presidential election win in May 2012, for example, but continued muted coverage of the repression in Bahrain, and virtually nothing on Saudi Arabia at a time of important palace developments in the kingdom.[48]

In addition to Al Jazeera and its relations with Islamists, Qatar's balancing act between its primary military protector and major trading partner, the United States, and its northern, restive neighbor Iran offer a textbook example of hedging. This is not to imply, however, that the nature of the bilateral relationships that Qatar maintains with Iran and the United States are identical. In fact, Qatari-Iranian and Qatari-American relationships are qualitatively different, though, one might argue, each in their own way quite strong. Qatar's relationship with the United States is anchored in three central pillars: military and security arrangements; commercial and economic interests; and educational and cultural initiatives. Qatar's relations with Iran, however, feature at best minimal elements of each of these three pillars. Instead, they revolve around what might be termed "expressions of friendship" and the frequent official visits that political leaders and high-ranking officials from each side pay one another.

As a subordinate state in relation to the United States, some aspects of Qatari foreign and domestic policies fit patterns consistent with other countries in comparable positions. These include, most notably, reduced defense needs, increased open trade, and a willingness to join wartime coalitions. Leaders who perceive their countries to be under security threats are more likely to enter into security hierarchies in which dominant states provide buffers against potential aggression.[49] And Qatar certainly feels threatened not so much by possible Iranian or Saudi expansionism but by consequences for its own safety should those giants, or another constellation of regional belligerents, such as Iran and Israel or Iran and the United States, come to blows.

But being subordinated to the United States in economic and security hierarchies has also brought the two into regular friction, at least on the margins, in an ongoing process of dialogue and tension over defining and redefining the scope and contours of their respective positions vis-à-vis one another.[50] Released Wikileaks cables show Doha-based American diplomats often perplexed by Qatar's deviance from the desired US position on various issues, frequently trying to make sense of the country's seemingly contradictory policy pursuits. A 2009 cable from the US State Department, for example, brands Qatar as "worst in the region" when it comes to cooperation with the United States in counterterrorism efforts.[51] Similarly, in reference to relations with Iran, Qatar prefers engaging with the Islamic Republic rather than isolating it, as the US ambassador to Qatar was reminded by the heir apparent in one of their meetings.[52] Another case in point is Qatar's patronage and guarded tolerance of the Egyptian-born cleric Yousef Al-Qaradawi, who is often outspoken in his support for Hamas and his condemnation of American and Israeli policies in the Middle East and elsewhere.[53] When in November 2009 the US ambassador to Qatar delivered a letter from the US Treasury Department to the Qatari foreign ministry complaining about Al-Qaradawi's alleged financial support for the Hamas, his interlocutor responded that "Qaradawi is not working as a terrorist" and balked at putting pressure on him to alter his views and activities.[54] Underlying such specific instances of friction is the whole question of Al Jazeera television network, which has long been a subject of criticism and objection by Washington and by the US embassy in Doha.[55]

In addition to security arrangements, trade and investments form another key pillar of the US-Qatari relationship. Qatar's currency, the Rial, is pegged to the dollar, and Qatar has consistently refused to de-peg despite occasional falls in the dollar.[56] Having signed a Trade and Investment Agreement in 2004, which was meant to create a formal dialogue to promote bilateral trade, by 2008 the US and Qatar were trading $3.5 billion in goods.[57] By 2008, American exports to Qatar amounted to $3.1 billion, up 11.6 percent from the previous year, and imports from Qatar were $484 million, up 1.5 percent compared to 2007. In 2008, 9 percent of Qatar's total imports came from the United States.[58] According to the US embassy in Doha, American exports to Qatar surged by 340 percent between 2003 and 2008, to a total of $3.2 billion.[59] US foreign direct investment in Qatar has also grown steadily in recent years, amounting to $7.1 billion in 2007, up from $5.4 billion in 2006. According to the US Census Bureau, the volume of trade between Qatar and the US shot up from $838.1 million in 2001 to more than $3.3 billion in 2011.[60] For its part, Qatar Investment Authority, the primary investment arm of the country's sovereign wealth fund, has often considered investing in US banks, although it has shown a preference for the perceived stability of European markets as compared to the United States.[61]

There is no comparable data on Qatari-Iranian trade, largely because trade and investment between the two countries is negligible. In fact, official trade documents issued by each of the governments fail to register any notable trade of any kind between the Islamic Republic and its southern neighbor, with neither country ranking as a major trading partner for the other one.[62] Also, while generally supportive of the idea, Qatar has shown coolness to an Iranian initiative to create a cartel of gas-exporting countries modeled after OPEC.[63]

In addition to placing itself firmly under the protection of the American security umbrella and having quite extensive commercial and trade relations with the United States, Qatar has also embarked on a massive, concerted effort to embrace and to import—or, more aptly, to incorporate within itself—a number of American educational institutions and cultural practices. In 2003, the Santa Monica-based Rand Corporation was invited to open a branch office in Qatar—the Rand-Qatar Policy Institute—in order to advise the Qatar Foundation more systematically on a host of demographic and social issues, including wide-ranging reforms in the country's K-12 educational system.[64] Based on a Rand study conducted in 2001, the following year the emir declared the establishment of "Independent" primary and secondary schools based on the US charter school model.[65] In addition to English becoming the language of instruction across the K-12 curriculum, except for courses on Arabic language and literature, American-style curricula and pedagogy are steadily becoming the norm in all Qatari primary and secondary schools.

The Rand-Qatar Policy Institute also recommended major reforms at the postsecondary level, as a result of which from 2003 to 2007 Qatar University underwent a comprehensive restructuring process.[66] At the same time, the Qatar Foundation invited a series of American universities to open branch campuses in Qatar and to bring American-style higher education to the country. In less than ten years, six US universities set up campuses in Qatar and were admitting students in specific fields of study: Virginia Commonwealth University (1998) in design; Weill Cornell Medical College (2002) in medicine; Texas A&M University (2003) in engineering; Carnegie Mellon University (2004) in computer science and business; Georgetown University (2005) in international politics and economics; and Northwestern University (2007) in journalism and communication. In 2012, the Foundation announced plans for the establishment of a joint graduate law program with the Harvard Law School. As of 2012, Sheikha Moza, the chairperson of the Qatar Foundation, had received honorary doctorates from Virginia Commonwealth, Texas A&M, Carnegie Mellon, and Georgetown universities.

The guiding principles behind these reform initiatives were outlined in the *Qatar National Vision 2030*, which the emir unveiled in 2008. The document, which "aims at transforming Qatar into an advanced country by 2030,"[67] pays particular attention to the role of education in the country's future economic development. It calls for the creation of "a world-class educational system that equips citizens to achieve their aspirations and to meet the needs of Qatar's society."[68] This will in turn lead to the development of "a knowledge-based economy characterized by innovation; entrepreneurship; excellence in education; a world-class infrastructural backbone; the efficient delivery of public services; and transparent and accountable government."[69]

There have been a number of other state-sponsored or state-supported cultural initiatives with strong normative implications. Such cultural initiatives invariably pay homage to a broadly defined "Arab culture," but most also have highly pronounced Western and American underpinnings. For example, the Qatar Philharmonic Orchestra, established in 2008, mounts performances that are much more firmly rooted in the Western musical tradition than anything resembling Qatari culture and heritage.[70] For its part, the Doha Tribeca Film Festival, established in 2009 by one of the emir's daughters, has sought to "create bridges between the past and present, East and West"[71] by featuring both Arab and Western independent films. But, as of 2013, there is not even a nascent Qatari film industry. The Washington-based Brookings Institution, through its Doha office, has also been sponsoring an annual US-Islamic World Forum since 2004 in the Qatari capital, bringing together a number of regional political leaders and prominent American policymakers, diplomats, and artists.[72] The Forum's stated goal has been to foster dialogue and mutual understanding. But its strong American character and flavor are lost on few who are familiar with it.

Intentions aside, the Qatari state has emerged as a major proponent of spreading Western and especially American cultural norms and practices. This is as evident in the arts as it is in the educational arena. In fact, despite the *National Vision*'s promise to strike a balance between "modernization and preservation of traditions,"[73] the widespread encouragement of Westernization—and more specifically Americanization—of the cultural arena is palpable. This is in marked contrast to the lack of any official sanction or support given to promoting aspects of Iranian culture. In fact, Qatari authorities keep a deliberate, careful distance from most things Iranian. For example, they have consistently refused permission to the one Iranian bank operating in Qatar, Bank-e Saderat-e Iran, to have more than one branch office in Doha. Iranian citizens cannot acquire tourist visas to Qatar without formal invitation by a Qatari entity, and many Iranian restaurants in Doha complain about their inability to bring chefs from Iran to help run their restaurants. These and other similar restrictions are largely a product of official sensitivity to the ethnic background and the historical connections of many Qataris to Iran.[74]

What Qatar-Iranian relations lack in military, commercial, educational, and cultural dimensions they more than make up in personal and "fraternal" relations between the leaders of the two countries. The traffic between Doha and Tehran, only an hour and a half apart by airplane, features frequent trips by high-ranking officials calling on one another for the expressed purpose of strengthening ties. As table 3.1 indicates, in the twenty-four months between February 2008 and February 2010, the international press reported no less than seventeen official visits between the two countries, among them two visits to Tehran by the emir, one visit by the heir apparent, one visit to Doha by President Ahmadinejad, and other visits involving the Iranian foreign and defense Ministers as well as the Qatari chief of staff, information minister, and others. Each visit has been rich in symbolism, entailing much pomp and ceremony, and has been accompanied by grand declarations of enduring friendship and fraternal ties.

The United States is not unaware of the superficial nature of Qatari-Iranian relations. In a classified memo penned in December 2009, the US ambassador to Qatar assessed the sheikhdom's relations with the Islamic Republic as follows:

> Close consultations with Iran are necessary since Qatar shares a mammoth natural gas field with Iran. As a result, Qatar carefully maintains with Iran a high tempo of top-level contacts, which have increased since the protests following Iranian presidential elections in (June 2009). Qatar does this because it is convinced that such a close relationship with Iran is a key to safeguarding trillions of dollars in potential wealth. We are convinced that Qatar will not be dissuaded from maintaining those ties. . . . That said, Qatar's leaders—while careful not to say it publicly—do not trust Iran; and Qatar does not want Iran to have nuclear weapons.[75]

The cable was written for the benefit of the State Department in advance of Prime Minister Hamad Ben Jassim's visit to Washington in early 2010. In a separate cable, the prime minister is shown to be significantly blunter about Qatar's approach to his country's relations with Iran. The Iranians, he is reported to have said, "frequently press the Qataris to have dialogue

TABLE 3.1. Qatar-Iran relations (January 2008–April 2010)

Official visits	Expressions of friendship	Commercial and economic ties	Military cooperation	Friction
Qatari PM visits Tehran, February 2008	Ahmadinejad calls for expansion of ties, February 2008	Iran, Qatar, Russia announce hope for gas exporting organization, October 2008	Iran, Qatar discuss enhanced border security, August 2009	Tehran's *Hezbollah* newspaper criticizes Qatar-Israeli relations, April 2008
Iranian justice minister visits Qatar, April 2008	Emir urges dialog with Iran, March 2008		Iran, Qatar sign defense pact, February 2010	*Etemad-e Melli* criticizes Qatar for LNG extraction from South Pars field, November 2008
Qatari Delegation to Int'l Islamic Unity Conference, April 2008	Emir expresses friendship toward Iran, March 2008			*Aftab-e Yazd* criticizes Qatar for excessive gas extraction, January 2009
Qatari prime minister visits Tehran, May 2008	Iran supports Qatar's Lebanon mediation efforts, May 2008			*Al-Rayah* urges Iran to adopt positive relations with Arab neighbors, February 2009
Qatari finance minister visits Tehran, June 2008	Emir-Ahmadinejad phone conversation, May 2008			Islamic Republic News Agency warns against spread of artificial islands in Persian Gulf, May 2009
Emir visits Tehran, August 2008	Qatari labor minister calls Iranian counterpart, June 2008			Members of Parliament concerned over Qatar's LNG extraction from South Pars, January 2010
Iranian defense minister visits Qatar, September 2008	Emir invites Ahmadinejad to GCC summit, August 2008			Qatar installs enhanced US anti-missile system, January 2010
Ahmadinejad visits Doha, November 2008	Iranian foreign minister praises friendly relations with Qatar, Nov. 2008			Tehran's *Javan* urges demilitarization of Persian Gulf, February 2010
Iranian foreign minister visits Doha, March 2009	Emir-Ahmadinejad phone conversation, December 2008			

(continued)

TABLE 3.1. *(continued)*

Official visits	Expressions of friendship	Commercial and economic ties	Military cooperation	Friction
Qatari minister of information visits Tehran, April 2009	Emir expresses friendship with Iran, March 2009			
Qatari assistant foreign minister visits Tehran, May 2009	Ahmadinejad sends "friendship message" to emir, May 2009			
Majles speaker visits Doha, July 2009	Qatari prime minister expresses friendship toward Iran, June 2009			
Qatari chief of staff visits Tehran, July 2009	Iranian ambassador calls Iran-Qatari relations "best and finest with the sisterly Qatar," September 2009			
Iranian foreign minister visits Doha, November 2009	Deputy emir calls Iran-Qatari relations "long-standing and brotherly," February 2010			
Emir visits Tehran, meets Khamenei, November 2009	Ahmadinejad, others, praise Qatar's active diplomacy, February 2010			
Heir apparent visits Tehran, February 2010				
Iranian defense minister visits Qatar, February 2010				

on their shared natural gas field and attempt to expand dialogue to include other subjects." But the Qataris "are always throwing cold water on their ideas." The PM is quoted as having summarized Qatar's relations with Iran as ones premised on less than trust: "They lie to us, and we lie to them."[76] In a similar vein, according to another released US embassy cable, when the heir apparent paid a highly publicized visit to President Ahmadinejad in Tehran in February 2010, he limited his visit to only half a day and declined Iranian offers to visit cultural sights outside the capital.[77]

In solidifying the international regimes that ensure their positions of dominance, hegemonic powers seek to persuade others to buy into their vision of the world order and to defer to their international leadership in various arenas of concern, especially in the areas of security and international trade and finance.[78] At the same time, hegemonic leadership must constantly recreate the conditions of its own existence in order to avoid collapse, complementing the relationship between the hegemon and its subordinates with healthy doses of cooperation and protection.[79] In Qatar's case, the country's approach to the United States also reflects its leaders' cultural, political, and commercial preferences. The emir and his inner circle have made a deliberate decision to pursue a US-centric path of economic development and cultural change, one that is given official sanction through various forms of royal patronage, and is guaranteed by the US security umbrella. This is reflected in the plethora of institutional arrangements that underwrite the three primary pillars of Qatari-US relations. At the same time, the Qatari state strongly resists the development of in-depth institutional ties with Iran, mindful that such arrangements might, intentionally or unintentionally, resonate with the sensibilities of the country's otherwise compliant Shi'a population. Nevertheless, Qatari leaders maintain quite warm and friendly personal relations with their Iranian counterparts, with the primary motivator on the part of the Qataris appearing to be fear. This fear appears to be rooted in two possible scenarios: first, that Tehran's frictions with Washington do not translate into frictions with Doha despite the deep and multifaceted nature of Qatari-US relations; second, that in the event of Iran somehow finding itself attacked or under increased pressure, the Qataris of Iranian background would not fault Qatar for being complicit in an anti-Iranian front. Ultimately, Qatar's warm relations with Iran appear to be a direct byproduct of—or, more accurately, a reactive impulse to—its wide-ranging and institutionally ingrained relations with the United States.

Given the preponderant US military presence in the Persian Gulf, irrespective of Qatar's security concerns, the sheikhdom to a large extent benefits from "free riding," while maintaining a significant amount of structurally rooted cooperation that characterizes the relations between the two countries. We know that "the longer one's time horizon, the greater the rewards from mutual cooperation are in comparison to fleeting benefits from free riding."[80] As the narrative here indicates, Qatari-US cooperation is systematic, multidimensional, and built on long-term assumptions. As such, despite occasional differences over priority and policy, it is likely to remain resilient and robust for the foreseeable future.

An effective survival strategy, Qatar's carefully balanced hedging has served it well. Apart from Oman, Qatar is the only other Persian Gulf state with whom Iran has not had any contentious issues since 1979.[81] The sheikhdom has cultivated an image of evenhandedness and balance that few of the other states in the Middle East can claim to have. As such it has emerged as a trusted "honest broker" that is well positioned to mediate conflicts. Its alliance and friendship is not taken for granted and is actively courted by both Iran and the United States. And, correspondingly, despite its strategic position at the mouth of the Hormuz Strait, it enjoys perhaps the largest immunity from any intentional or unintentional spillover of a military conflict involving Iran and other international actors, most notably the United States and Israel.

Military Security and Protection

Military and security arrangements underwrite the larger context within which US-Qatari relations unfold. Unlike many of its regional neighbors, particularly the UAE and Kuwait, Qatar does not have a credible military force of its own. It has an estimated total of 12,000 individuals in uniform, plus an additional 8,000 employed in the public security forces. Of these, an undisclosed but disproportionately large number are non-nationals from Yemeni and Pakistani backgrounds. Part of the problem is demographic: there simply are not enough Qataris of a militarily significant age to address the country's growing military needs. At the same time, military service is not a career path to which most young Qataris aspire, drawn instead to the private sector and the prospects of secure, prestigious white collar positions fattened by the state's labor Qatarization policies.

Equally important appear to be deliberate decisions, made at the highest levels of the state, to relegate the country's defense to the much more powerful, and in the Persian Gulf omnipotent, United States. According to one of the cables from the US embassy in Doha, "the QAF (Qatar Air Force) could put up little defense against Qatar's primary perceived threats—Saudi Arabia and Iran—and the U.S. military's presence here is larger and far more capable than Qatar's forces."[82] In the Americans' assessment, Qatar lacks a comprehensive national military strategy, and the Qataris have been cool to the US military's proposal to draw up one for them.[83] Similarly, unlike its regional neighbors, Qatar's requests for the purchase of advanced US weaponry have been modest over time, and at times the Qataris have backed out of weapons deals with the United States.[84]

Precisely why the Qatari leadership has chosen to pursue an apparently minimalist military policy is hard to answer. Part of the calculation must surely involve the country's small size as compared to Iran and Saudi Arabia—why start an arms competition that cannot possibly be won? Another reason appears to lie in the emphasis on domestic infrastructural development and on international investments. Knowing there is the US protection to rely on, the Qatari leadership appears to have made a strategic decision to focus its financial resources on other endeavors. And, lest the Americans take the Qataris for granted, there is always hedging to remind them otherwise. The US embassy appears to have read the Qatari strategy correctly:

> We believe Qatar wishes to make incremental improvements in all components of its military, with the caveat that such investments will remain subordinate to the primary national goal of economic and human development.... Qatar's desire to be the "friend of everyone and enemy of no one" means that politics will remain a crucial factor in any defense purchase decisions.[85]

Qatar is home to two large US bases, the Al Udeid air base, which is estimated to house as many as 10,000 US military personnel and more that 120 aircraft, and the As Sayliha, which houses the Army component of the US Central Command.[86] Al Udeid, which has the longest runway in the Persian Gulf, was built by the Qataris in 2000 at an estimated cost of more than $1 billion. The two facilities constitute the largest pre-positioning bases outside of the United States.[87] From 2002 to 2011, the United States is estimated to have spent more than $459 million in the expansion and upgrading of the Al Udeid Air base alone.[88] For 2012, the US administration requested another $37 million from Congress to continue the base's construction projects. In 2012 the Pentagon was reported to be building a missile-defense radar station at a secret location in Qatar at a cost of $12.2 million.[89]

As part of its overall foreign and security policies, the Qatari state is committed to "a broad strategic partnership with the United States."[90] American officials are therefore repeatedly assured that for Qatar "maintaining strategic relations with the United States is the 'number one priority' and that Qatar 'will never change' that alignment."[91] What appears to be neglect on the part of state elites of a key component of national defense is, in fact, part of a deliberately calculated decision to rely on an outside, far more powerful patron. But reliance on the US for defense and security ought not to be conflated with a policy of bandwagoning and aligning foreign policies and priorities in a way to match those of the United States. Qatar needs and likes the American military protection; it would be otherwise defenseless on its own. But it also likes its foreign policy independence, as manifested in its hedging, as a way of maintaining open lines of communication with as many disparate international actors as possible, friend and foe alike.

Branding and Hyperactive Diplomacy

Qatar's diplomatic hyperactivism, made possible by an efficiently run and cohesive state, occurs concurrently with—and is reinforced by—an intense campaign of branding the country. In the ultra-competitive era of globalization and in the race to attract ever-greater levels of direct foreign investment, states often embark on aggressive campaigns of branding in order to acquire positive reputations both generally and in specific areas. The explosion of the international media and the accessibility of global communication networks have made a country's image and reputation central to its economic and diplomatic success. According to one observer of the phenomenon, "branding has emerged as a state asset to rival geopolitics and traditional considerations of power."[92] In fact, maintains another, "the unbranded state has a difficult time attracting economic and political attention."[93]

Since the mid-1990s, Qatar has emerged as a "brand state" par excellence, with concerted efforts underway in multiple areas of politics, economics, sports, and culture.[94] Slick advertisements in glossy magazines and on TV screens across the world often showcase Qatar Airways (billed as "the world's five-star airline"); Qatar Foundation, which is said to "help the world think";[95] the Museum of Islamic Art, with its world-class art collection; and the country's business-friendly environment. Securing a place for itself as a hub for major world sporting events, the country hosted the 2006 Asian Games, unsuccessfully bid for the 2016 Summer Olympic Games, hosted football's Asian Cup in 2011, and shocked the sporting world by winning the bid to host the 2022 FIFA World Cup. Despite the scarcity of Qatari-born athletes, Doha frequently hosts international tournaments in handball, football, track and field, and gymnastics. In November 2012, meanwhile, Sheikha Moza announced the creation of a global program in collaboration with the United Nations designed to educate 61 million children worldwide who have no access to formal schooling.[96]

In these respects, Qatar's branding efforts are not greatly different from those undertaken by the other small Persian Gulf states. It is all but impossible to be a soccer fan anywhere in the world and not know of Dubai and its airline, Emirates, which is a key sponsor of teams and has a major soccer stadium in London named after it. The Bahrain Rally, New York University-Abu Dhabi, and the planned Louvre Abu Dhabi are all meant to solidify respective reputations as havens for auto racing, culture and learning, and modernity and globalization. There are two unique forms of branding, however, that set Qatar apart from other regional actors and, in fact, from much of the rest of the world. One is the Al Jazeera satellite television station, and the other is diplomatic mediation and conflict resolution efforts.

Al Jazeera owed its genesis to a desire by the then heir apparent sheikh Hamad bin Khalifa in 1994 to modernize Qatari state television and to broadcast its programs via satellite.[97] Soon after assuming power, he issued a decree in 1996 establishing Al Jazeera, whose broadcasts expanded quickly from six to twelve and eventually to twenty-four hours a day. Benefiting from the premature demise of the BBC's Arabic news service due to editorial differences with the venture's Saudi financiers, and an unexpected open slot in the Arabsat satellite, Al Jazeera's popularity grew as rapidly as Arab audiences could tune in. The key was the station's radical departure from what had been the norm across the Arab world by offering news that went beyond mere presentation of doctored government statistics and data and instead offered what were raw, often unvarnished, facts. Controversial guests and even Israelis speaking in Hebrew, once shocking for Arab audiences, became regular features of the network's often piercing news stories. Soon the network began to rival, and in some areas even surpass, the BBC and CNN as a recognized international source of information.[98] Far more popular were the many news talk shows, hosted by colorful personalities and tackling political, social, and even religious topics long considered taboo across the Arab world.[99]

The launching of Al Jazeera was inspired by the effort to brand Qatar as a pioneer on several fronts, ranging from dialogue and discussion to openness and debate, communication technology, and a news trailblazer. Equally important was the desire to project Qatar's image as a serious regional and global player. In the process the network has managed to attract the ire of countless Arab and Western governments that have either harassed or altogether barred its correspondents from reporting from their territories, or, as is the case with the Saudis, have pressured advertisers to stay away from the network.[100] Few inside Al Jazeera believe that the US military's bombing of its facilities in Afghanistan in November 2001 and in Iraq in April 2003 were, as the Americans claim, accidental, pointing instead to the leaked 2004 memo between the Bush White House and former British prime minister Tony Blair concerning the bombing of its headquarters in Doha.[101]

While in the short run such incidents are likely to complicate the job of Qatari diplomats, who often find themselves addressing complaints from around the world about Al Jazeera broadcasts, in the long run the station serves Qatar's diplomatic interests well.[102] Al Jazeera has gone beyond simply giving "a big voice to a tiny country." The network's reach across the globe expanded dramatically in 2006 when it established Al Jazeera International, a twenty-four hour satellite channel delivering the news in English. Beginning in 2003 the network started adding a number of sports channels, complemented with additional channels devoted to public affairs (Al Jazeera Mubasher, in 2005), children's programs (Al Jazeera Children's Channel, also in 2005), and documentary shows (the Al Jazeera Documentary Channel, launched in 2007). By 2010, according to the annual Arab Public Opinion Poll, some 78 percent of individuals across the Arab world claimed to rely on Al Jazeera as their main source of international news.[103] In 2011, the network announced planned expansions of broadcasts to Turkish, Swahili, and Balkan audiences. At the same time, with advertisers few and far in-between, and with mounting expenses as it expands the reach and variety of its offerings, the network continues to rely overwhelmingly on the Qatari government for its operating budget. As mentioned earlier, the ambiguous nature of the relationship between Al Jazeera's editorial choices and Qatari diplomacy remains a subject of debate and controversy.[104] Protestations regarding its uneven coverage of the Arab Spring notwithstanding, the rebellions engulfing the Middle East solidified the network's indispensability to the region's—and indeed the world's—communication revolution. In the words of one of its chief officers, the network "experienced rebirth" through the Arab Spring,[105] and, in the process, surpassed its original goal of helping put Qatar on the map.

A second, rather distinctive, branding strategy that Qatar employs is through proactive attempts at regional conflict resolution. Over the past decade, Qatar has become one of the world's most active mediators in international conflicts across the Middle East and parts of Africa, and in the process it has actively cultivated an image of itself as an honest broker interested in peace and stability. These have included mediation efforts in Yemen, Palestine, Sudan, Djibouti and Eritrea, and, most notably, in Lebanon. Qatar has not had much success in its efforts to bring about peaceful resolutions to the conflicts between Hamas and Fatah in Palestine in 2008, and between the Huthis and the central government in Yemen in 2009–2010. But its successes in hosting substantive talks aimed at ending or at least curtailing the Sudanese civil war and the border dispute between Djibouti and Eritrea, both in 2010, are quite notable. Even more significant was Qatar's successful mediation of a serious political crisis in Lebanon in May 2008 that threatened to reignite the country's civil war. In this particular instance, Qatari mediation succeeded where previous efforts by the Arab League, the United Nations, and France had all failed. Even in relation to cases where lasting peace has been elusive, successful mediation is often measured in terms of the reduction of hostilities rather than the effectiveness of a lasting agreement.[106] As such, the value of Qatari efforts at mediation, regardless of their yield, should not be underestimated.

In a region known for its cross-border crises and intra-national sectarian strife, Qatar has quickly emerged as an actor adept at diffusing and mediating conflicts. Doha's "niche diplomacy" has led to its reputation as a reliable peace broker.[107] An integral part of its foreign policy pursuits, Qatar's insistence on playing a mediating role has at times provoked the ire of other regional actors hoping to assume such a role for themselves. For instance, Egypt, which has long viewed itself as Sudan's primary patron, initially sought to take the initiative away from Qatar in solving the Darfur crisis. In the end, Qatar's richer pockets and less of a history in relation to Sudan won.[108]

As far as international mediation efforts by state actors are concerned, several aspects of Qatari mediation efforts stand out. By and large mediation often takes place under the aegis of one of the major powers such as the United States (Secretary of State Henry Kissinger's "shuttle diplomacy" designed to bring the Arab-Israeli 1973 War to a conclusion), the former Soviet Union (Moscow's 1966 efforts to end the Indo-Pakistani conflict), France, or Britain. Sometimes "middle powers" also involve themselves in international mediation efforts, as was the case with Austria during the premiership of Bruno Kreisky (1970–1983), Algeria and its role in the freeing of American hostages in Iran in 1981, and, in 2010, Brazil and Turkey in relation to the Iranian nuclear program. Rarely do small states involve themselves in international mediations as a principal mediator, with Norway's role in sponsoring the secret talks that led to the 1993 Oslo Accords being a major exception.[109] In specific relation to the Middle East, the role of mediator has traditionally been played by the regional heavyweights, in particular Egypt and Saudi Arabia, each of whom views itself as the protector of the regional status quo.[110] For their part, none of the other GCC states have ever engaged in mediation efforts. Qatar's prolific mediation efforts are unique both regionally and, given its size, globally.

Qatar's motivations for emerging as a serious mediator of international conflicts are not that different from those of other states wishing to shine on the world stage. As early as the seventeenth century, diplomats at the court of Louis XIV advised him of the prestige attached to mediating international conflicts, and, today, the spread of the global media has only added to the veracity of that advice.[111] States may also engage in mediation because the potential costs of standing by as a conflict rages on are seen as greater than the risks involved in becoming a mediator. The dangers of spillover, particularly for conflicts that are nearby or may directly affect a state's interests, often serve as powerful motivators for mediation efforts.

Similarly important are calculations of regional or global power politics that are perceived as enhancing the mediator state's position within the international system.[112] Moreover, for many mediator states, mediation is not simply a response to emerging developments. Rather, mediation *is* foreign policy; it is a "broader framework of strategic action within the international and domestic political systems."[113] In the case of Qatari diplomacy, mediation appears to be an integral part of its toolbox.

In addition to these broad objectives, for Qatar mediation efforts serve specific purposes related to branding. Qatar is seeking to carve out for itself the image of an experienced mediator with a proven track record, a regional diplomatic powerhouse, an honest broker, a wise and mature player interested in peace and stability. The fanfare with which Qatari mediation efforts are often accompanied bespeak of their importance to the country's carefully crafted image. Secrecy is often considered to be one of the central elements of any mediation effort. "If elements of secret negotiations are leaked," according to the diplomatic historian R. P. Barston, "difficulties occur in that possible concessions by one party are exposed, thus weakening its position; the credibility of the mediator may be called into question; or an incorrect or misinterpreted version of the 'contract' discussions or negotiations may be presented by the media."[114] Invariably, Qatar's mediation effort have taken place in the limelight and often before the local and regional media outlets, with high-ranking Qatari diplomats frequently granting media interviews as the process is still underway and reflecting on the country's role in positive, often glowing terms.[115] Keenly aware of the advertising value of their mediation efforts, long after the mediation process is over Qatari leaders continue to refer to it as one of their major accomplishments and an important contribution to regional stability. They cannot, after all, be blamed for being proud of having successfully positioned their country as a peace broker in a region so rich with warriors.

Effective diplomacy of crisis management and conflict termination requires in-depth knowledge of other states and nonstate actors, especially those in alliance or in opposition, and their perceptions of the issues at hand and the world in general.[116] Given the lack of depth in Qatar's diplomatic bureaucracy—a structural condition arising from its demographic limitations—and the resulting dearth of skills and knowhow, as well as resources necessary for sustained, on-the-ground presence, it is far from clear how sustainable and lasting Qatar's mediation efforts are in the long run. Take, for example, the crowning achievement of Qatar's mediation efforts, namely its astounding success at bringing Lebanon's contentious factions to the negotiating table in 2009.[117] What came to be known as the Doha Accord, and was accompanied by the customary fanfare, nearly unraveled a year later once the Lebanese factions were faced with the difficult realities of translating signatures and handshakes into action on the ground. When in Beirut the rubber of the agreement hit the rocky road, it was not the Qataris who managed to salvage the agreement, but instead the Saudis and the Syrians, and, if rumors are to be believed, also the Iranians. Qatar's mediation efforts, it seems, are at best only partially successful; at worst, they are expensive and glitzy media events. Their overriding objective of putting the country on the map and solidifying its brand image as a peacemaker is brilliantly successful. But, for now at least, their value in bringing meaningful peace and stability to the region is far from clear.

International Investments

Another means through which Qatar seeks to enhance its influence regionally and internationally is by international investments through its sovereign wealth fund (SWF). In this respect Qatar is by no means alone, and, with its SWF, the Qatar Investment Authority (QIA), established only in 2005, it actually entered the game relatively late. The earliest SWF dates back to 1953, with the pioneering work of the Kuwait Investment Authority, set up before Kuwait was even an independent country. Following precipitous rises in oil prices beginning in 2002, Russia and the Persian Gulf oil produces started accumulating massive reserves, which they invested through their SWFs. These funds are generally set up with aim of helping facilitate macroeconomic stabilization, seeking higher returns on investments, creating a pool of wealth for future generations, and helping the growth of domestic industries.[118] It was only at that point, in the politically charged atmosphere of the post–9/11 era, that the size and operations of SWFs began garnering attention and, in many cases, suspicion.[119] The negative attention directed at the secretive SWFs operating out of the Persian Gulf, especially the Abu Dhabi Investment Authority (ADIA) and Mubadala, also of Abu Dhabi, was particularly intense.[120]

In reality, the estimated size and influence of Persian Gulf SWFs has often been exaggerated, with countries such as Malaysia, Algeria, Mexico, and Thailand having significantly more foreign reserves excluding gold.[121] Within the Persian Gulf region, the QIA's estimated assets of $85 to more than $100 billion is relatively modest compared to the holdings of Abu Dhabi Investment Authority (ADIA) and the Kuwait Investment Authority (KIA), both of which are thought to be into the hundreds of billions of dollars.[122] But for Qatar, international investments assume particular significance for two primary reasons. First, these investments take place in a dynamic context within which mutually reinforcing relationships are forged with the three other aspects of the country's foreign policy—military security, hedging, and especially branding. By and large, "sovereign wealth fund portfolios appear to act as economically driven investors."[123] In Qatar's case, according to a high-ranking official within the QIA, the Qatari fund is engaged in a "drive to build up a diversified portfolio globally of the highest quality assets across a broad spectrum of asset classes."[124] Also important for the QIA is fostering technology transfer to Qatar through encouraging the companies it acquires to set up branches or subsidiaries in the country. When in 2009 the QIA purchased a 10 percent stake in Porsche, for example, the luxury automaker agreed to set up testing and research and development facilities in Qatar.[125] Diversification and technology transfer notwithstanding, an important direct and indirect aspect of Qatar's international investment strategy is its close alignment with the country's foreign policy initiatives.

This alignment is both actual and perceived, supported by numerous examples.[126] When in the spring and summer of 2011 Qatar had dove headfirst into the Libyan conflict by throwing its full diplomatic and military support behind the National Transitional Council (NTC) in its fight against Colonel Qaddafi,[127] the emir is reported to have promised Tunisia a resumption of its investments in the country in return for Tunisia's recognition of the NTC.[128] Interestingly, although its prior investment commitments in Libya amounted to $10 billion, the QIA was initially reluctant to return to post-Qaddafi Libya because of the country's risky investment environment.[129] It thus chose to invest in Tunisia instead. A second example is the rapid increase in the volume of trade between Lebanon and Qatar, from $55 million to $93 million between 2005 and 2009, when the Doha Agreement was signed saving Lebanon from civil war, and also safeguarding Qatari investment in Lebanon in infrastructure, water and power, communications, and the health-care sectors.[130] A third example comes from Syria, whose acquiescence was necessary to make the Doha Accord possible, where in 2008 the Qatari Diar announced plans to invest as much as $12 billion in the country over a five-year period.[131]

Second, Qatar tends to be somewhat uncharacteristically aggressive in its investment strategies compared to the other Persian Gulf SWFs, particularly when it comes to investments in Europe. Similar to the QIA, other funds have also been investing heavily in Europe. But the Qatari fund stands out for the broad range and diversity of its European investments across multiple sectors.[132] In the process Qatar has acquired a reputation as "the most deal-hungry of the Gulf states."[133] In 2012, a QIA official, who boasted about the fund's more than $30 billion assets for investments that year alone, referred to the fund's investment strategy as "opportunistic" and maintained that whenever "anything (comes) at the right price, we are willing to buy."[134] As a 2010 report put it, none of the other sovereign wealth funds "can match the speed and scale with which Qatar has set about spending its surplus cash to acquire, either in whole or in part, some of the oldest and biggest companies in markets from Britain and France to Morocco, Sudan, the Seychelles and Indonesia."[135] According to the Qatari prime minister Hamad bin Jassem Al Thani, who is also the QIA's chief executive officer, in 2011 alone Qatar intended to invest some $30 billion abroad, making QIA "one of the world's most acquisitive sovereign wealth funds."[136] The fund's aggressive investment strategy suggests that the "QIA is trying to make up for lost time."[137]

As "a fast-moving, active, strategic global investor," the QIA has quickly emerged as an important and influential actor in global real estate, financial services, health care, and construction industries.[138] A 2009 report added energy, commodities, food, and water to the list of QIA's interests.[139] In a 2010 confidential conversation with the US ambassador to Qatar, a member of the QIA Executive Board outlined an investment strategy focused on three areas: "acquire distressed businesses that have cash flow problems but are otherwise healthy; invest in a broad range of commodities; and purchase, in the second half of CY 2010, commercial real estate in prime locations, principally in the United States and Europe."[140] The QIA seeks long-term and geographically diversified investment strategies.[141] Although in recent years the primary focus of the QIA has been the acquisition of prime real estate in London, it has projects in Cuba, Eritrea, Indonesia, Morocco, Oman, Qatar, Sudan, the United States, and Vietnam.[142] Altogether, the Qatari Diar, the real estate investment arm of the QIA, is present in thirty-two countries around the world, making Qatar one of the largest overseas property investors in the world in 2010.[143] In recent years, the QIA has also entered into strategic partnerships with other SWFs to cooperate on joint investments and takeovers, as it did in 2009, for example, when it joined the China Investment Corporation to purchase $448 million worth of shares in Songbird Estates, the owner of much of London's Canary Wharf.[144]

The global financial crisis that began in 2008, resulting in a serious contraction of Dubai's financial prowess and massive slowdowns in Europe and the United States, turned out to be an investment bonanza for Qatar. The emir himself went on record on the issue: "With the current financial crisis, many countries prefer to keep their money instead of investing it abroad. For us, though, this is an opportunity that will not be repeated in the next 20 years."[145] The emir's words cannot be neglected, at least not insofar as the QIA is concerned. The fund began to aggressively invest in stressed financial institutions in the West, spending some $8.2 billion in just the first quarter of 2008, and investing another £1 billion in Barclays Bank.[146] The QIA also purchased a 24 percent share in the London Stock Exchange along with a 10 percent share in OMX, the Nordic Stock Exchange based in Stockholm.[147] In 2011, as the Greek banking system teetered on the verge of collapse, Qatar agreed to the purchase of a number of stressed Greek assets, adding to the $5 billion in Greek assets and investments it had already acquired by 2010.[148] In 2012 the QIA acquired a 5.2 percent stake in Tiffany's, the US jewelry maker, becoming its largest stakeholder, adding to its stakes in the French media company Lagardere, of which it owns 10 percent, and the construction giant Vinci, of which it owns 5.6 percent.[149] That same year the QIA emerged as the biggest buyer of European property, reportedly spending $4.3 billion on eight major deals that included the London Olympic Village and a shopping mall on Paris's Champs Elysees.[150] To varying degrees, Qatar's European investments appear to have been quite profitable, having yielded more than $630 million in profits by the first quarter of 2011.[151]

The 2011 Arab Spring provided another investment opportunity for Qatar, with the Qatar Investment Authority investing some $543.8 million in Egypt, for example, and creating 4,000 jobs in the country's hard-hit economy.[152] As continued political instability in Egypt eroded the prospects of a speedy recovery of the country's economy throughout 2011, Qatar announced its willingness to increase its Egyptian investments to $10 billion.[153] Moreover, in August 2012, Qatar announced depositing $2 billion in the Egyptian Central Bank to help the country's economy stabilize.[154] Before the start of Libya's 2011 civil war and Colonel Qaddafi's eventual overthrow, Qatari investments in Libya reported amounted to $10 billion. With an estimated $700 billion needed for infrastructural repair and investment,[155] Libya finds itself greatly dependent on the financial largess of the one Arab country so publicly involved in Colonel Qaddafi's collapse. Qatar's influence in Libya is only likely to increase over the coming years.

In 2009, Qatar invested some £2 billion in Britain, a sum that shot up to £10 billion in 2010.[156] By 2012, nearly 80 percent of the QIA's property purchases were in either London or Paris.[157] These investments included some of the most prized showpieces of Britain's economy. The *Times* of London could hardly contain its resentment:

> In 1868 Colonel Lewis Pelly, Britain's man in the Persian Gulf, arrived on a wind-blasted peninsula and struck a deal with Sheikh Mohammed Bin Thani, "a shrewd, wary old man" according to a contemporary account, with "the air of [an] avaricious pearl-merchant."
>
> The British Empire was merely seeking to keep peace, and the Sheikh appeared to be "the most influential man in the area," but that simple act of recognition helped to secure his leadership and that of his heirs in Qatar. One hundred and forty years later, the scales have shifted and the sheikh's descendants now call the shots in their dealings with the British: the Government pays homage to Qatar, peers fly there, royals seek the Emir's favour.
>
> We are all in his power. Without Qatar and its vast reserves of natural gas Britain would suffer power cuts or fuel rationing. Qatar, via its fleet of investment vehicles, has also invested tens of billions in Britain. It owns a quarter of our third-biggest supermarket (Sainsbury's), a chunk of one of our biggest banks (Barclays), a stake in the London Stock Exchange, the US Embassy in Grosvenor Square, part of Canary Wharf and most of the showpiece skyscraper The Shard that is taking shape close to London Bridge.[158]

The article goes on to wonder if there will be a Doha branch of Harrods, Britain's most well-known department store, which the Qataris also bought in 2010.

It seems befitting to conclude this section with a reminder of the relationship between Qatari international investments and the country's foreign policy, one which, it must be remembered, is neither linear nor one-dimensional. On the one hand, the QIA appears to be a highly professional, and by all accounts highly successful, investment vehicle. In addition to drawing on local expertise, the QIA has attracted some of the most talented, and expensive, international bankers, who have turned it into one of the world's most active SWFs. Given expectations of uninterrupted revenue streams from the sale of liquefied natural gas in the coming years, the QIA is expected to "grow exponentially" in the coming years.[159]

On the other hand, the QIA's strategy is closely aligned with the objectives and interests of the country's foreign policy. The work of the QIA is immensely critical to the larger domestic and international trajectory and profile of Qatar. The QIA itself is seen as one of the country's most important institutions, as evident by its choice of leadership; Sheikh Tamim bin Hamad Al Thani is its chairman, and Sheikh Hamad bin Jassim bin Jabr Al Thani, holding the dual posts of Qatar's foreign minister and prime minister, serves as its chief executive. Its board of directors also includes some of the Qatari regime's most trusted, and capable, figures. Although highly opaque and secretive, the QIA's works and operations tend to be highly politicized. According to one former employee, "People get on with their jobs but are always looking over their shoulders thinking of the implications: will it upset the Emir? Will it upset the PM? . . . To understand the role of the Emir and the workings of the upper reaches of Qatari Diar, you need to look at it as being more akin to the court of the Turkish Sultan c1700 than the boardroom of (a modern corporation)."[160]

What upsets the emir and the PM is the QIA's underperformance. What pleases them is more money, more visibility, and more influence. In that, it has succeeded. And there is little reason to believe this success will not continue into the future. In the process, the monarch is likely to collect his share of criticisms and unsolicited advice. "Qatar's strutting on the world stage," wrote one particularly cranky commentator, "would seem more savvy if the QIA was half as transparent about its strategy for managing its existing wealth as it is for domestic development."[161] But, Byzantine opacity aside, the QIA has done what it was meant to do—to make Qatar, a small, young state in a rough neighborhood a key and highly consequential player in the world of global finance and diplomacy.

Finally, mention must be made of Qatar's agricultural land purchases abroad, about which even less is known as compared to the workings of the QIA. In 2008 the QIA established a company for the specific purpose of purchasing lands and investing in food production companies around the world. With an initial capitalization of $1 billion, by 2012 Hassad Food was reported to have invested more than $2 billion in the agricultural sector worldwide.[162] Preliminary research indicates that, along with the rest of the GCC states, Qatar is a major investor in and purchaser of agricultural lands aboard, especially in many parts of Africa, most notably in Ethiopia, Gambia, Ghana, Kenya, Sudan, and Mozambique, and also in a few countries in Southeast Asia, including the Philippines and Cambodia.[163] Hassad has also purchased sizeable plots of land in New Zealand and Australia—in the latter just under 250,000 hectares by 2012[164]—as well as in Argentina, India, Pakistan, Georgia, Ukraine, and Uruguay.[165] The company is also reportedly a major stakeholder in agricultural corporations in Kenya, Brazil, Argentina, and Turkey, among others. The primary purpose of these purchases and investments is to guarantee the country's food security through ensuring supplies and access to agricultural resources.[166] One of their major consequences is to enhance Qatar's global financial status and, especially insofar as other developing counties are concerned, their dependence on continued investments and revenue flows from the small Sheikhdom.

Conclusion

Since 1995 Qatar has steadily emerged as one of the major players in Persian Gulf and Middle Eastern politics as well as in global finance. Under the energetic leadership of Sheikh Hamad bin Khalifa Al Thani and his trusted lieutenants, Qatar has successfully employed a combination of diplomatic hyperactivism and hedging, the American security umbrella, economic prowess, and branding to position itself as an influential actor in the region and beyond. By turning hedging into a science, it has set itself apart from the rest of the region by pursuing a foreign policy that at first glance seems maverick but is actually well thought out. In the process not only has it broken out of the mold in which small states are generally cast but it has indeed thrown into question existing assumptions about the types of power and influence that may be generated in international politics.

Despite the pervasive influence of Al Jazeera on Arab public opinion across the globe, Qatar may not really be said to have soft power; Al Jazeera may have brought Qatar worldwide acclaim and admiration among Arabs and many others, but it has not, at least for now, led to the widespread salience and appeal of Qatari values and a sense of Qatariness. Al Jazeera is primarily a mechanism for branding the country; the residual admiration that it generates for Qatar is at best marginal. More than anything else, as yet another element in the country's branding arsenal, Al Jazeera has helped Qatar, as one observer has somewhat cynically noted, create "an extremely digestible narrative."[167]

Neither does the country have hard or smart powers. Yet its negotiating skills are sought after by those disputants eager to exit their conflicts in face-saving ways.[168] Its diplomatic self-confidence in dealing with the Americans, the Iranians, the Israelis, Hamas, the Sudanese and the Yemenis, and with everyone else, has been extremely high, betraying a sense of can-do optimism that is indeed rarely found anywhere else in the today's Persian Gulf and the larger Middle East. What Qatar has is a subtle form of power—a quiet, steadily accumulating type of power that has resulted from a combination of financial affluence, diplomatic activism, self-confident and cohesive leadership, effective self-advertizing, and a sense of indispensability to peace and stability when others busy themselves with conflicts. What Qatar has done is to generate and to benefit from what is by all indications *subtle power*.

A *Times* journalist captures the essence of Qatari foreign policy perfectly:

> Since the invasion of neighboring Kuwait in 1990, Emir Hamad bin Khalifa Al-Thani decided that anonymity is no form of defense. With energetic diplomacy he has established an unrivalled contacts book straddling regional tensions and has alliances with the United States, and Israel, Hamas, and Iran.
>
> Underpinning all this is money . . . The attraction of Western economies struggling out of recession is obvious.
>
> This financial clout keeps countries coming back. And the emirate has grown more daring, mediating in Lebanon, Darfur, Yemen and Eritrea.
>
> In Washington, the Obama Administration has recognised the value in Qatar's relationship with rogue states and terrorist groups.
>
> As the US tries to ensure regional stability while extricating itself from two foreign wars, Doha's willingness to engage America's enemies on its behalf in invaluable.[169]

Is this increasing power of Qatar sustainable in the long term? The question of what the rise of Qatar's power and influence means for the long-term geopolitical alignments of the Persian Gulf in general and Qatar in particular is difficult to answer. In sultanistic regimes such as Qatar, one heart attack can change everything. Especially in Qatar where there is no parliament, no meaningful armed forces to speak of, no institutional bastions of the state, only an army of imported functionaries who implement the decisions made by a few Qataris. In Qatar individuals have not just replaced institutions. They have become institutions. If Louis XIV were alive today, he would have felt at home in Qatari politics. And, just as the forced transition of power in 1995 radically changed the direction and tenor of Qatar's domestic and international politics, it is conceivable that the next power transition would also usher significant shifts in Qatar's perceptions of itself and the global position it is seeking to carve out for itself.

Although conceivable, several indicators point to the unlikelihood of dramatic alterations in Qatar's ambitious diplomatic pursuits and its far-reaching programs of domestic social change. Even if the country's next emir wishes to pursue fundamentally different domestic and international priorities, by now path dependency makes such possible developments as retrenchment from the global economy, moving away from the US security umbrella, or abandoning hedging extremely difficult and at best highly incremental. At any rate, for a future emir to steer the country too far from what has become the norm in each of these areas would require substantial political capital, which neither the current heir apparent, nor anyone else within the royal household possesses. Qatar is likely to pursue its current domestic and geopolitical trajectories for generations to come.

The Stability of Royal Autocracy

Qatar can capitalize on its resources and its strategic location only if it has its domestic house in order. While larger structural developments in the Persian Gulf region and in the larger Middle East may have played important roles in creating leadership opportunities for Qatar, the deliberate policies and priorities of the Qatari leadership have been instrumental in capitalizing on those opportunities and in maneuvering developing circumstances to their advantage. Qatar's current regional and international ascent cannot last without a visionary and determined leadership that feels secure in its domestic position.

More than forty years after the country's official independence, and more than two hundred years after its birth as a country, Qatar is still undergoing a process of state formation. Successive rulers have proliferated state institutions as a means of expanding their patronage resources and thus ensuring their own tenure in office, and Sheikh Hamad, perhaps the country's most energetic and transformative leader, has been no exception. He has staffed existing and new institutions of the state with younger cohorts sharing his vision of the country's future, dismantled some institutional bastions of conservatism, and, when necessary, created parallel institutions meant to compete with and eventually eclipse older ones.[1] In the process, he has streamlined and brought under control internal family politics, has effectively monopolized the political process under his consolidated rule, and has ensured that succession remains within his own branch of the family.

Al Thani rule per se was never threatened, as from the earliest days of its move into the city the family was able to establish its dominance in Doha and to marginalize potential competitor families. While the family's monopoly on political rule was secure, the personal position of the emir was not, thus compelling each successive emir to grant more concessions and patronage rewards to family members to ensure their acquiescence to his rule. This chapter examines the twin processes of state formation and political consolidation in Qatar, analyzing the means and methods through which power has been contested, captured, and secured by one ruling sheikh after another. Qatar's political history has been anything but peaceful, featuring repeated contested successions. But today the sources of that drama appear to have subsided, and there are multiple reasons to believe that the next succession will be a comparatively smooth one. This, I argue, is the product of a system that has finally reached a comfortable degree of political consolidation.

I begin with a brief political history of Qatar, chronicling the steady consolidation of Al Thani rule throughout the country and, commensurately, the ruling family's increasing and overwhelming domination of emerging and proliferating state institutions. Creating and then staffing new institutions of the state has been one of the most favored means of ensuring political consolidation, with the inadvertent result of simultaneously fostering state formation. From humble beginnings as late as the 1960s and 1970s, the Qatari state's explosive growth continues to this day, as much in order to accommodate new and emerging social classes into its employ as to direct the phenomenal development of the country's economy and infrastructure.

All states rely on a combination of means and methods to maintain themselves in power. I conclude this discussion with an examination of the central pillars on which the Qatari state relies for ensuring its political longevity, focusing specifically on expansive patronage networks, the emir's successful balancing of multiple, countervailing trends and influences within Qatari society, and instruments of coercion. These, of course, are in addition to the ruling family's monopoly over the institutions of the state, which give them unsurpassed organizational, political, and economic superiority over the rest of society. The outcome has been a consolidated and comparatively powerful state, enjoying a remarkable level of elite cohesion, power, and, with the emir Hamad bin Khalifa Al Thani as its head, palpable popularity. Qatar's political system may be autocratic, but it is stable and popular as well.

A Political History

Qatar's political history features two prominent characteristics: by comparative standards, it is brief; and it is also marked by a fair degree of instability and turmoil. Qatar did not have the tradition of centralized authority and strong leadership that was the case in Kuwait and Bahrain. It is not surprising that the alliances and settlements found throughout the country were highly fluid.[2] In fact, the country acquired permanent settlements only in the late nineteenth century. Although technically under Ottoman suzerainty until 1914, Qatar was often Ottoman only in name and remained a restless territory during much of the period of Ottoman rule. The Ottomans, in fact, could hardly afford to bring it under their full control. According to Frederick Anscombe, "throughout the last period of Istanbul's sovereignty over Qatar, the Ottoman position in this dangling *kaza* [administrative district] varied from poor to woeful."[3] Requiring large, permanent civil and military posts, beginning in the 1880s the maintenance of Qatar became a costly drain on the Ottomans.[4] Besides Kuwait, which they viewed as strategically especially important, the Ottomans in fact paid little sustained attention to their Persian Gulf territories.[5] The Al Thani were able to employ this hands-off policy to their advantage by accepting Ottoman suzerainty, thus protecting themselves from the possible wrath of Istanbul and other nearby tribal adversaries, while at the same time building up their own powerbase and patronage network.[6]

The Al Thanis were somewhat latecomers to the Qatari political scene. Throughout the 1700s they played no major role in the events that shaped Qatar's history, such as the conquest of Bahrain, in which other notable families such as the Al Sulaithis, the Jalahima, al-Bu Kwara, al-Musallam, and the Al Khalifa were involved, the latter eventually establishing their rule over the island.[7] It was not until the 1820s that power, whatever of it there was, shifted from the western city of Zubara to Doha in the east.[8] The Al Thanis moved to the city in the 1850s and, under the leadership of Sheikh Muhammed bin Thani, steadily emerged as one of its dominant and influential clans. The Al Thanis viewed the acceptance of Ottoman suzerainty as strengthening them against rivals in Bahrain, Abu Dhabi, and Najd.[9]

Al Thani rule in Qatar received the all-important British recognition in November 1868, when Sheikh Mohammad bin Thani was acknowledged by the British Resident in the Persian Gulf as the "principal Chief of Katar."[10] Signed onboard HMS *Vigilant* on 11 September 1868, the treaty took the form of a pledge by Sheikh Mohammed to the British Resident not to "put to sea with hostile intensions," to refer any possible disputes with others, especially the al Khalifa of Bahrain to the British Resident. In return, two days later the British Resident issued a note to the other leading clans of the city informing them that Sheikh Mohammed "has bound himself to live peaceably there and not to molest any of his neighbouring tribes. It is therefore expected that all the Sheikhs and tribes of Gutter should not molest him or his tribesmen."[11]

Despite British assurances, by the beginning of the twentieth century, both the coastal and interior parts of Qatar were still riven with conflict, most of which was due to pearl fishing disputes. Compounding the country's difficulties were depressed economic circumstances throughout the early 1900s because of poor pearl fishing and financial mismanagement. Al Thani rule remained on tenuous ground, and Qatar sought the same kind of treaty relationship with Britain that the Trucial States had had since 1892. British protection gave emerging ruling elites significant power. According to Nazih Ayubi, "the state was separated from its socio-economic base and given a specifically political/strategic underpinning within newly defined, 'rigid' and often artificial borders."[12] Qatar was, in fact, the last of the Arabian Peninsula states to enter into a treaty relationship with Britain, which it did in 1916, whereby Qatar was given protections similar to those granted earlier to the Trucial States in return for placing the country "firmly within the British orbit."[13] Abdullah Al Thani (r. 1913–1949) was promised protection from sea and land attacks in return for privileged diplomatic and trade relationships, and abstention from piracy, arms trafficking, and slavery.

By giving international recognition and military support by the superpower of the day to a ruling sheikh and his clan, the treaty greatly strengthened processes of political consolidation and, eventually, state building.

The early decades of the twentieth century brought little change to Qatar, and it was only with the arrival of the oil era that the country began to witness rapid and profound transformation of its social and economic landscapes. Besides Britain, which essentially played the role of a quasi-colonial power in Qatar, the ruling family was the only other agent of change in the country, and its default position was conserving the status quo and preventing change. The Great Depression and the collapse of the pearling industry in the early 1930s had decimated Qatar's already sclerotic merchant classes, leaving only two families, the Al-Darwish and Al-Mani, with any meaningful wealth derived from commerce before the oil era.[14] Social change remained conspicuously absent from Qatar.

According to one contemporary observer, "even by the late 1950s, most ordinary modern amenities had not yet arrived. Water was brought in by tanker.... There was no drainage of any kind.... The weekly plane which brought the mail often did not bother to land; it would circle around two or three times and then drop its load by parachute. In the harbor there were only two small jetties. One belonged to the ruler."[15] Social services were not widespread. Thanks to Ottoman efforts to modernize the country toward the end of the nineteenth century, in 1891 Qatar was estimated to have a population of 20,000, fifteen schools, and thirty-four mosques.[16] By the mid-1950s, the number of literate Qataris was estimated at only about 630. There were an estimated 3,000 slaves in Qatar in 1951.[17]

Even more resistant to change was the political system, which remained highly personalist and was essentially summed up in the person of the emir and, at times, the heir apparent. Beginning in the 1950s, Britain introduced the establishment of fiscal and coercive state institutions. Throughout the decade, while factionalism within the ruling family increased in scope and intensity, so did British influence within the internal affairs of Qatar, especially as far as the ruling family and the court were concerned. By the end of the 1950s, "a security apparatus of sorts" was in place but most other state institutions had yet to emerge. Nevertheless, there were some state services, especially the provision of health care, education, and drinking water that were established in the 1950, with the number of state employees increasing from six in 1949 to forty-two in 1954.[18]

By the late 1950s and 1960s, Qatar had experienced little in the way of political development. Throughout, the emir sought to redress his own fragile power base by buying the support of the sheikhs with allowances, land grants, and state jobs, policies that inadvertently helped create a large and bureaucratic state. Oil had the paradoxical effect of increasing tensions among the Al Thanis while at the same time making them the undisputed rulers of the realm. In fact, claims for sheikhly allowance by another prominent family, the Al Attiyah, were denied, leaving the Al Thani as the only sheikhs throughout the country.[19] At the same time, however, with the stakes exponentially higher, bitter rivalries within the ruling family continued and in fact intensified. Sheikh Ali, who ruled from 1949 to 1960, developed policies for allowances derived from oil revenues for members of the ruling family. These allowances varied based on the recipients' proximity to the person of the ruler. But these and other similar efforts brought the emir little respite from family tensions, and as he kept giving more and more privileges to members of the ruling family, few were placated and wanted more, in turn raising the resentment of the population.

The arrival of oil hastened the transformation of the Qatari state from a quasi-tribal institution to a comparatively more bureaucratic one. Prior to oil wealth, one of the primary means of securing patronage had been through land distributions—a practice that continues to this day—resulting in the emergence of the Al Thanis as large landowners as early as the 1950s. Oil added proliferating state offices into the patronage mix, enabling the Al Thanis and their loyal allies to monopolize new and expanding levers of power. In the process, tribal identities were increasingly subsumed under state-sponsored ones, but they were hardly replaced altogether. Unwritten tribal rules and customs, commonly referred to as *urf*, still dominate the societies of the Arabian Peninsula, including Qatar.[20] Although designations such as "tribe" or "tribal" are largely problematic, tribes, according to Allen Fromherz, remain "the major self-identified groupings of Qatar's society, imagined or not." "One's *qabila*, one's extended 'tribe' or family" remains the fundamental determinant of an individual Qatari's social position and future. This remains true even if that ancestry is in some ways imagined, created, or politically repositioned.[21]

In their approach to tribes and tribal identity, all states of the Arabian Peninsula rely on a combination of enticement as well as enforcement to ensure tribal loyalties and, ultimately, national cohesion. Depending on context and circumstances, this mixture of the *saif* (sword) and the *mansaf* (bedouin banquet) can take a variety of forms and degrees of intensity, but often occurs through the provision of employment opportunities and state services with the intent of deepening patron-client relationships and the tribal groups' dependence on the state.[22] Throughout the Arabian Peninsula, kinship, oil, and religion have coalesced to produce what appears to be a "tribal ideology" that permeates most institutions and practices. Though never formally articulated, this tribal ideology is not openly criticized either.[23]

The nexus between tribe and state remains nuanced and complex, with the Al Thanis maintaining an uneasy relationship with what is purported to be the country's largest tribe, namely the Al Murrah, who occupy vast expanses of territory in northern and eastern Arabia. In 2005, as Qatar's relations with Saudi Arabia steadily darkened, more than 5,000 Qataris belonging to the Al Ghafran branch of the Al Murrah tribe were stripped of their citizenship because of their alleged involvement in the failed 1996 coup attempt, which was supposedly backed by Saudi Arabia and the United Arab Emirates (UAE).[24] The official reason given was that the tribe was of Saudi origin and held dual citizenship, which is banned under the Qatari constitution. A year later, as Qatari-Saudi relations began to improve, most of the Al Murrah except about two hundred regained their Qatari citizenship. Nevertheless, twenty-one prominent members of the tribe remained in prison for fourteen years, until their release in 2010 in response to a personal request from King Abdullah of Saudi Arabia. Upon their release, the former prisoners were flown to Saudi Arabia.

The state's efforts aimed at marginalizing the Al Murrah have ironically led to their increasing self-awareness and, at times, expressions of grievance against the state. Ultimately, it has been the emergence of state institutions, and their growing consolidation, that has shaped the destiny of the Al Murrah along with the rest of Qatar. As I discuss later, Qatar's tribal society had a direct impact on the nature and direction of the evolution of the Qatari state. Although oil created a wide gap between the ruler and his subjects that did not exist before, the state—or, more specifically, the person of the emir—still considers itself a natural extension of society, its grand patriarch and protector. Processes of political consolidation and state-building particularly in a tribally rooted country like Qatar, must necessarily take into account the state's ongoing entanglement with forces found in society.

Political Consolidation and State-Building

State institutions and social actors engage in multiple processes of negotiations, interactions, and resistance toward each other, and in the process they have significant constitutive and transformative consequences on one another.[25] It is important to focus on the processes of interaction between state and society and how each transforms and influences the other through ongoing interactions. As Joel Migdal has convincingly demonstrated, while states transform societies in multiple ways, "the state is hemmed in—indeed transformed—by" a mélange of social forces within its territory, just as it is by international forces. Society's structure affects politics at the highest levels of the state, just as it does the implementation of state policy at the lowest level. The structure of society can deny the state its ability to carry out its intended agendas in relation to particular social actors and groups. At multiple levels and in multiple arenas, states struggle to dominate society, at times with complete success while at other times only partially successful, and still at other times with no success at all.[26] Rejecting "the false primacy of institutions," Sangmpam similarly argues that "society-rooted politics determines institutions even if one recognizes the latter's effect on politics in return."[27]

This mutually transformative process of state-society interaction is most evident in efforts to construct a state and consolidate political rule in Qatar. State-building in Qatar took place under circumstances that are largely unique in relation to most other parts of the Arabian Peninsula. Unlike in Saudi Arabia, Kuwait, or Bahrain, Qatar's ruling family did not have to contend with other groups in their vicinity who had collective identities or corporate interests. In Qatar, lack of easily accessible ports and an underdeveloped pearling industry resulted in the comparative weakness of the merchant class, and an absence of vibrant urban centers impeded the growth of a robust religious establishment. This left the large Al Thani clan as the only organized group to vie for power and freed it from the need to offer concessions to other, potentially competing groups. Political competition was thus limited to within the ruling family.

The flow of oil revenues further consolidated Al Thani rule, though it did little to foster cohesion and unity within the family. If anything, internal family competition over political power and influence intensified. The emir was not always successful in resisting demands of the family members for revenues accrued from oil sales. In 1952, British officials in the region reported that the Al Thanis received one-third of the proceeds from oil revenues, a sum that was raised to 45 percent of the total by 1958. At the same time, throughout the 1950s and 1960s, following the advice of the British to involve more family members in the state administration in order to "blunt the edge of the succession issue," the emir gave more concessions to unhappy family members and allies and potential rivals alike, therefore deepening the Al Thanis' hold over the various offices of the state.[28]

Only beginning in the 1990s, with the ascension to power of Hamad bin Khalifa following yet another palace coup, were the internal politics of the Al Thani family streamlined and were the rules of succession codified. Preoccupation with political consolidation took place at the expense of state-building processes, thus resulting in the absence of many of the institutional accouterments of a modern state. Institutional underdevelopment has been reinforced by the pervasiveness of rent revenues, which have freed the state from the need to give concessions to any potential opposition groups. Since the mid-1990s, the state has undertaken a frantic effort to proliferate much needed institutions for modern governance. But the underlying personalism of the sultanistic system remains intact. The emerging system of benign despotism has so far not encountered any serious difficulties, but its continued viability in the post-oil era, at least in its present form, is open to question.

Although it has been an ongoing process, the process of political consolidation started in earnest with the emir Ali (r. 1949–1960), during whose reign state institutions proliferated thanks to oil revenues and, more important, who organized and codified, as much as possible, the allocation of allowances to members of the ruling family. The process of consolidation continued, and deepened, during the rule of the two subsequent emirs, Ahmad (r. 1960–1972) and Khalifa (r. 1972–1995). Neither of them, however, was able to rein in the fractiousness that had long divided the Al Thanis and which had intensified in recent decades due to the increasingly higher financial windfalls at stake. In fact, the successions of 1949, 1960, and 1972 were all contested, and the 1995 succession was made possible through a palace coup. In an effort to secure his reign, Khalifa placed family members in key positions, including his son Hamad, as the heir apparent, in 1977. The emir initially promised reforms, but instead centralized power. Upon taking over, he had immediately set out to expand the existing institutions of the state and to build new ones. To expand the reach and authority of the state, he increased the size of the armed forces, and established public housing benefits, old age pensions, housing units, and food cooperatives. Qatar University was established in 1974.[29] But no institutionalization occurred and dissent remained. The emir then resorted to the establishment of alternate institutions as means of consolidating his power, a practice used extensively by his son and successor. Despite a proliferation of bureaucratic institutions, Khalifa remained personally involved in the minutiae of government, personally singing all checks above $50,000.[30] It was largely only during the reign of Hamad (1995–) that political consolidation put an end to the bitter divisiveness that had characterized the Al Thanis since before their assumption of power.

In reality, Hamad started the process of political consolidation before he formally assumed power, when, in his capacity as heir apparent, in 1989 and then again in 1992 he instigated two major cabinet reshuffles that progressively cast aside old guard Al Thanis and replaced them with a crop of younger and more like-minded family members. From then on, and with unprecedented speed after his formal assumption of power in 1995, the emir has gone about consolidating his own rule—and by extension Al Thani longevity—simultaneously constructing a supportive state edifice. Historically, Qatari rulers' control over various states institutions, which were controlled by their family members, were weak. Sheikh Hamad appears to have effectively reversed this and to have consolidated his own hold, and that of his immediate family members, over the various institutions of the state. Previous emirs initiated moves toward political consolidation and state-building, but only haltingly and under pressure (from Britain and family members). But Hamad has taken both endeavors, particularly state-building, to new heights. In this sense, his reign has been truly transformative.

The proliferation of state institutions in Qatar was a remarkably late and also remarkably rapid phenomenon. Only in 1964 did Khalifa attempt to form "a family proto-cabinet" by announcing the formation of a *majlis al-shura* made-up of fifteen sheikhs of the Al Thanis. The *majlis al-shura* never met, however, and it was not until 1970—when under pressure from family members and the British—the ruler announced the formation of a cabinet of ten, with seven sheikhs from the Al Thanis, coming from the different branches of the family.[31]

The consequences of oil on processes of state formation in Qatar cannot be overemphasized. Oil changed both the Qatari state as well as society. It broke down old ruler-merchant coalitions and enhanced the autonomy of rulers. With the arrival of the oil era, the merchants were reincorporated into the state once more, this time in a "more subservient capacity as commercial agents and importers of commodities from the capitalist world."[32] As a class, they were "bought off" by the state.[33] Traditional forms of interaction with society, meanwhile, especially the institution of the *majlis*, were maintained, thus helping gauge opinion, preempting grievances, providing a channel for "venting" or participation, and helping maintain a certain measure of "social pluralism."[34]

Similarly, the growth of the petro-state and the resulting financial windfalls afforded ruling families the opportunity to expand, and in many ways institutionalize, their control over the state and its expansive organs. The creation of cabinets provided positions and offices suitable for sheikhs and princes, and internal family bargains over these and other similar positions within the state afforded the ruling family the opportunity to expand its control over the state. In other words, internal family politics and jockeying for position led to the political consolidation of the ruling family and its expanded hold over the state. "The ruling family captured the new bureaucratic state in its infancy and its corporate authority, in comparison with other clans in society, grew at a dizzying pace alongside the explosive growth of the modern state, which the ruling families virtually came to own."[35]

The resulting political system that has emerged is a hybrid of traditional institutions and practices coexisting alongside ostensibly modern ones. Hisham Sharabi uses the concept of *neopatriarchy* to describe the consequences of distorted changes that have "deformed" Arab society over the past hundred years. Through partial and incomplete modernization, the patriarchal structures of Arab society have been deformed, then strengthened, and have resulted in a hybrid condition called neopatriarchy.[36] The concept perfectly describes the traditional modernizers of Qatari politics. Similar to its neighbors in the Arabian Peninsula, Qatar has a "post-traditional state" that uses "neo-traditionalist forms and methods."[37] In the absence of consolidated power in such systems, leaders resort to "elite *asabiyya* [communal and kinship ties] to control state institutions, which result in *neo-patrimonialism* in which participation narrows to cronies and clients. Leaders are both empowered and constrained by modern institutions, resulting in rather durable hybrid regimes."[38]

Throughout the 1980s and the early 1990s, as economic underperformance resulted in mounting pressures on wealthy Qataris, and as Khalifa busied himself with the pursuit of worldly pleasures in Europe, his popularity plummeted. In 1991, fifty-four prominent Qataris presented a petition to the emir demanding a series of reforms, such as the establishment of a meaningful legislature and improvements to the health and education services. The 1995 coup, in fact, came at a time of serious downturn in Qatar's economic fortunes and therefore had considerable support among many Al Thanis.[39]

Hamad also had a strong support base within the armed forces thanks to his reputation, however mythologized, as a war hero. He had commanded a mobile battalion during the 1990–1991 Persian Gulf War and had been responsible for the liberation of the Saudi town of Khafji.[40] His efforts to modernize the armed forces had won him much popularity among Qatari military commanders.

After the 1992 cabinet reshuffle, Hamad was widely perceived to be running the country. During the next three years, until he formally assumed power, there were considerable tensions between Hamad and Khalifa, who retained control over the country's finances.[41] While Khalifa was in Geneva in June 1995, Hamad informed him that he was no longer the emir and would not be allowed back into the country. Hamad had earlier secured support from most senior members of the Al Thanis and—following the dispatch to Washington of one of his trusted cousins, Sheikh Hamad bin Jassim—the support of the United States in overthrowing his father. Hamad bin Jassim later assumed the positions of foreign minister and prime minister.

In a brief television appearance, Hamad told his countrymen: "I am not happy with what has happened, but it had to be done and I had to do it." Khalifa for his part denounced the "an abnormal behaviour of an ignorant man" and reminded Qataris that "I am still their legitimate emir, whether it is for the royal family, for the people, or for the army and I will return home whatever it costs."[42] Senior sheikhs and other family members soon gave *bay'a* to the new emir, whose cabinet, formed two weeks after the coup, included thirteen Al Thanis.[43] An attempted coup in February 1996 to restore the former emir to power fizzled out with the arrest of a group of men at the border with Saudi Arabia.

Once in power, Hamad moved quickly to consolidate power within an inner circle of trusted family members. In one of his first official acts, the new emir decreed a change to the country's constitution limiting the line of succession to his sons. By thus codifying succession through the constitution, in one stroke Hamad eliminated a whole host of uncles, cousins, and brothers as potential contenders to the throne. He then retired or otherwise marginalized many of the older Al Thanis whom he suspected of loyalty to his father—and to his father's more relaxed approach to Qatar's future—and steadily replaced them with younger and more ambitious Qataris with ideals closer to his and on whose loyalty he could more reliably count. These types of appointments have continued well into Hamad's reign. In a cable sent to Washington around 2009–2010, the US embassy in Doha noted the rise to power of "a new generation of capable, Western-educated and energetic Qataris whose role in influencing and shaping foreign policy we expect to increase."[44] Some of these appointments of younger, highly educated Qataris included the minister of state for international cooperation, Khaled Al Attiyah, and the PM's new foreign policy adviser Sheikh Mohammed Al Thani, the youngest son of the emir.

The burgeoning state bureaucracy continues to open up new venues for royal patronage and for incorporating newly emerging elites into the orbit of the state. While a relatively recent phenomenon, as early as the 1980s and 1990s the Al Thanis' dominance of the key positions within the state ranks among the highest across the countries of the Gulf Cooperation Council (GCC).[45] Within a short few years, Hamad had placed enough trusted family members and allies in key institutions to feel secure in his reign. Some of the emir's trusted allies and relatives, who often simultaneously hold multiple salaried positions in the state machinery and on the boards of several organizations, have enjoyed remarkable durability in their official government positions. Abdullah Al Attiyah, one of the regime's key figures and the emir's cousin, has for example at various times served as minister of energy and industry (1992–2011), deputy prime minister (2007–), and head of the Emiri Diwan, the emir's executive office (2011). He has also served as the director of Qatar Petroleum and on a number of other corporate boards. Yousef Hussain Kamal, the minister of finance since 1998, has—according to a Qatari website—some thirty-three other additional, mostly paid positions in state agencies and private organizations.[46] The emir's children, especially those born to Skeikha Moza, occupy positions of particular importance: Tamim is the heir apparent; Hind is the emir's chief of staff; Mayassa runs the high-profile Museums Authority; and Mohammad (b. 1988), who successfully ran the Qatar 2022 Bid committee, is often mentioned as a future foreign minister or heir apparent, or both. In the process, the emir has managed to impose a measure of discipline and unity within the family that has been unprecedented in Qatari history. In fact, one of the major political accomplishments of Hamad's reign has been to bring cohesion and order into internal family politics.

Insofar as the institution of the monarchy and the larger system are concerned, ruling families play several key functions. Members of the ruling families continue to hold the *majlis* in which citizens can have an audience and present complaints.[47] This enables the ruler to survey the opinion of key elites, solicit their support, and cement his ties with them. To this day, Hamad holds regular audiences with ordinary Qataris in the Emiri Diwan executive offices, during which attendees can present petitions. At the same time, the family acts as "a large intelligence-gathering network" through which information is collected and is circulated at the highest levels.[48]

For analytical purposes, the Al Thanis can be divided into three broad, overlapping groups. The first group includes an inner circle of top policymakers, made up of a handful of individuals. Among them, several decision makers comprising the leadership of what may be conceived as Qatar, Inc. stand out. These individuals include the emir; his son Tamim, who is the deputy emir and heir apparent; Sheikha Moza, the emir's second wife and officially his consort; Abdullah bin Hamad Al Attiyah, the emir's childhood friend and current deputy prime minister and minister of energy and industry; and Hamad bin Jassim Al Thani, the prime minister. With the emir as the supreme overseer of the whole operation, each of the other four individuals has assumed responsibility for a different and distinct area. United by multilayered personal, financial, and political ties, they collectively form the policymaking inner circle responsible for articulating and overseeing the country's domestic, foreign, energy, financial, and security policies.

A man of considerable physical stature, Sheikh Hamad bin Khalifa is loud and gregarious, resembling more a prankster favorite uncle than the calculating politician with finely honed political instinct that he is. Doha is unique in Middle Eastern capitals for its paucity of larger-than-life portraits of the emir hung by the municipality on every street corner and roundabout, betraying the comparatively low-key—and politically highly astute—nature of the emir's personalized rule. Instead, Sheikh Hamad is often spotted in the city driving an old Land Cruiser, or smoking the shisha at a favorite hangout in the *souq*, or, when the weather permits, unassumingly strolling with Sheikha Moza among other Friday night window shoppers in one of Doha's growing open-air markets. Though his powers are unrivalled in the land, and his wealth imagined as astronomical, Sheikh Hamad remains a man of the people, an emir who personifies the romanticized image of the Arab ruler who is at once gracious and magnanimous, just and down-to-earth, worldly and wise, visionary but keenly aware of his past. Compared to his counterparts next door—be it the outlandishly image-conscious rulers of Dubai and Abu Dhabi, or the less-than-beloved emir of Kuwait, the unpopular king of Bahrain, and Saudi Arabia's aloof and distant ruler—the emir of Qatar appears to be much more genuinely loved by the couple of hundred thousand subjects he has, and the unease that the country's rapid social changes has unleashed among the more conservative quarters of Qatari society has yet to be directed at him personally.

By far the second most visible face of the Qatari state after the emir is Sheikha Moza.[49] A woman of impressive intellect and drive, Sheikha Moza primarily concerns herself with the domestic arena, focusing in particular on education, culture, and medical care. As the chairperson of the Qatar Foundation, Sheikha Moza has overseen the introduction and expansion of American-style higher education in Qatar, the undertaking of several cultural initiatives such as the assembling of the Qatar Philharmonic Orchestra, and the building of a new, $2.3 billion medical facility named Sidra. She has also encouraged reforms at Qatar University and in the country's biggest hospital, Hamad Medical Corporation. According to her website,

> Her highness shares the Emir's vision to make Qatar a prosperous, developed and sustainable society. She has been instrumental in setting up centers of excellence to enhance opportunities for the people of Qatar and to build the nation's resources in regard to education, science, community development, health and other areas. She is also actively involved in preserving and protecting Qatar's cultural heritage . . .

In all aspects of her work, Her Highness is guided by her faith in Islam, dedication to the Emir's vision for the future, a deep respect for traditional values, and a commitment to the highest possible standards.

The website reiterates Sheikha Moza's "commitment to progressive education and community welfare in Qatar and her strong advocacy for closer relations between the Islamic world and the West."[50]

Moreover, since the early 2000s Sheikha Moza has emerged as an international personality, the face not just of modern Qatar but also of the modern Arab woman. Self-assured and confident, she is one of the few wives of contemporary Middle Eastern rulers with highly visible public profiles.[51] Younger Qatari women get their cues from her not just on fashion and attire, for which she is universally praised and admired, but, more important, on how to navigate the modern world by reconciling the often irreconcilable demands of tradition and modernity, family expectations and personal aspirations, individual expressions and social strictures.

Somewhat less visible and only slightly less influential is Abdullah bin Hamad Al Attiyah, a maternal cousin and close friend and confidante of the emir since childhood and one of his most trusted and loyal advisers. In a 2011 cabinet reshuffle, Al Attiyah became the director of the Emiri Diwan, reportedly in order to oversee important changes in the emir's executive offices. Known for his fierce loyalty to the emir, Al Attiyah is the chief architect of Qatar's oil and gas policy, which is the cornerstone of the country's frantic drive toward development domestically, and survival, recognition, and respect internationally. Qatar's oil and gas policies are especially critical elements in its relations with Iran and Saudi Arabia. With Iran, the sharing of the lucrative North Field/South Pars gas field leaves open the chronic possibility of friction. In relation to Saudi Arabia, Qatar has already used its gas reserves, through the Dolphin project, to supply gas to the UAE and Oman in order to strengthen its ties with them at the expense of Saudi Arabia.[52]

Another key member of the policymaking inner circle is Hamad bin Jassim Al Thani. The emir's trust in his prime minister is based more on respect for his professional judgment and his tactical acumen than their family ties. A person of significant means and multiple business interests, Hamad bin Jassim largely oversees the country's international finances through his chairmanship of the Qatar Investment Authority (QIA) and one of its primary investment vehicles, Qatar Holdings. Sheikh Hamad bin Jassim, or HBJ as he is often referred to by the army of expats working in the country's financial sector, is known for his banker's reserve and a fine sense of personal and global diplomacy, a product no doubt of his many years of service as Qatar's chief diplomat. The prime minister has been credited with several of Qatar's major international accomplishments and so-called diplomatic coups, not the least of which was bringing peace to warring Lebanese factions in 2008, and also with several of QIA's high-profile acquisitions.[53]

Sheikh Tamim bin Hamad Al Thani is the youngest member of the policymaking inner circle. Born in 1980, the heir apparent has been increasingly more visible in his public profile and his official responsibilities, including service as the deputy commander-in-chief of the armed forces and chairman of the board of QIA. While keenly interested in sports, the heir apparent currently appears to be on apprenticeship, shadowing his father and the prime minister in preparation for eventual ascension to rule. The ultimate decision maker remains the emir, who oversees each of the functional areas described above and whatever else is left. In this sense, the emir's role is similar to that of a chief executive officer to whom four functional deputies report. As it happens, the deputies are both highly loyal and competent. It is no surprise that Qatar, Inc. often runs remarkably efficiently.

Although these individuals forming the emir's inner circle may change offices from time to time, and their numbers may vary by one or two over the years, so far the concentration of power and decision making in their hands appears to have served them—and perhaps Qatar at large—well. Clearly, agency matters, and the specific decisions made by these key individuals at critical junctures in present-day Qatar have been consequential to the course of the country's political direction and economic development. Ordinarily, this pervasiveness of personalism in lieu of institutional depth could seriously undermine state capacity and erode its ability to carry out developmental and other transformational agendas.[54] In the case of Qatar, however, the particularities of the country—its small size and massive wealth, and the singular determination of the small elite of policymakers—have greatly helped rather than hindered the state's capacity to affect change. Elite factionalism or even discord has been either nonexistent or minimal; the small size of society has not required a large bureaucracy that would be more prone to inefficiency; and the state's huge supply of cash has enabled it to import wholesale talent and international enterprises that perform many of the functions which would have otherwise been left to domestic entities and institutions. A case could be made that in Qatar the centralization of power and decision making among a few personalities has helped enhance state capacity rather than undermine it.

In this respect, the Qatari policymaking machinery is completely different in its composition and nature. Even by the highly personalized standards of political systems in the Arabian Peninsula, despite a proliferation of institutions in recent decades, the Qatari system stands out for its comparative lack of institutional depth and the continued centrality of individual personalities as the founts of power. The closest regional comparison to the Qatari system is the absolutist monarchy in Oman, where Sultan Qaboos has ruled since 1970. But even in Oman there have been moves to expand at least the superficial powers and responsibilities of various participatory state structures since the early 1980s, culminating in the inauguration of a parliament in 2001.[55] In 2011, to abort the spread of protests that had shown surprising resilience in one town after another, the sultan gave the largely symbolic, consultative assembly some actual delegatory powers.[56] But in Qatar the 1990s' promises of political liberalization have come to naught so far, and, fifteen years into the emir's reign, there are no indications that the fundamentally personalized modus operandi of the state is about to change anytime in the near future.[57] At the same time, the system remains remarkably stable. No Arab Spring, no liberating revolutions of any kind, appear to be in the offing in Qatar anytime in the near future.

The second group of Al Thanis, also very senior and often with intimate ties to members of the ruling inner circle, are usually made up of highly skilled technocrats who occupy important positions within the state bureaucracy, especially in the Foreign Ministry (generally as ambassadors or other high-ranking diplomats) and in the oil and gas sectors. These Al Thanis tend to number in the tens—by most accounts around fifty to sixty—and often work closely with members of other key families, such as the Al Attiyah and the Al Kuwari, who have reached equally prominent positions within the state machinery. Although less powerful than the first tier, the key positioning of these members throughout the state apparatus ensures the ruling family's presence, and therefore its information-gathering abilities, at the different levels of policymaking and implementation. Together with the top leadership, they help ensure the family's continued dominance over the system.

The third and remaining group of Al Thanis are concentrated in the private and semiprivate sectors. Some may be occasionally asked to join a specific government agency or one of the ministries at relatively high levels. But most are interested in the pursuit of commercial interests and run their own businesses. Many own commercial and residential real estate, especially the towers and large residential compounds in and around central Doha in which Western expats live. Many also occupy senior positions in enterprises owned wholly or partially by the state, such as the Qatar Stock Exchange, Qatar Telecom, Qatar National Bank, Qatar Petroleum, Qatar Museum Authority, and Qatar Foundation. Of this latter group, many continue to pursue business interests on the side.

In addition to placing loyal and like-minded Al Thanis in key institutions of the state, Hamad set out to address two additional, important aspects of state formation that had hitherto remained neglected. The first, and by far the most important of the two, was to create a "civic myth," a set of symbols based on Qatari tradition and heritage that justified Al Thani rule as a natural extension of the country's cultural history and national tradition. In the 1980s, to compensate for and divert attention from mounting economic difficulties, Sheikh Khalifa had started to place greater emphasis on the regime's normative socialization. But, during Khalifa's reign, "no clear symbols were evoked for none were evocative. Qatar was sadly lacking a civic myth; it was a polity suffering from a severe shortage of symbols."[58]

Sheikh Hamad started to address this exigency in a hurry, quickly giving rise to one of the region's busiest and most prolific heritage industries. National symbols were dug up, some invented, and held up as symbols of Qatari pride and identity. Falconry and camel races were promoted as national sports with deep historical roots, and soccer tournaments named the Emiri Cup and the Heir Apparent's Cup were launched with great fanfare. In 2006, in preparation for the hosting of the Asian Games, Doha's old *souq*, known as Souq al-Farsi, or the Iranian Souq for the background of its merchants, was redone in traditional Gulfi style and renamed Souq Wakif. In 2007, 18 December—the day in 1878 when "national unity" was supposedly achieved under Jassim Al Thani—was declared the National

Day, with state-sponsored nationwide celebrations that tend to become increasingly more grand and feverish year after year.[59] In 2008, the world-class Museum of Islamic Art, headed by one of the emir's daughters, was inaugurated. The following year, under the patronage of one of the emir's sons, Katara Cultural Village opened with a purported endowment of $1 billion. In 2010, no doubt to Cairo's bemusement, Doha was declared as "the cultural capital of the Arab world." As the increasingly boisterous and spontaneous National Day celebrations show every years, under Hamad Qatar has developed a sense of identity and a heritage of its own. This emergent national identity has only been reinforced, and is continuously regenerated, by Qatar's high-profile foreign policy and its active presence in the international arena.

Complementing efforts to bestow the regime with normative depth and symbolic legitimacy have been moves to enhance the institutional accouterments of the state. The first municipal elections were held in 1999. A draft constitution with 150 articles was presented to the public in 2002, approved in a 2003 referendum by 96 percent of the voters, and became effective in July 2005. According to official statistics at the time, out of a total of 650,000, the national population numbered 150,000, of whom 71,400 were eligible to vote.[60] Given the small number of eligible voters, it is easy to achieve high voter turnout rates. Subsequent municipal elections were held in 2003, 2007, and 2011, with the last witnessing a voter turnout of 43 percent, or about 13,000 of the estimated 32,000 registered voters.[61] The promised parliamentary elections of 2007 never materialized, with official explanations that the country was not yet ready.[62] But in a speech to the Advisory Council in 2011, the emir made the following announcement:

> From the podium of this Council, I declare that we have decided that [new] Advisory Council elections would be held in the second half of 2013 . . . ? We know that all these steps are necessary to build the modern State of Qatar and the Qatari citizen who is capable of dealing with the challenges of the time and building the country. We are confident that you would be capable of shouldering the responsibility.

In a sign of his awareness of his surroundings, he continued,

> Moreover, we emphasise that the only guarantee for the stability of Arab States, in the short and long terms, lies in the adoption of continuous reforms

to meet the aspirations of their people, for reality affirms that no country can isolate itself from the current political movement. The people have discovered their strength and their ability to claim their rights and to consolidate the values of freedom, dignity and social justice. This requires their courage to open channels of positive dialogue with their people in order to carry out the required reforms in a safe and gradual manner without upheavals.[63]

Michael Herb attributes the regime's lack of interference in the country's municipal elections to the pliant nature of the elected municipal council. The regime, he maintains, "probably will continue this tradition in the upcoming parliamentary elections, if only because the deputies will have little power to constrain the monarchy beyond using the parliament as a soapbox."[64]

Significantly, the 2003 constitution stipulates near-absolute powers for the emir (Articles 64–75), who remains—as the head of state—the commander-in-chief of the armed forces, will draw up "the general policy of the State" and appoint the prime minister, and "may take all urgent necessary measures to counter any threat that undermine the safety of the State, the integrity of its territories or the security of its people and interests or obstruct the organs of the State from performing their duties" (Article 69). At the same time, the document outlines a parliament that has little actual legislative powers (Articles 76–116), with the emir ultimately retaining veto power over the laws it passes (Article 106.3). Of the body's forty-five members, thirty are to be elected through direct vote, while "the Emir shall appoint the remaining fifteen Members from amongst the Ministers or any other persons" (Article 77). Even when Qatar does finally get its much-heralded parliament, there is little indication that its fundamentally autocratic underpinnings will be altered in any meaningful way.

This raises two related questions: exactly what kind of a political system does Qatar have, and to what extent is it politically stable? At the risk of stating the obvious, the Qatari system appears to be an archetypical form of traditional authority as conceptualized by Max Weber. According to Weber, authority can be justified on traditional grounds when it rests on "an established belief in the sanctity of immemorial traditions and the legitimacy of the status of those exercising authority under them." Weber places the person of the leader at the center of such an authority. "In the case of traditional authority," he writes, "obedience is owed to the *person* of the chief who occupies the traditionally sanctioned position of authority

and who is (within its sphere) bound by tradition. But here the obliga-
tion for obedience is not based on the impersonal order, but is a matter of
personal loyalty within the area of accustomed obligations."[65]

The Qatari system also fits in perfectly with classical definitions of
authoritarianism. Juan Linz defines authoritarian regimes as those featuring a number of distinctive characteristics: limited political pluralism; devoid of a guiding ideology but with "distinctive mentalities"; relying on
the political apathy and demobilization of the populace; and a leader or a
small clique whose powers have "formally ill-defined limits but are actually quite predictable ones."[66] In lieu of an ideology or a cult of personality,
these regimes feature "mentalities [that] are ways of thinking and feeling,
more emotional than rational, that provide noncodified ways of reacting to
different situations. . . . Mentality is intellectual attitude; ideology is intellectual content. Mentality is psychic predisposition, ideology is reflection,
self-interpretation; mentality is previous, ideology later; mentality is form-
less, fluctuating—ideology, however, is firmly formed."[67]

Although Linz distinguishes between monarchies that rely on traditional sources of legitimacy and modern authoritarian systems, which he
sees as avaricious and arbitrary, his description of the prototypical authoritarian system bears close resemblance to Qatar's:

> The personalistic and particularistic use of power for essentially private
> ends of the ruler and his collaborators makes the country essentially like
> a huge domain. . . . The boundaries between the public treasury and the
> private wealth of the ruler become blurred. He and his collaborators, with
> his consent, take appropriate public funds freely, establish public oriented
> monopolies, and demand gifts and pay-offs from business for which no
> public accounting is given; the enterprises of the ruler contract with the
> state, and the ruler often shows his generosity to his followers and to his
> subjects in a particularistic way. The family of the ruler often plays a prom-
> inent political role, appropriates public offices, and shares in the spoils. It is
> this fusion between the public and the private and the lack of commitment
> to impersonal purposes that distinguishes essentially such regimes from
> totalitarianism. The economy is subject to considerable governmental inter-
> ference but not for the purposes of planning but of extracting resources.[68]

More than just an authoritarian system, Qatar's may be called, in the
words of Daniel Brumberg, a "total autocracy." Brumberg distinguishes

between what he calls "liberalized" and "total" autocracies. Liberalized autocracies are characterized by "an adaptable ecology of repression, control, and partial openness," whereas total autocracies feature hegemonic state institutions that seek to "absorb or repress rival political voices" and "spread the idea that the state's mission is to defend the supposedly unified nature" of the nation and the community.[69] Although total autocracies tend to be the exception rather than the rule,[70] Qatar appears to fit the category neatly. The inner-circle of policymakers remains small and limited to a handful of individuals; even if and when a parliament is inaugurated it is likely to remain peripheral and devoid of much political meaning; and the mission of economic growth and enhancing wealth continues to trump all other preoccupations.

Despite its personalist and autocratic underpinnings—or perhaps because of them—the Qatari political system is remarkably stable. This stability is rooted first in the overall nature of Arabian Peninsula monarchies and, second, in the particular mechanisms of rule at the disposal of the Al Thanis in Qatar. In broad terms, the monarchical states of the Arabian Peninsula have been able to draw on a combination of oil revenues, tribal heritage and other traditional sources of legitimacy, and corporate family rule to portray themselves as natural extensions of historical and social dynamics that sustain them in power. This is in sharp contrast to the monarchies once found in Libya, Egypt, Iraq, and Iran, where the state's failed attempts at carving out a supportive "civic myth" on which it could rest its legitimacy resulted in its ultimate collapse.[71] Along similar lines, Lisa Anderson has argued that given some of their prominent features—such as being centralized, personalized, and coercive—Middle Eastern monarchies are particularly adept at fostering and navigating through processes of state formation.[72] The very personalism of these regimes is a source of strength. Especially in the early phases of state-building, when institutions are tenuous and there is uncertainty about their future prospects, personal networks and relationships enable states to better cope with internal and at times even external challenges.[73] Once oil revenues flowed into the coffers of the state, and the pockets of the ruling family, state institutions became the personal fiefdoms of ruling family members, thus consolidating the ruling family's dominance—in Qatar's case monopoly—over state institutions. As a small polity with strong personal and kinship networks, politics can more easily be managed in a place like

Qatar. "Such links and networks tend to take some of the edge off political conflict—arguably making for evolutionary rather than revolutionary
responses to tensions."[74]

In addition to the state's institutional features and its comparatively successful cultivation and reliance on sources of legitimacy, several features in
the societies of the Arabian Peninsula also help sustain monarchical states
in power. Unlike most other parts of the Middle East, in arid regions and
desert areas the relatively small size and weakness of nationalist-minded
middle and working classes has helped keep monarchic legitimacy mostly
intact. According to Raymond Hinnebusch, in these polities "the small size
of the indigenous working class, overdeveloped atomized tertiary sectors,
and traditional political technology—clientalism—relieves pressures for
inclusion. The male citizenry, who, enjoying welfare entitlements while
temporary workers without rights do most of the manual or skilled labor,
is a privileged minority with a stake in regime survival."[75] Some observers
have gone as far as to suggest that the state has deliberately avoided policies that may foster the birth of a vibrant working class for the very reason
of not wanting to inadvertently undermine its own legitimacy, preferring
instead to rely on imported labor with no chance of becoming naturalized
citizens.[76]

Oil-dependent, personalist monarchies tend to encounter their most
serious crises during two particular junctures—at times of precipitous
decline in oil revenues and during disagreements over succession. Oil
exporters are not necessarily prone to regime breakdown during periods of economic downturn. The critical variable is how leaders respond.
State responses to economic crises can either hasten the state's collapse or
ensure its persistence. As Miriam Lowi states, "outcomes turn on leaders'
decisions relative to their particular context—the 'structured' environment
composed of resources, institutions, social systems, and social forces—they
find themselves in."[77] Much depends on how states respond to such downturns. In fact, if economic downturns lead to market reforms and privatization, new forms of rent are often generated through the privatization of
state-owned enterprises, thus prolonging authoritarian persistence. Even
under conditions of economic decline, privatization can provide a social
base for autocracy and foster a "domestic social structure unfavorable to
democratic outcomes."[78]

Equally problematic are contested or unplanned successions, during which dissention and divisions within the ruling family tend to be at their highest and when the family's corporate identity is at its nadir. Nevertheless, as Qatar's political history has amply demonstrated, succession crises need not be fatal. In fact, because each succession has been followed by a slew of concessions by the ruler to family members in the form of appointments to state institutions, contested successions tend to result in a strengthening of the ruling family's grip over the state. At the same time, there is a built-in incentive within the family to form internal coalitions that protect its power monopoly. In order to preserve their privileges and the ultimate longevity of the ruling family, those family members who are not in direct competition with the ruler tend to bandwagon rather than resort to balancing. "Able to regulate its own internal disputes, and indisputably in control of its state and national territory, such dynasties display a remarkable resilience."[79] Those family members who lose out on succession often receive lofty "compensation prizes" and are free to pursue "their moderate desires."[80] Reflecting on Qatar in the 1980s, Jill Crystal commented that "the regime is stable; its leaders are not."[81] Given Hamad's deft handling of family politics since the mid-1990s, today the position of Qatar's leader appears to be equally secure as that of his regime.

Pillars of Political Rule in Qatar

In his seminal study Michael Mann identified four primary sources of power: ideological power, economic power, military power, and the power of political organizations that constitute the state. According to Mann, these sources "generate overlapping, intersecting networks of power relations with different sociospatial boundaries and dynamics; and their interrelations produce unanticipated, emergent consequences for power actors."[82] Thus ensued a nonlinear and at times incongruent political process involving trial-and-error negotiations and renegotiations on the part of those in possession of political power—the state, and those subject to it—society. Mann's focus is state formation in Europe and how the continent's institutions of central power interacted with constituencies in civil societies. Broadly similar parallels may be found in the Arabian Peninsula, and particularly in Qatar, though with adjustments and adaptations resulting from economic resources, the predominance of tribal and clan affiliations and networks, and the role of agency. In specific relation to contemporary Qatar, four central pillar of political power may be identified. They include the power derived from control over state institutions, which is the overwhelming preserve of the ruling family; the power of patronage and clientelism, derived from control over economic resources; the power of balancing, a product of Sheikh Hamad's careful maneuvering between countervailing tendencies and forces within Qatar and also internationally; and, when necessary, the power of surveillance and suppression.

By far the most central pillar of state power in Qatar is the power of patronage, with the country today being a rentier state par excellence thanks to revenues from hydrocarbon exports. The establishment of patron-client relations have deep roots in the political history of the Arabian Peninsula, with contemporary GCC states relying on their tribal impulse, and, through the establishment of extensive welfare systems, seeking to "re-enact the traditional tribal system of allegiance for economic support."[83] Sheikhly and patrimonial patterns of rule, under the auspices of the Al Thani ruling family, had been firmly established between the 1930s and 1950s. It was only after that that the flow of oil revenues into the coffers of the state—or more specifically to the ruling clique within the Al Thanis—kicked in, thus consolidating existing patterns of patrimonial rule. Rentierism did not create new patterns of rule from scratch; it reinforced existing ones.

Throughout the Arabian Peninsula, patronage is part of a broader state effort to foster a corporatism that is meant to bring into its ambit existing or potential corporate groups in society: tribes and the sheikh to which they have allegiance; the major commercial families; the religious establishment, whether of the dominant groups (the Sunnis) or the major sects (the Shias, the Ibadis, the Zaidis, etc.), and the middle classes. What ensues is a system of "political tribalism" closely modeled after the clannishness of a tribe (*'ashariyya*).[84] Although inclusionary in its communal and tribal makeup, this corporatism does not include "less authentic" citizens—in Qatar's case, those who immigrated to the country after the 1930s—and foreigners.

Unlike most other rentier states, in which the state funnels rent revenues into society only indirectly and in the form of state employment or the granting of licenses, the Qatari state is one of the few in the world that engages in multiple forms of direct rent distribution.[85] This of course is in addition to various indirect means of ensuring that there is an uninterrupted flow of money into the pockets of Qataris. Upon getting married, for example, each Qatari couple is eligible to receive a free plot of land that is at least 600 square meters and an interest-free loan of QR1,200,000 (approx. US$329,000 in 2012), payable in twenty-five years, in order to develop the land. This rule, which previously excluded Qatari women who were married to non-Qatari men, was amended in 2007 to extend to those Qatari women who were divorced or who were past the age of thirty-five. As if to deliberately reinforce patronage ties between the emir and his people, this land distribution is done directly by the Emiri Diwan. All Qataris are also guaranteed state employment with salaries starting—in 2012—at QR16,000 (US$4,400) a month if they have a high school diploma or QR22,400 (US$6,100) if they have a bachelors degree. Few Qataris rely on state salaries as their sole source of income and most have multiple business interests. Because non-Qataris are not allowed to have controlling shares in local businesses, most Qataris are silent partners in stores and shops of all sizes that are run by migrant workers from the Philippines or from South Asia.

The state also provides comprehensive, cradle-to-grave services for all Qatari citizens free of charge or for a nominal fee. Education and health services are free for all Qataris who wish to avail themselves of the expanding choices available in universities and hospitals. Qatari nationals also have the highest per capita GDP in the world, estimated at just under US$450,000 a year in 2008.[86] Qataris do not pay for water and electricity usage; and the price of petrol is among the lowest in the world. Not surprisingly, Qataris have the highest per capita carbon footprint and water and electricity consumption rates in the world.[87] According to a 2012 report by the World Wildlife Fund, Qatar has the world's highest ecological footprint, measured as the number of global hectares demanded per person, while at the same time having one of the world's lowest "biocapacities" in terms of the number of global hectares available per person.[88]

As the prime minister stated in a 2011 interview with a US television network, making Qataris wealthy is the state's top domestic priority.[89] The General Secretariat of Development Planning, one of the state agencies charged with the implementation of the National Development Strategy, boasts about the government's "generous social protection system that is funded through abundant hydrocarbon resource revenues."

There is no personal income tax or value added sales tax. . . . Pensions are given to retired government servants. The Ministry of Social Affairs provides a range of welfare benefits for disadvantaged groups. . . . Civil service employment is seen as part of Qatar's social protection through the provision of social allowances over and above actual wages received. Hence government employment tends to be the first choice for Qataris.[90]

All this amounts to an absence of poor Qataris. According to a 2006–2007 survey by the General Secretariat of Development Planning, "less than 5 per cent of Qatari households have equivalized incomes or expenditures below 40 per cent of the median" and "just over 9 per cent of Qatari households receive income less than half the median."[91]

Qatar has entered what Matthew Gray calls "late rentierism." Gray attributes several features to late rentierism, some of the more prominent of which include a maturing of the state and its view toward rents; the state's widespread engagement with the global economy; new economic and development imperatives; and population and employment pressures.[92] According to Gray, state maturity is reflected in the careful management of state capitalism. Characteristics of state capitalism in late rentierism include the professional operation of state-owned industries, continued state control over strategic industries, and preferential treatment of certain actors.[93] The late rentier state is "more entrepreneurial, supportive of development, and responsive than it was previously. However, the fundamental characteristics of rentierism remain."[94]

Two of the more important consequences of advanced or late rentierism, which happen to be interrelated, include the weakening of traditional merchant families, and the emergence of new, state-dependent classes. The Qatari merchant classes have historically lacked the political influence of Kuwaiti merchants and have constituted a politically—or, for that matter, economically—relative marginal group in society. With structural transformation in the country's macroeconomy resulting from globalization, such as the expansion of the stock market, the widespread introduction of large, one-stop retailers (e.g., Carrefour), and the entry of new, globally savvy local entrepreneurs into the market, "the merchant clans of the Gulf are facing unprecedented challenges."[95]

It so happens that some of the most prominent merchant families in Qatar have been Shia, and, presumably for their own protection and self-preservation, traditionally they have often been among the most influential supporters of the country's rulers.[96] Historically, the Qatari Shia have enjoyed relative religious freedom and have even participated in government institutions.[97] Therefore, the mutually reinforcing phenomena of globalization and late rentierism have further strained whatever power the traditional merchant families had managed to retain.

Distributive policies have also enabled the state to foster the creation of and to in turn forge ties with new social classes. Expanded and free educational opportunities have resulted in the upward mobility of a number of highly educated Qataris—especially women—who are the beneficiaries of the state's labor nationalization campaign. Educated Qataris are in extremely high demand by the countless Western and local companies with operations in the country, eager to meet demands in the media and among influential Qataris for the Qatarization of their workforce.[98] Graduates of imported Western universities with fluency in English are especially valuable. Cosmopolitan and upwardly mobile, these young professionals are aware that they owe their positions to state policies. They constitute a new base of support for the state that did not exist in the past, eclipsing potential rivals within and outside the ruling family.

A second pillar of political power is based on the emir's ability to balance between multiple countervailing tendencies and forces within Qatari society. In many ways, Sheikh Hamad is the supreme balancer. This balancing occurs in the form of navigating, as carefully as possible, the processes of change and modernization while at the same time appearing respectful to the forces of tradition and cultural heritage. In both personal conversations and public appearances, Hamad reiterates the need to manage change in measured and careful ways, no doubt mindful of the fate that befell the Shah of Iran in 1979. The first article of *Qatar National Vision 2030* points emphatically the need to foster "modernization and preservation of traditions" together. According to the document,

> Preservation of cultural traditions is a major challenge that confronts many societies in a rapidly globalizing and increasingly interconnected world.
>
> Qatar's very rapid economic and population growth have created intense strains between the old and new in almost every aspect of life. . . . Yet it is possible to combine modern life with values and culture. Other societies

have successfully molded modernization around local culture and traditions. Qatar's National Vision responds to this challenge and seeks to connect and balance the old and the new.[99]

There are multiple examples of this type of balancing by the emir personally and by the state he heads at large. In 2011, a group of extremist Wahhabis, purportedly with backing from individuals within the Awqaf Ministry, tried to bulldoze a Shia cemetery in the outskirts of Doha. Learning of the incident, the emir is said to have expressed outrage and to have made a rare appearance at a Shia funeral as a sign of his displeasure with the extremists. At the same time, to the surprise of most outside observers, Doha's newest attraction, and its central place of worship for the country's Muslims, is a mosque named after the founder of the Wahhabi movement.

The naming of the visually stunning new national mosque, whose construction started in 2009 and which was inaugurated in December 2011, as the Imam Muhammad Ibn Abdul Wahhab Mosque, is another example of careful balancing. In a highly publicized ceremony, the emir's remarks seemed to be carefully calibrated to highlight his and the system's observance of Wahhabi principles:

> We named the mosque after the great reformer and a renowned reviver Imam Muhammad Ibn Abdul Wahhab in honor of the Muslim scholars, who still carry his thought and call for revival to serve Islam and Muslims. . . .
>
> His walk all through life in the path of light spread throughout the Arabian Peninsula, guides people to the right path according to the Holy Quran and *Sunnah*, removes confusion from the minds and deviations that confounded souls. . . .
>
> We, as we meet today to open this mosque and name it after Imam Muhammad bin Abdul Wahhab, are honoring scholars who still carry his thought and his message to serve Islam and Muslims. I'm honored along with you to open this mosque and I pray to Almighty Allah to help us now and in the future to keep this mosque a platform to light and a torch of guidance.[100]

The expression of such sentiments is often as puzzling to outsiders as is Qatar's apparent "maverick" and "enigmatic" foreign policy. But balancing is to domestic politics what hedging is to foreign policy. It is a deliberately calculated policy of keep an eye on the forces of tradition and culture as cherished and represented by the more conservative members of society, while advancing a broadly defined modernization and becoming a central hub for globalization. The clash of the two, of the amorphous and often incoherent pulls and pushes of tradition and modernity—however vaguely conceived and perceived by those experiencing them—inevitably places the state in difficult and at times contradictory positions. Once again, however, the state's agility, rooted in the centralization of its decision-making processes and the small size of society over which it governs, enable quick and seemingly successful responses to occasional pushbacks and backlashes. In late 2011, for example, after complaints by Qatari nationals about intoxicated expats on the Pearl-Qatar, an artificial island and one of Doha's main attractions, the sale of alcohol on the island was suddenly banned. The ban came shortly after pork was made available for sale at the country's only legally licensed alcohol shop for foreign nationals. That the state responded swiftly and in such a dramatic manner—with several high-end restaurants and eventually shops closing up due to dried up business—is an indication of its careful attention to and its responsiveness to social pressures. For now, the state's maneuverability—and at its core Sheikh Hamad's careful balancing act—between countervailing forces and dynamics is important to bear in mind.

A final pillar of the state's political power is its security apparatus. Qatar is, after all, governed by an authoritarian system, and the monarchical regime is autocratic and absolutists. But Qatar is far from the typical *"mukhaberat* state" for which Middle Eastern political history is infamous. By all standards, Qatar's total autocracy is uniquely benign, and, somewhat counterintuitively, relatively popular. This popularity derives from the manner in which the state in general and the emir in particular have positioned themselves in relation to Qatari society.

Driving around Doha one is impressed not only by what one sees all around—dramatic and often outlandish manifestations of the country's extraordinary physical transformation—but also by what one does not see, namely larger-than-life statutes and portraits of the emir. Such contrived symbols of brotherly love for the leader are routine if often resented features of the urban landscape in the Middle East, especially before the Arab Spring brought down the seemingly omnipresent—and supposedly invulnerable—Ben Ali and Qaddafi. To this day, especially across the Persian Gulf, photos of kings and rulers adorn major boulevards and public buildings from Kuwait City to Manama, Riyadh, Abu Dhabi, Dubai, and Muscat. But not in Qatar. The emir's countenance is conspicuous in its absence from the streets of Doha and from the nation's flagship institution of higher learning. Instead, in Education City, large sculptures in English and Arabic exhort students to "think," "explore," and "discover." When at a matriculation ceremony in 2011 in Education City Sheikha Moza declared the establishment of the Hamad bin Khalifa University, the emir, who was in attendance, seemed genuinely surprised.[101]

This is not to imply that the emir, or more accurately his state, is not omnipresent. But the emir's portraits are not a product of the careful pattern of rule and a deliberately cultivated image of humility and of being "of the people." Being everywhere and yet in not too many places is one of the key reasons that account for Sheikh Hamad's genuine popularity among an overwhelming majority of Qataris.

The state does not have the same laissez faire attitude toward surveillance that it seems to display toward economics. In fact, the eyes of the state are everywhere. "Smart Cards," rolled out by the Interior Ministry in 2011, now double as residency permits, national identity cards, and electronic gate passes at the airport. Technically meant to help cardholders avail themselves of government e-services, they are generally seen as more efficient means of state control and surveillance. More ominously, not-so-hidden cameras are everywhere. Hotels, malls, parks, and the popular Doha Corniche are all filled with closed-circuit television cameras. Literally all major boulevards and thoroughfares are lined with what are officially called speed cameras but are popularly assumed to be for more nefarious purposes. Some of the more important highways, such as the one leading to Wajba Palace, the emir's official residence, show visible signs of the latest surveillance equipment. Even if these are indeed speed cameras meant for checking Qataris' obsession with speed, and even if Smart Cards do mean to make life easier, the general assumption that their actual purposes are different serves as means of inducing compliance.

Qatar's is a highly refined, high-tech authoritarianism. It does not rely on oversized policemen with batons to frighten the population into compliance. It does not hoist larger-than-life photos of a smiling emir approving of his subjects' daily lives as they pass through major intersections and squares. There are few uniformed policemen visible anywhere other than those manning traffic in Doha's chronically congested roads. The ubiquitous private security guards found in the shopping malls and elsewhere are all migrant workers, mostly from Nepal, and dare not even look straight at Qatari nationals, never mind keep a watchful eye on them. One of the emir's first official acts when he took over in 1995 was to disband the despised Information Ministry, seen as an archaic, outdated symbol of his father's dilapidated dictatorship. He was praised for his foresight and his liberal leanings. But censorship then steadily developed a new look. It is now more subtle.

All states watch their citizens, and some do so more intently than others.[102] Qatar's modus operandi for doing so has important consequences for the state itself and its relationship with social actors, both Qatari citizens and expatriates. For purposes of mass consumption, both domestically and internationally, the state presents itself as progressive, deeply concerned with social welfare and issues of human security. The state's official narrative, as articulated in the *National Vision 2030*, promises to move the country forward while maintaining respect for tradition and heritage. Combined with the emir's benevolent image and his palpable popularity, the perceptions created by the state's official narrative do appear to have gained widespread currency among Qataris at large. Qatar's dictatorship, in other words, is genuinely popular. The state, of course, takes nothing for granted, remaining ever vigilant about potential signs of dissent. But it takes great care not to needlessly antagonize its subjects by outlandish displays of royal grandeur or its corollary of extensive police presence. The result has been a generally stable, and largely popular, system of royal autocracy.

According to a 2009 cable from the US embassy in Doha, Qatar's intelligence services have four top priorities. They include "a) regime protection; b) the existential threat from Iran; c) threats of increased criminal and/or collective labor activity by third-country workers; and d) counterterrorism."[103] The cable went on to state that "Qatar's State Security (QSS) simply does not see a credible terrorist threat here." QSS is far from complacent, however. Because the printed media seldom publish articles or letters to the editor challenging the official narrative, expressions of discomfort often find their way into Qatari cyberspace, and therefore cyber-policing by the authorities is commonplace. Qataris posting blogs deemed unacceptable have been visited by the authorities and warned to desist. None, to my knowledge, have been jailed for their blogs; the cautions appear to be sufficiently intimidating.[104] Similarly, in public spaces such as shopping malls and in Qatar University, undercover QSS agents are assumed to keep their ears open for politically sensitive conversations, resulting, if need be, in a visit to their headquarters in central Doha. Qatar remains perhaps the only country in the Arab world without any political prisoners.

Conclusion

Throughout the Middle East and North Africa, the one common thread that unites disparate political systems is their bureaucratic inefficiency and their all too-frequent policy discords at the highest levels of state power.[105] Although the sheikhdoms of the Arabian Peninsula are by nature less prone to policymaking inefficiency because of their comparatively smaller sizes, their greater financial resources, and the family-centered nature of their political decision-making processes,[106] none comes anywhere close to Qatar in the levels of cohesion and unity among the country's top elite. In Saudi Arabia there are frequent disagreements among influential princes over a number of key policy choices. The Bahraini and Kuwaiti states both feature parliaments that, although often pliant, can at the very least slow-down the policymaking process. In Kuwait, the parliament at times has brought the political process to a grinding halt over contentious policy issues. And, as the "freedom revolutions" of 2011 starkly demonstrated—rocking the Al Khalifa to their very foundation in Bahrain and bringing unrest into Eastern Saudi Arabia—the Arab Spring made a shy appearance as far as the southern shores of the Persian Gulf. But Qatar's shores remained calm. Perhaps because of its benign nature, the personal popularity and political savvy of the emir, and its ability to foster unimaginable personal riches for most Qataris, the country's autocracy remains remarkably stable.

That Qatar is the world's wealthiest nation has much to do with its stability and the power of its state. By itself, however, wealth is an insufficient ingredient of state power. It is undeniable that the Qatari state has significant financial resources at its disposal and that it employs these resources in ways meant to optimize its power and stature domestically and internationally. But it also has an incredibly effective policymaking apparatus.

More specifically, today Qatar has a highly centralized, streamlined, and cohesive elite of policymakers who are united in their vision of the country's regional and global roles. Particularly since the ascension to power of Hamad bin Khalifa in 1995, the Al Thanis' domination of the state has become overwhelming while intra-family tensions have precipitously declined. In addition to tremendous wealth, today the Qatari state benefits from a level of elite cohesion that is comparatively rare in the Persian Gulf region and is almost unique across the Middle East.

But does power, or, more specifically in this context, state capacity, also mean complete state autonomy? It is this question that is the topic of the next chapter.

5

STATE CAPACITY AND HIGH MODERNISM

A critical factor in the Qatari state's ability to pursue its international and regional agendas is its considerable capacity in relation to society. In fact, the state has pursued domestic social engineering—an ambitious project of "high modernism"—with the same enthusiasm and determination characterizing its foreign policy behavior. In the process, the state has managed to expand and deepen its ties with important social actors and to bring them into its orbit through forging lucrative financial ties, maintain and enhance its own autonomy and its domestic and international maneuverability, and to continuously expand its capacities to pursue ambitious developmental agendas.

State capacity and autonomy are two key ingredients of developmental states. Whereas capacity is the general ability to articulate and implement developmental agendas, autonomy rests in the state's ability to "formulate and pursue goals that are not simply reflective of the demands or interests of social groups, classes, or interests."[1] I argue that in the past decade the Qatari state has been able to maximize both its capacity and its autonomy, having in the process become a successful developmental state. Moreover, through reliance on publicly owned real estate companies, the state has, on the one hand, pursued a project of high modernism while, on the other hand, deepened the dependence of social actors and private capital on itself. Augmentation of state capacity and political consolidation have gone hand in hand, with the state both penetrative of and densely linked with society. What domestic constraints there are on the state are of a relatively minor nature and are not sufficient to necessitate course alterations or even meaningful concessions to social actors.

Building on the arguments of the previous chapter on the consolidation of Al Thani rule, the chapter begins with an examination of the financial resources at the disposal of the Qatari state and the resulting, ambitious infrastructural projects that have dramatically changed Qatar's physical landscape over the past few years. Doing so has required considerable capacity on the part of the state, broadly defined as its ability to meaningfully penetrate the various levels of society and to carry out its transformative, developmental agendas with great success. The primary vehicles for the country's phenomenal growth have been publicly owned corporations, almost all highly profitable, and all used as important vehicles for the incorporation of technocrats and other skilled members of the middle and upper classes into the orbit of the state. An important resulting consequence has been a deepening embeddedness of the state in society and the expansion of its linkages with social actors. The domestic stability of the Qatari state rests not just in the consolidation of Al Thani rule. Just as significantly, it derives from expansive and deepening commercial and institutional linkages with society. A mutually reinforcing and empowering relationship develops between state and society in which the state relies on its societal allies to carry out its manifold developmental agendas, while social actors rely on the state for a continuation of their economic status and enrichment.

The chapter then examines the capacity of the Qatari state in relation to Qatari society. It looks in particular at the state's efforts to bring about what James C. Scott has termed "high modernism." It specifically explores the state's efforts to create a parallel, alternate reality with its projects of modernism. That these projects have little resemblance to anything remotely Qatari, and that they often directly undermine and contradict the state's own vibrant heritage industry efforts, matter little. The state is determined to modernize Qatari society—to rationalize and to upgrade its life through the creation of futuristic cities and public spaces—and it claims to be doing so while simultaneously preserving Qatari tradition.

Change is never easy and is often accompanied by a certain degree of unease and discomfort. Rapid and profound social change can have particularly destabilizing effects in dictatorships with few or no outlets for public debate and discussion. The state remains autocratic and allows for no dissent. But its intolerance appears to be more a product of dictatorships' knee-jerk reaction to any signs of nonconformity rather than the existence of widespread dissent in Qatari society. In fact, political dissent in Qatar is relatively benign, a product of inordinate wealth, supported by carefully crafted state policies. The outcome, ultimately, is a state with tremendous capacity to foster development and an insatiable appetite for reaching for the stars.

State Capacity and Autonomy

The ability of the Qatari state to engage in its domestic and international endeavors with the same level of zeal and enthusiasm is sustained and reinforced through two mechanisms: the massive revenues accrued by the state through the sale of hydrocarbons, and the cohesion of the ruling elite. A member of OPEC, Qatar is an important producer and supplier of oil. Compared to other OPEC members, however, it is not a major player in the global oil markets. With its oil production at 1,569,000 barrels per day (bpd) at the end of 2010 (1.7 percent of total), it ranks far below Saud Arabia (10,007,000 bpd; 12 percent of total), Iran (4,245,000 bpd; 5.2 percent of total), the United Arab Emirates (UAE: 2,845,000 bpd; 3.3 percent of total), and Iraq and Kuwait (each with approximately 2,500,000 bpd; 3.1 percent of total).[2] But what Qatar lacks in terms of oil reserves and production, it more than makes up for in natural gas. In fact, starting in 2007 Qatar began earning more from gas exports than from oil exports. The country has the world's third largest reserves of natural gas (13.5 percent of total), after Russia and Iran (with 23.9 and 15.8 percent of global total each), and is the world's largest exporter of liquefied natural gas. In 2010, Qatar produced some 116.7 billion cubic meters of LNG, almost all of which was exported and brought the country billions in earnings.[3]

The financial windfalls resulting from Qatar's oil and gas sales are considerable by any standard, but all the more so given the small scale of the society over which the state rules. As the data in tables 5.1–5.4 indicates, from 2002 to 2012, Qatar's oil and gas exports saw an increase of more than 631 percent, to a total of $98.8 billion. From 2002/3 to 2011/12, the state's revenues increased by 711 percent, shooting up from $8.1 billion to approximately $57.3 billion. State expenditures in the same period grew by 717 percent, from $6.2 billion to $44.8 billion. From 2004 to 2012 the foreign assets of the country's Central Bank saw an increase of over 726 percent to over $24 billion. Qatar's nominal gross domestic product was reported at a $172 billion in 2011, equating to 2.5 percent of global GDP and 12.5 percent of the countries of Gulf Cooperation Council (GCC).[4] In the meanwhile, the state has had to support a workforce of no more than about 149,000 at most, about half of which worked for mixed venture companies with private sector partners.

On top of the reserves accrued from the sale of oil and gas, the Qatari government has access to additional revenue streams resulting from its multiple domestic and international investments. The actual size of Qatar's sovereign wealth fund, similar to most others across the GCC, is a closely guarded secret and is therefore difficult to determine with great accuracy.[5] However, as of 2012 it was generally estimated at approximately $85 billion,[6] with stakes in companies, banks, and various development projects in Asia, North America, and Europe, including the London Stock Exchange, Volkswagen, Sainsbury supermarkets, and the Harrods Group. Established in 2005, the primary objective of the Qatar Investment Authority is to diversify the state's revenue sources and to mitigate the risks associated with the country's reliance on global energy markets.[7] As such, most of its domestic and international investments are outside of the energy sector. Although the rate of return on these global investments is difficult to determine, they do provide a significant source

TABLE 5.1. Qatar's select economic indicators: Hydrocarbon exports (millions of USD)

	2002	2003	2004	2005	2006	2007	2008	2009	2010	2011	2012
Crude oil	5,628	6,716	8,528	12,843	16,299	19,181	26,270	18,384	29,099	35,249	35,534
Non-oil exports	4,327	5,436	7,728	10,018	14,901	20,707	32,630	23,947	43,535	61,938	61,330
Total	9,955	12,152	16,256	22,861	31,200	39,888	58,900	42,331	72,634	97,187	96,864

TABLE 5.2. Qatar's select economic indicators: Government revenues and expenditure, 2002/3–2011/12 (millions of US)

	2002/3	2003/4	2004/5	2005/6	2006/7	2007/8	2008/9	2009/10	2010/11	2011/12
Total revenue	8,069.3	8,415.9	15,086.3	17,995.9	23,578.6	32,271.2	38,492.3	46,327.3	42,714.5	57,387.3
Total expenditure	6,246.3	6,809.4	9,891.2	13,909.0	18,396.4	23,213.1	27,083.6	31,390.1	39,005.4	44,783.5

TABLE 5.3. Qatar's select economic indicators: Foreign assets of Qatar Central Bank (millions of USD)

2004	2005	2006	2007	2008	2009	2010	2011	2012
3,351.5	4,559.7	5,401.4	9,519.7	9,805.4	18,301.3	30,635.8	20,645.7	24,345.2

TABLE 5.4. Qatar's select economic indicators: Economically active population by nationality, gender, and sector (October 2007)

	Qatari			Non-Qatari			Total		
	Males	Females	Total	Males	Females	Total	Males	Females	Total
Government department	29,099	16,315	45,414	27,957	5,021	32,978	57,056	21,336	78,392
Government Company/ Corporation	5,982	3,274	9,256	26,935	8,086	35,021	32,917	11,360	44,277
Mixed	2,714	597	3,311	16,693	6,359	23,052	19,407	6,956	26,363
Private	2,590	1,086	3,676	584,394	16,156	600,550	586,984	17,242	604,226
Diplomatic/International/ Regional	18	17	35	1,517	212	1,729	1,535	229	1,764
Domestic	15	—	15	28,958	43,807	72,765	28,973	43,807	72,780
Total	40,418	21,289	61,707	686,454	79,641	766,095	726,872	100,930	827,802

Source: IMF, *Qatar: Statistical Appendix.*

of funds for the state that further enrich its coffers and enables it to act as an important actor on the global stage.

All of this has amounted to the country's phenomenal growth in recent years. According to the Institute for International Finance (IIF), Qatar's economy grew at 18.8 and 18 percent in 2010 and 2011, respectively.[8] Accordingly, Qatar is witnessing an unprecedented building bonanza. Estimates of the government's projected expenditure on infrastructure in the 2011–2016 period vary from $150 billion to $225 billion.[9] In the first half of 2011, Qatar was estimated to have a budget surplus of $13.7 billion.[10] The Qatar Stock Exchange also saw a 20 percent rise in its value during the same period.[11] By late 2011, international financial analysts were proclaiming Doha rather than Dubai as the region's preeminent financial hub.[12] In 2012, for the second year in a row, a global survey found Qatar to have the most innovative economy in the GCC, placing it a respectable thirty-third out of a total of 141 countries surveyed.[13] Although the IIF estimates that the growth will decelerate to 6 percent in 2012 and then to 4 percent in 2013, the country's massive growth and infrastructural development is expected to continue in the foreseeable future. In fact, as a confident sign of more good times yet to come, in 2011, the Ezdan Real Estate Company, one of the country's oldest publicly owned companies with 2010 profits in excess of $33 million and assets of $8.7 billion, announced plans for building the world's largest tower in Doha.[14]

In Qatar, state capacity has manifested itself in multiple ways in both the domestic and international arenas, ranging from the creation of a cradle-to-grave welfare state to continuously transforming the physical landscape and architecture of the country.[15] Although private corporations have played an important role in the country's physical transformation, most major urban development projects are wholly or largely funded by the state.[16] As is the case in much of the GCC and elsewhere in the Middle East, the Qatari state continues to remain by far one of the largest players in the construction sector, with significant stakes in major capital projects such as the new Doha International Airport ($11 billion[17]), Energy City ($2.6 billion[18]), the Pearl artificial island (estimated at $10 billion[19]), and Dohaland (the first phase out of six phases of which costs $4.5 billion[20]), not to mention countless high rise towers in downtown Doha and other similar projects around the country. Tellingly, this rapid physical transformation shows no signs of slowing down in the foreseeable future.

There is, of course, more to state capacity than mere wealth and generous expenditure on infrastructure. Just as important are the institutional characteristics of the state and the specific policy instruments at its disposal needed to pursue its goals in particular areas.[21] State capacity should be assessed through the "identification of specific organizational structures the presence (or absence) of which seems critical to the ability of state authorities to undertake given tasks."[22] This, in simple terms, has to do with the *strength* of state power and its ability to plan and execute policies.[23] As Linda Weiss points out, state capacity is derived from both *institutional depth* and *institutional breadth*. Institutional depth refers to "the degree to which the boundaries of the state and the orientations of state actors define a public sphere distinguishable from larger society." Institutional breadth, meanwhile, describes "the density of the links between state activities and those of other social entities."[24]

It is important to note that state capacity is not generated in a vacuum but is formed in relation to social actors and socially rooted dynamics that empower the state in relation to society. In fact, state capacity may be viewed as "a form of socially produced power [that] reflects the particular patterns of relationship current in a sociopolitical formation at any point in time."[25] Thus socially situated, an important aspect of state capacity revolves around the state's ability to effectively promote certain interests while marginalizing others.[26]

Equally important, regime goals are central pillars of state capacity and should not be taken for granted. How policymakers choose to utilize the wealth and resources at their disposal makes a difference, with some states being "simply more purposive and better organized than others."[27] "Choices still exist," reminds us Dan Breznitz, and "states and societies, through the political process of crafting and picking alternative modes of action, can follow diverse paths and still achieve industrial success."[28] Similarly, Meredith Woo-Cumings points to the centrality of ambition— "the will to develop"—as a constitutive feature of developmental states irrespective of their economic performance.[29]

Some of the key ways in which state capacity is increased include initiating changes to state structures; the creation of new economic instruments at the hands of the state; and new patterns of state-class relations.[30] More specifically, states enhance their powers and capacities through international and domestic alliances, for example with business groups. Weiss calls these states "catalytic," as they "seek to achieve their goals less by relying on their own resources than by assuming a dominant role in coalitions of states, transnational institutions and private-sector groups."[31] In order to adapt to new challenges, states are relying more and more on collaborative arrangements with international allies and domestic stakeholders to enhance their own capacities and to create more control over their economies. Qatar has emerged as a prototypical catalytic state.

Capacity is the key ingredient of developmental states. Qatar's catalytic state is also developmentally successful. T. J. Pempel identifies several characteristics of developmental states in East Asia—most notably South Korea, Japan, and Taiwan—most of which can also be found in the Qatari state. Ideally these features include strength of state institutions; lack of a sharp dichotomy between state and society; open to entry based largely on merits; engaged in "hegemonic projects"; actively manipulate domestic markets; have had overall success in fostering economic growth and increasing national income and living standards; and are closely linked with the United States in economics and security.[32]

Developmental states often articulate a carefully devised strategic industrial policy and invest considerable resources to ensure its success.[33] It is important to note that they are not always successful at delivering on their intended economic goals, nor, according to Michael Loriaux, do they always necessarily intend to foster rapid economic growth and development. Instead, Loriaux claims, the state is interested in delivering a kind of "moral good." Premised on such goals as social stability, social cohesion, and self-sufficiency, such goals are not merely economic and "correspond to a customary good or social norm that has been constructed historically within a particular society."[34]

The notion of "moral good" is particularly applicable to Qatar, where the state makes little or no pretensions of wanting to become a modern, industrial powerhouse, in the same way, for example, that the late Shah of Iran wanted to turn his country into the "Japan of the Middle East." Instead, what the Qatari state is after, and what it seeks to promote domestically and internationally, is a particular *vision*, a conception of Qatar that is materially and infrastructurally modern yet remains respectful of and steeped in its tradition and heritage. The modernity of the Qatari state has its own unique attributes and characteristics: gleaming buildings, world-class venues and showcase projects, artificial islands, the diplomatic limelight, regional and international power, domestic wealth and prosperity, capped with political autocracy.

Rivaling capacity in importance to developmental states is autonomy. Turning broad national goals into state policy requires two central features that all developmental states need to have: "an unusual degree" of bureaucratic autonomy on the part of the state, and a robust level of public-private cooperation that is carefully engineered by the state.[35] State autonomy should not be seen solely in terms of the state's isolation from social forces and social currents. State autonomy and capacity are not zero-sum games and involve complex interactions between state and society.[36] In fact, the two are mutually enforcing. A completely autonomous state lacks sources of information and intelligence. Only when autonomy is coupled with embeddedness, can a state be called truly developmental. Corporate coherence gives state apparatuses a certain kind of autonomy. But states also need to be embedded in a "concrete set of social ties" that bind them to society and "provide channels for continual negotiation and renegotiation of goals and policies."[37] "Connectedness complements autonomy," Peter Evans writes. Moreover, "internal cohesiveness and dense external ties should be seen as complementary and mutually reinforcing. Efficacious states combine well-developed, bureaucratic internal organization with dense public-private ties."[38] This is the case in Qatar, with publicly owned corporations providing a key linkage between the state and key social actors.

In most developmental states, finance is the bond that ties industrialists to the state.[39] In Qatar, real estate development companies perform this task. The links thus established enable the state to create and maintain ties with social classes. The developmental state is "a partner with the business sector in a historical compact of industrial transformation."[40] In South Korea, for example, by channeling capital to industrialists, the state created political interest groups that could be molded into a developmental coalition.[41] The Qatari state similarly channels capital to its own base, made up of wealthy merchants and investors, skilled technocrats, and members of the upwardly mobile middle classes. Mutual reinforcement by state and society—derived from the state's embeddedness in society—lies at the heart of successful developmental states.[42]

In the Qatari context, the state's embeddedness has taken the form of establishing and funding publicly owned real estate companies, which are in turn tasked with carrying forward the multiple projects of modernity as defined by the state. Partly out of necessity and partly by design, the state in essence has privatized many of its modernization functions by relegating them to parastatals. Some of the most important and biggest of these publicly owned companies include Barwa, United Development Company (UDC), the Ezdan Real Estate Company, and Musheireb, all in charge of some of the country's most noteworthy real estate development projects. By delegating its real estate development projects to these companies, the state bypasses the often inefficient government bureaucracy and creates what Evans calls "pockets of efficiency" by addition rather than transformation.[43]

More important, the state uses these companies to funnel wealth into society and to tie itself more effectively to various social actors. As the late Nazih Ayubi argued, rentier states have a higher degree of autonomy from certain social classes, and are able to "create new classes and/or to dismantle and reassemble existing ones."[44] This class engineering of sorts is achieved through devices such as general public expenditure, employment in the state bureaucracy, and specific public policies pertaining to economic subsidies and land allocation. What Ayubi did not foresee was attempts such as those of the Qatari state aimed at creating new wealth among the upper and middle classes by employing them in management positions in publicly owned companies or making them shareholders in extremely lucrative ventures.

In Qatar, the state appears to have made a deliberate effort to use publicly owned corporations to both create new public wealth and to establish and deepen its financial ties with the commercial classes. The top management and senior decision makers of these enterprises—their boards of directors and senior management teams—are often made up of a combination of technically skilled Qataris who acquired their positions because of their qualifications or merits, along with prominent businessmen with influence. Significantly, few of the major decision makers and senior managers in the publicly owned corporations are from the Al Thanis, though, naturally, members of the ruling family are not far from the decision-making process or the commercial advantages accrued through such commercial activities. That comparatively few Al Thanis are involved in the publicly owned companies is not due to lack of qualified or trusted ruling family members. In fact, state positions are used with great effect as a means of patronage for the larger Al Thani family, and Qatar tends to have the highest percentage of ruling family members in senior cabinet positions as compared to the rest of the GCC states (for more on this, see chapter 4).

Information from two of the larger of such companies, Barwa and the UDC, helps to better illustrate the point being made here (see table 5.5 on some of Qatar's other major publicly owned companies and their projects). In its 2010 *Annual Report*, none of the five members of Barwa's Board of Directors are Al Thanis. The company's net assets totaled more than $20 billion that year, and its annual net profits jumped by 15 percent, reaching $386.6 million. Over the previous three years, Barwa's profits had grown by an average of 13 percent, each year yielding an average net profit of more than $147 million.[45]

Barwa's stockholders were no doubt happy, but perhaps not as happy as those owning stocks in the United Development Company. The UDC, in charge of developing the Pearl artificial island, is an equally significant state-owned enterprise in establishing critical links with influential social actors. In 2011, the company's nine-man board of directors included only one Al Thani. There were two members of the Al Attiyah family, generally acknowledged to be the country's second most prominent and powerful clan, as well as two Al Fardans—including the family patriarch Hussein Ibrahim and one of his sons Omar—which are one of Qatar's wealthiest, if not the wealthiest, merchant families. The elder Al Fardan, in fact, served as the chairman of UDC's Board of Directors in 2011. Coincidentally, the Al Fardans are generally assumed to be Shia. The company boasts that its board members are "among Qatar's most successful investors and developers." According to the company's *2011 Annual Report*, its profits in 2011 grew by an astounding 511 percent, to a total of $1.03 billion, up from $169 million in 2010. The company's assets grew by 75 percent, from $2.98 billion in 2010 to $5.22 billion in 2011.[46] Some 75 percent of the company's shareholders are reportedly Qataris, with the remaining 25 percent being made up of international investors.[47]

The state's developmental capacity depends largely on the denseness of state-society relations. The state's own internal corporate and policy coherence enhances the cohesiveness of societal networks. It also empowers those social groups that share its vision, and also solidifies institutional, normative, and financial ties with them.[48] Given the international nature of Qatar's development projects, and its manifold and in-depth financial and economic global engagements, globalization plays an important role in the capacity and strength of the Qatari state. In fact, developmental states' capacities and their embedded autonomy in society tend to benefit from globalization.

TABLE 5.5. Real estate development enterprises in Qatar

Real estate project	Name of developer	Parent company	Year established	Assets/Endowments	Features
The Pearl Island	United Development Company (UDC)	UDC	1999	$5.2 billion (as of 2011)	18,000 luxury residences; 41,000 residents; 3 five-star hotels; 3 marinas with mooring for 1,000 boats; 2,000,000 square meters of space for retail, leisure, and restaurants
Lusail City	Qatari Diar	Lusail Rear Estate Development Company	2005	$4 billion (as of 2012)	38 square kilometers & four islands; 28 kilometers of waterfront devel opment; 19 multipurpose mixed use, residential, & commercial districts; 200,000 residents, 170,000 employees, and 80,000 visitors; 22 hotels
Barwa (includes Barwa City, Barwa Village, Barwa Al Sadd, Baraya Center, Baraha Motor City)	Barwa	Barwa	2007	$20 billion (as of 2010)	2.5 million square meters; 10,000 residences; 193 buildings; 1 five-star hotel; 918 retail units; 1 shopping mall; 1 cinema complex
Dohaland	Musheireb Properties	Qatar Foundation	2009	$5.4 billion (as of 2011)	35 hectares; rebuilding and development of historic Doha downtown; Amiri Diwan annex; 13,700 underground car park spaces; 5 "character zones": Amiri Diwan quarter; residential quarter; residential & mixed use quarter; Heritage Quarter; and, retail quarter

Engagement and collaboration with global forces enables states to draw on one another's strengths and to augment their conventional powers.[49] At the same time, as states become more involved in their transformative roles domestically, they often tend to look internationally for a division of labor, and therefore the connections between internal accomplishments and the external context become stronger and more robust.[50] The Qatari state's embrace of globalization, and especially its assertive presence on the global financial and diplomatic arenas, only adds to its domestic strengths and to the density of its ties with actors in Qatari society.

The Qatari state's social allies have been pivotal in advancing its various developmental agendas. David Waldner has argued convincingly that the timing of the state's incorporation of social allies is key to its success in furthering developmental goals. When state formation occurs simultaneously with the political incorporation of the popular classes, economic outcomes tend to reflect the elite's political concessions rather than their own preferences. But when state-building precedes the incorporation of popular classes, the state has a comparatively freer hand to pursue its desired economic goals and agendas. These two paths of state development can result in the emergence of what Waldner calls "mediated" and "unmediated" states, with the former being those in which "state elites rule through an alliance with local notables," whereas the latter are those "in which institutions replace notables to link state, economy, and society."[51] Transformation from mediated to unmediated state requires the establishment of institutions that supplant local notables. Most transitions from mediated to unmediated states occurred at a time when new institutions were not established sufficiently firmly to effectively supplant elites. Thus power-holders sought to enhance their powers by incorporating the masses into the orbit of the state.[52]

In Qatar, new institutions have been created, but old ones continue to be kept alongside new ones. The state remains in a hybrid stage, in-between a mediated to an unmediated state. But the older institutions—the Ministry of Education, for example, remain relatively insignificant in the state's new overall trajectory. They are mere offices for salary-drawing, patronage-dependent, older and relatively marginalized Al Thanis, where they can hang their hats until retirement. Actual power and influence lies elsewhere, in key ministries staffed by the emir's allies, and in parastatals whose technocratic management shares the emir's vision of modernity, and who are only too grateful to get rich, or richer, in the process. According to Waldner, "levels of elite conflict determine whether state formation occurs simultaneously with or before popular incorporation."[53] In Qatar, the consolidation of power within Hamad's immediate inner circle was secured first—in the mid- to the late-1990s—and then, beginning in the 2000s, the state started expanding its incorporation of social actors, including non-Al Thanis, through fostering rapid and globally oriented economic growth and expansion. Qatar may be in an in-between stage in its transition from a mediated to an unmediated state, but the particular nature of its hybridity appears to have done little to undermine its developmental capacities.

Qatari High Modernism

In addition to its pursuit of subtle power in the international arena, the Qatari state has employed its enormous capacity to bring about what James C. Scott has called a high modernist society. Scott has defined high modernism as

> a strong (one might even say muscle-bound) version of the beliefs in scientific and technical progress that were associated with industrialization in Western Europe and in North America from roughly 1830 until World War I. At its center was a supreme self-confidence about continued linear progress, the development of scientific and technical knowledge, the expansion of production, the rational design for social order, the growing satisfaction of human needs, and, not least, an increasing control over nature (including human nature) commensurate with scientific understanding of natural law. *High* modernism is thus a particularly sweeping vision of how the benefits of technical and scientific progress might be applied—usually through the state—in every field of human activity.[54]

The core assumption of high modernism is the creation of a new society, by force if need be. In achieving its goal, the state sets out to "conceive of an artificial, engineered society designed, not by custom and historical accident, but according to conscious, rational, scientific criteria." It undertakes social engineering with zeal and determination, with the hope that "every nook and cranny of the social order might be improved upon."[55]

The project of high modernism is often carried out by authoritarian states that need to rely on coercive practices to accomplish their self-ascribed missions of pulling their societies out of the dark ages and into a new era. Often times, high modernism is premised on a radical break with the past. Insofar as the state is concerned, "the past is an impediment, a history that must be transcended; the present is the platform for launching plans for a better future." This better future is often most dramatically manifested through spatial and geographic forms that are meant to make life, and governance, easier. Ordinary people, the assumption goes, do not have the necessary intelligence, skills, and experience to fully grasp the superior logic that underlies the high modernist project. But they will buy into it once they see its impressive results at work. As Scott puts it, a key characteristic of the discourse of high modernism is heavy emphasis on "visual images of heroic progress toward a totally transformed future." High modernism is meant to make a visual statement. "The new city has striking sculptural properties; it is designed to make a powerful visual impact as a *form*."[56] As an ultra-modern city, however, the high modernist city can be anywhere; it lacks context and individuality.

Qatari high modernism differs from Scott's ideal type in three important respects. First, although the Qatari state is autocratic, it is of a milder, more benign sort that, so far at least, has not had to rely on force to carry out its modernization projects. In fact, the state has managed to expand and to solidify its base of support through—and at the same time as—fostering high modernism. Critically, instead of being implemented solely by the state, Qatar's high modernism project is being mostly carried out by state-owned corporations, which incidentally serve as venues for deepening state-society's linkages through mutually empowering, and financially enriching, ties. Far from being corrosive in the long term of the state's underpinning authoritarianism, the manner in which Qatari high modernism is unfolding appears to be strengthening the political status quo and adding new dimensions to its already robust clientelistic networks across Qatari society.

A second important difference between Qatari high modernism and the type of high modernism that Scott describes, drawing mostly from South American and former communist East European examples, is the role of tradition. Due largely to its youth and the historical and geopolitical conditions in which its formation occurred, heritage and national identity—the myth of historical resonance and continuity—are central to the traditional legitimacy on which the Qatari state rests. Moreover, by virtue of the nature of the very position he occupies, the emir can ill afford to ignore Qatari tradition and not to continuously pay lip service to it even if the projects he patronizes undermine it. In reality, what has ended up happening is the state carefully walking on a tightrope, fostering high modernism, on the one hand, and a vibrant if contrived heritage industry, on the other.[57]

As the new cities and islands being built are concerned, their connections with Qatari culture—even if only in name—are emphasized by the state and by private developers. In one of the promotional materials for Lusail, a city being built north of Doha, the emphasis on mixing Qatari traditions and futuristic aspirations is prominent:

Lusail goes beyond the usual concept of a modern city; it is, in fact, a futuristic reflection of wonderful aspirations, technologies and ideas. Simultaneously, Lusail is characterised by a rich history that captures the authentic heritage and values of the remarkable Qatari culture. The unique name "Lusail" is not only derived from the rare flower that grows in Qatar, it is also a symbol of the authenticity of the place where the late Sheikh Jassem Ben Mohammad Al Thani built the Lusail Castle, previously the centre for governance. In the vicinity of this significant castle lies Lusail, a modernistic city, yet one that has innovatively preserved the traditional aspects of Qatar.[58]

Qatari Diar, Lusail City's developer, further elaborates on its guiding philosophy:

We have a strong desire to ensure the cultural fabric of society is woven into every one of our developments across the world. . . . Guided by the progressive and forward-looking vision of His Highness the Emir Sheikh Hamad Bin Khalifa Al-Thani and His Highness the Heir Apparent Sheikh Tamim Bin Hamad Al-Thani, Qatar has developed the Qatar National Vision 2030, which provides for the long-term benefit of its people and future generations by creating an advanced society capable of sustaining its development and providing a high standard of living for all.

Since its launch in 2005, Qatari Diar has been dedicated to bringing these ambitious goals to life. More than just a real estate investor and developer, Qatari Diar is the organization proudly entrusted with realizing our country's vision for a beautifully built environment, new sustainable communities and developments that catch the imagination of a world audience.[59]

This, in fact, is where Qatari high modernism most closely approximates Scott's ideal type. The most visible manifestation of high modernism is the construction of entire cities anew, with Brasilia as a prime example, and the Qatari state has been busily encouraging the proliferation of newly built, modern cities across the country's sandy cost. The four biggest of such projects are the Pearl artificial island, Barwa, Lusail City, and Dohaland, which, combined, are changing the face and the very urban geography of Qatar, all at a cost of tens of billions of dollars and in the process generating profits in the billions as well. Table 5.5 offers a snapshot of the scope and magnitude of these projects. Considering that greater Doha has an approximate size of only 50 square miles, once on line, these projects will substantially change the spatial life and geographic look of the entire country. The Pearl is an artificial island being built north of Doha and, when completed, is meant to comprise two separate islands each with their own string of smaller islands. Lusail is being modeled as a futuristic, environment-friendly city. Barwa comprises several mega-projects to provide everything from luxury to low-cost housing and a motor speedway. And Dohaland is an urban planning project undertaken by the Qatar Foundation designed to rebuild large swathes of downtown Doha in the form of modern, multipurpose areas. The government has also announced plans for planting a billion trees across the country. Where there is sand today, there will soon be glass, concrete, and greenery.

All of this is meant to transform Qatar into a showcase example of an ultra-modern, advanced country. Barwa's mission statement is emblematic of what all these projects represent and what they hope to accomplish: "Barwa's creation was a demonstration of the vision of the country led by His Highness the Emir and the government of the State of Qatar to build a modern country with a diversified economy for the benefit of future generations. We seek to contribute to the government's over-arching development plan for the State set out in *Qatar Vision 2030*."[60]

Constraints on the State

What, then, are the constraints on the Qatari state? With its enormous capacity, and with seemingly endless financial resources at its disposal, does the state face any constraints in carrying out its projects of high modernism and social change? There are, in fact, two sets of constraints the state has to contend with—one structural and the other political—though neither appears to require an inordinate amount of energy to overcome. Structurally, by far the biggest set of constraints on the state arises from the consequences of rentierism. But these constraints are not of the political-economic kind generally associated with rentier systems. Elsewhere I have argued for a more nuanced conception of rentierism in the Persian Gulf, in which the relatively resource-rich, direct rentier polities of the GCC are distinguished for the much larger, and much poorer, political economies of Iran and Iraq.[61] In those countries, the state's rentier linkages with society tend to be indirect and are primarily in the form of state salaries and price subsidies. Fluctuations in oil revenues, and therefore in the state's ability to buy off socially based opposition, is more constricted. In GCC countries, state-society rentier ties are far more direct, with a relationship of dependence having emerged between private capital and the state, with the former dependent on the latter for continued state-generated or state-supported contracts and commercial advantages. Even in times of downturn, in these rentier polities private capital is unlikely to break with the state and to form a contesting block against it. If anything, its dependence on the state grows even deeper, eager for more support and patronage to weather the storm.[62]

This has been especially the case in Qatar, in which private capital and the professional classes are intimately tied to the state through the latter's establishment and sponsorship of publicly owned companies charged with implementing its projects of high modernism. As the scope and pace of these phenomenally ambitious development projects have picked up, there has been a commensurate deepening of the links between social actors and the state. Private capital now needs the state more than ever to continue to grow and prosper and, in lean times, to get protection from severe adversity. Far from breaking away from the state in times of downturn, private and state-dependent capital tries to seek shelter under the state's protective wings.

High modernism appeals most to those who have the most to gain from it and its worldview—bureaucratic intelligentsia, technicians, planners, and engineers.[63] According to Ayubi, "bonanza modernization" in the Persian Gulf has fostered the birth of what may be called a "new middle class" of professional administrators, army officers, and other technocrats. A product of the rentier political economy, bonanza development relies on rent revenues generated from hydrocarbon exports to develop other economic sectors, to create lucrative positions within the state bureaucracy, to foster extensive public works projects, and to provide generous welfare services. "Opportunities for upward mobility are opened to ambitious societal elements, especially members of the middle classes who are capable of mounting serious threats to the status quo if frustrated by a situation of blocked ascent. The ruling stratus does not therefore have to be 'unpleasant' either to the owning classes by taxing their profits or to the working classes by extracting part of their surplus labour."[64]

The kind of constraint that rentierism does pose on the Qatari state is not so much economic as it is sociopolitical. More specifically, it has to do with a general sense among the national population that attaining wealth is both possible and feasible in return for comparatively little effort. A "rentier mentality" can set in when "individuals can live well without having to commit themselves to any strict 'work ethic,'" and when no "distinction need to be made between income 'received' and income 'earned.' An 'easy come, easy go' attitude may inspire both individual and public spending—it is indeed a 'bonanza time' for all to enjoy."[65] Most Qataris have come to expect the state's generous allowances, which in 2011–2012 could reach as high as $7,000 a month, along with interest-free loans, free land, and guaranteed civil service employment.[66] As Ayubi put it, in rentier states, "a certain dependency may be promoted in the citizen whereby he will be disinclined to act economically or politically on his own behalf, let alone seriously to criticise or to challenge the state."[67] As one observer has commented,

> Gulf states use their wealth to buy political loyalties through public spending, including a generous subsidy system. This noneconomic utilization of resources socializes youth to believe that work has no inherent value and production is irrelevant, because salaries are paid in the bureaucracy without regard to work. These citizens look at income as their right, their fair share in the oil revenues. Because of entitlements, individuals and families

perceive no need to change the current position. Were they to try to bring pressure on the state, they might jeopardize these benefits. In a sense, they become "more royal than the king."[68]

Difficult to empirically quantify, the deleterious effects of massive wealth is particularly observable among the country's young male population, whose relatively easy wealth serves as a demotivating factor for hard work. Young Qatari males lag behind young females in most educational indicators. Guaranteed of a job in the public sector, fewer men are motivated to attend university as compared to women; for example, at Qatar University 75 percent of students are female. According to a 2007 report by the government's Planning Council, Qatari female workers have 14.1 years of education compared to 10.7 years for male workers.[69] According to the report, overall Qataris remain woefully unprepared for the management of the country's ambitious development projects. "If the current employment trends continue," the report states, "the future large investments [in education] will have little primary employment impact on Qataris. These investments are concentrated in sectors where Qataris do not work or are in jobs [for] which they cannot readily compete with expatriate workers." The report cited "an inadequately educated population" as "the most problematic factor in doing business in Qatar." Some 96 percent of all employed Qataris work for the public sector. "The combination of various benefits for Qataris and more generous working conditions in the broad public sector results in Qataris not working in the private sector."[70]

Meanwhile, the state's Qatarization schemes, through which private corporations operating in the country are encouraged, at times compelled, to hire and promote Qatari employees, have done little to help combat the phenomenon described here. The state has indeed undertaken major reforms to the country's educational system, spending upwards of 5 to as much as 9 percent of the national budget on education.[71] But these measures cannot produce results overnight. In the 2009 OECD Pisa rankings, the universally recognized measure of educational performance in 64 countries, which ranks countries by student performance in reading, mathematics, and science, Qatar scored fifth from bottom.[72] As Kristian Ulrichsen argues, there continues to be "a substantive disconnect between the educational system and the labor market" across the GCC.[73] Massive investments in infrastructure, and the erection of impressive buildings, are insufficient in addressing deep-seated issues, such as the emergence of a merit-based culture that directly links educational achievement to professional advancement. The pervasiveness of Western universities across the region, especially in Qatar, deepens the possibility that GCC societies become "consumers, rather than producers, of knowledge, which continues to be generated externally."[74]

What the long-term effects of the rentier mentality will be is hard to tell. Clearly, despite persistent pressures for Qatarization, the private sector's heavy dependence on foreign labor and expertise is unlikely to lessen anytime in the near future. Just as possible economic downturns are unlikely to negatively impact state-private capital relations, they are also unlikely to darken the state's relations with the country's middle classes, most of whom will continue to be employed in the state's bloated and inefficient bureaucracy. Development projects may be slowed down, and the expatriate labor may be squeezed in terms of salaries and employment opportunities, but the Qataris' life of relative comfort and affluence is unlikely to be seriously impacted. The state may cut back on its spending spree abroad, and it may even lose some face internationally, but that is far from confronting domestic challenges or crises.

A second set of constraints on the Qatari state may be broadly categorized as political. Qatari politics tends to be low-intensity and even dull by regional standards. This is due largely to a combination of the state's effective patronage of social actors, on the one hand, and the powerful and popular personality of Emir Hamad, on the other. Whatever there is of "chatter" tends to be of a generally moderate and benign nature, revolving mostly around the appointment of unqualified officials, the pace and direction of the social changes underway in society, and Qatar's hyperactive diplomacy. This chatter finds its most unfettered expression in cyberspace, which—given restrictions on press freedom and pervasive fears of talking in the open—has become a popular forum for expressing political grievances. Interestingly, despite the anonymity offered by the Internet, there are no posts that attack the emir or other members of the ruling family directly.

"Oppositional talk" in Qatari cyberspace is relatively tame compared to most other regional cyberspace chatter. One of the main topics of discussion is the appointment of apparently unqualified individuals to multiple and at times powerful positions. An example is Aisha Al Khater, who in 2011 was appointed as the director of the Museum of Islamic Art. Al Khater, who does not wear the traditional *abayya*, is often criticized as unqualified for the job and is said to have been appointed to this high profile position solely because of her friendship with Sheikha Mayassa, the emir's daughter and chair of the Qatar Museums Authority. Minister of Health Abdullah Khaled Al Qahtani (b. 1970, appointed in 2009) is similarly criticized for not having the right credentials for the position. It is not uncommon to find the same individual simultaneously holding multiple paid positions, often in one of the sports federations or in other private or state-owned companies. Given that the country considers itself a major sporting hub, a high premium is attached to positions in the field of sports management, though many of the individuals with such positions are often criticized as unqualified and overpaid.[75] The powerful minister of finance and economy, Yusof Hussain Kamal, was reported in a 2011 article by a local newspaper to hold no less than thirty-three other positions at the same time, including paid membership on corporate boards, committees, and councils.[76]

An even more lively topic of discussion in Qatari cyberspace is the pace and direction of the social and cultural changes promoted by the state. One such topic is the serving of alcohol outside of hotel bars and restaurants and the government's decision in late 2011 to allow the sale of pork in the country's only, officially sanctioned liquor store.[77] The sale of pork soon gave rise to a flurry of unhappy chatter by Qataris in cyberspace.[78] According to one posting on Twitter, "Ppl don't get it. Its not about the pork—its about us feeling more and more like a minority—in our own country."[79] In December 2011, after the appearance of several critical blogs on the issue, the government abruptly declared a ban on the sale of alcohol at the Pearl. However, permission for the sale of pork was not reversed.

Qatar's hyperactive diplomacy has not escaped criticism in cyberspace, and the country's high-profile involvement in the Libyan civil war was the topic of several critical blogs. One blogger complained about Qatar's violation of international law, while another wished for Qatar to have been more like the UAE, where the government is not nearly as involved in international relations and instead "remains close to its people." "We are sick and tired of people mocking us," he went on to say.[80]

Ultimately, these and other similar sentiments trace their origins to expressions of nationalism. In recent years, an "inward-facing nationalism" has emerged throughout the Arabian Peninsula that measures national identity against internal demographic "threats."[81] Nationalism did not emerge in the region through protracted national liberation struggles. Therefore, the oil monarchies' intimate alliance with the United States is less unpalatable than it would have been otherwise. But it is a perception of domestic encirclement, of being a minority in one's own country, and of having a still-emerging national identity eroded, that is often a source of animated discussions in private *majlis*es and in cyberspace. For example, language is a key definer of national identity, but in countries like Qatar and the UAE, Arabic has effectively been reduced to a second language. Ongoing, feverish processes of state-building invariably include the invention of the national community, often "without regard to the sometimes contradictory elements that underpin authority and the differing sub-communities who are not being equally 'imagined.'"[82] So far, these and other similar attempts appear to have enabled the Qatari state to stay well ahead of whatever alternative, nonstate nationalist discourse that might emerge. Barring unforeseen developments that may radically change existing circumstances, there is no reason to believe that the state's abilities in this area will diminish precipitously.

Significantly, the political chatter seldom has an Islamic flavor to it. A number of factors have combined to impede the politicization of Islam in Qatar. Unlike Saudi Arabia, in Qatar religion historically did not play a role in the process of state formation. An absence of major urban centers also impeded the development of prominent centers of religious learning and philosophy. Today, most religious clerics in Qatar are actually from South Asia or from other Arab countries. They are, in effect, migrant workers whose residency permits can be revoked if they step out of line. More important, the state often uses the ministries of Awqaf, education, and justice for purposes of incorporating nationals with Islamist tendencies and to ensure the nurturing of a "government-friendly Islam" that finds expression in Friday prayer sermons across the country's mosques.[83] The state's patronage of Yusuf Qaradawi, one of contemporary Islam's most outspoken and most controversial clerics, has also done much to blunt possibilities of antistate sentiments from Islamic quarters.

Like all other states, the Qatari state faces constraints on its agendas and its policies by actors and currents in Qatari society, as well as from those emanating from the international arena. But the specific set of societal constraints faced by the Qatari state are relatively mild and deal mostly with issues of less direct significance to overall state policy. Qatari politics remain largely low-intensity, and state capacity is constrained by the availability of resources and the scope of ambition rather than by structural or political contractions narrowing the purview of state goals and agendas.

Conclusion

State capacity is far from constant and varies over time depending on the constellation of international and domestic forces with which the state has to contend. Neither is state capacity uniform in both the domestic and international arenas, nor across all areas of state operations domestically and internationally. In Qatar's case, state capacity has been increasingly on the rise since Hamad bin Khalifa's assumption of power in 1995, thanks largely to steady rises in oil and gas prices, growing cohesion and internal discipline within the Al Thanis, focused and carefully calculated policymaking, and the state's effective inclusion of private capital and social actors in its developmental projects and its larger agendas of high modernism. Increased state capacity and deepened political consolidation have gone hand-in-hand with the robustness of state-society ties, increasing as the state has worked with the private and semi-private sectors to implement its developmental agendas.

Throughout, the state has kept its ears close to the ground—whether through the state intelligence service monitoring chatter in public or in cyberspace or through the private *majlis*es, or both—listening to "the street" intently to ensure that its normative gap with society does not widen beyond comfortable levels. Whenever through newspaper articles or letters to the editor scattered voices are heard about the "threat" of being a minority inside Qatar, for example, a statement is usually soon issued by some government ministry or official concerning a new push for Qatarization. In the late 2000s, complaints began surfacing about Sheikha Moza's highly visible profile internationally and what it meant for the powers and influence of her large and influential family, the Al Misnids. In January 2011, she officially dropped Al Misnid from her last name and simply became Sheikha Moza bint Nasser. All state entities were subsequently instructed to use her new proper name. The state may be autocratic, and it may have had astounding success so far in bringing about high modernism, but it is also responsive to popular sensibilities.

That the state has the capacity to carry out high modernist projects of great ambition, and that in the process it has further cemented its ties to actors across Qatari society, is not questionable. What is open to question is the validity of the "build them and they will come" assumption underlying the state's aggressive pursuit of high modernism. Are the new cities and islands being built simply to keep up with Dubai and Abu Dhabi or are they being built in response to genuine needs and thought-out developmental trajectories? Does it matter why they are being built as long as they are changing the geography and the physical landscape of the country? There is no single correct answer to these questions. What is certain is that Qatar is now developing a robust domestic infrastructure to go with its high profile diplomacy and its emerging status as one of the Middle East's—and indeed one of the world's—most influential players.

6

QATAR'S MOMENT IN HISTORY

Are Qatar's powers and influence in the Middle East and elsewhere ephemeral or lasting? This was the question with which I started the book. This volume has demonstrated how the center of gravity in the Middle East has steadily shifted toward the Persian Gulf, and how within the Persian Gulf Qatar enjoys a number of comparative advantages that have propelled it to the top. This ascendance has been made possible through the acquisition and exertion of what may be called subtle power, arising from careful and strategic use of international investments, financial influence, and diplomacy. Qatar has been using this power to push through its agendas of buying international friends and allies, asserting its leadership role within the Arab world, setting agendas in international and even national forums, and, wherever possible—whether it is in Lebanon, Libya, Syria, or elsewhere—carving out for itself spheres of influence.

This subtle power in the international arena is reinforced by a solid domestic base thanks largely to the steady consolidation of Al Thani rule, increasing discipline and cohesion within the ruling inner-circle, and the

institutionalization and codification of Hamad bin Khalifa's vision of
Qatar's future. That future is one of ultra-modernism, continued hyper-
growth, and physical and infrastructural expansion, all accompanied by
and made possible through steadily expansive state capacity. Needless to
say, the Al Thanis see themselves and their continued rule as an integral
part of the future.

By all accounts, what has been accomplished so far in the fields of diplomacy, international finance, domestic politics, and economic growth,
have been remarkable and impressive. Ever-expansive oil and gas revenues have no doubt helped mask lingering inefficiencies in the state sector,
and chatter about nepotism and the appointment of incompetent paper
pushers to key civil service positions remains widespread. But the state's
accomplishments on multiple economic, political, and diplomatic levels,
and its overall efficacy and effectiveness in achieving the goals it sets for
itself, cannot be denied.

This concluding chapter tackles the question of the durability of Qatar's
power and influence. Qatar may not be a mere blip on the radar, but how
durable is its prominent regional and international position likely to be?
And, domestically, how viable is the "Qatar model" likely to be in the long
run? Does the consolidation of Al Thani rule and the increasing expansion
of state capacity equate with a continuation of, and ultimate success of, the
country's ambitious project of high modernism?

Lessons from Qatar

Before delving into the prospects of Qatar's fortunes, it may be worth re-
iterating some of the main theoretical conclusions that can be drawn from
my analysis of the country. Specifically, I believe my research has yielded
five significant conclusions. The first two conclusions have to do with the
size of a state and the form(s) of power it may come to acquire and project.
In international relations small size need not necessarily be a hindrance to
power and influence. Small states are not always on the receiving end of
international power. Some can become quite consequential and—under
the right set of circumstances—may in fact exert different kinds of power.

Second, this kind of power may not always square perfectly with our
preexisting conceptions of hard, soft, and smart varieties of power. Such

notions of power do not adequately capture the emergent power and influence of countries such as Qatar, whose investments are actively courted and which in subtle ways can influence and frame agendas. In today's international relations, subtle power may be as much of a factor in influencing outcomes as hard or soft power.

Third, the acquisition and exercise of subtle power is as much a product of carefully crafted use of available financial resources and diplomacy as it is due to context, opportunities, and structural conditions. Agency matters. And it matters even more in shaping outcomes in developing political systems, where personal initiatives directly influence the viability of such institutions as the ruling family, the state and its constituent organizations, and the nature, direction, and intensity of projects of high modernism meant to engineer entire societies.

A related, fourth conclusion has to do with the transferability of the developmental state model. With the developmental state seen as a product of specific historical and political developments in East Asia, it is often assumed that "there exist major constrains on its transferability to or replicability in alternative national contexts."[1] But the Qatari state exhibits all the characteristics of a classical developmental state, and so does its closest relative, the Emirate of Abu Dhabi.[2] Clearly, the Qatari state is unique in the inordinate amount of wealth it has at its disposal. But it also possesses seemingly single-minded vision, clearly articulated developmental objectives, tremendous intra-elite cohesion, and a robust set of linkages between strategically placed social actors and critical state or state-related agencies. Whatever its merits, Qatar currently possesses its own variety of a developmental state.

All of this points to a rather obvious fifth conclusion. Whether as a social science construct or an actual entity, the state is not about to dissipate anytime soon. In fact, far from rendering the state obsolete or eroding its powers, globalization has significantly strengthened some states by enabling them to carve out a specific niche for themselves in the international political economy. That the state is nowhere near being eclipsed was established as far back as the mid-1980s, when the historical sociologist Peter Evans and others successfully brought it back into the fore of analysis.[3] But what the Qatari case shows us is that even in the post–Arab Spring Middle East, an authoritarian state can be both quite durable and popular. It bears repeating that popularity appears to have much to do with durability, especially if it is rooted in strategic alliances with social actors whose positions of affluence and prestige and whose economic well-being are closely tied to the personalist state's policies and institutions.

Qatar's Future

What does all of this mean for Qatar in the coming years? The durability of Qatar's preeminent position within the larger Middle East and in the Persian Gulf in particular, and the viability and success of its high modernism project, pivot on two main factors: contingency and agency. More specifically, the question of Qatar's continued ability to capitalize on its strategic assets and opportunities, and at the same time to fulfill the promises of its high modernist projects, depend in large measure on several independent variables. These tend to fall into the two broad categories of domestic and international developments.

Domestically, the success or failure of Qatar's high modernist project depends overwhelmingly, if not entirely, on the vision, strategic priorities, and resourcefulness of the country's next generation of leaders after the current emir departs from the scene. Sheikh Hamad has not been just a wily, crafty politician. He has been the driving force behind what Qatar has become today. With multiple and expansive institutional and organizational accouterments being added to the state every day, Hamad may no longer personify Louis XIV's dictum of "L'Etat, c'est moi." But he does personify all that Qatar and its ambitions for rapid modernization and progress stand for. Will Sheikh Tamim, the heir apparent, share the same vision and drive, the same contagious enthusiasm, the same navigatory craftiness? Only time will tell.

What will become of the high modernist drive is less uncertain. The intensity and zeal of the multiple high modernist projects underway may change, but the facts on the ground will not. Qatar's physical landscape is being forever changed, and the cities going up in the sky and the islands being created in the sea will neither wither away nor sink. The very creation of infrastructures where none existed before—of roads and schools, water desalination plants and new public spaces—will permanently change the lives of Qataris, in the same way, for example, that the widespread introduction and use of air-conditioning did in the 1960s and the 1970s.

There is no reason to share the pessimism of James C. Scott with regard to the project of high modernism underway in Qatar. Scott contends that high modernist projects invariably end up in tragedies of national proportion or, at best, ultimately worsen the lives of those meant to benefit from them.[4] Undoubtedly, the physical and geographic changes underway in Qatar are only bound to aggravate the country's strained ecosystem.[5] Already, Qatar leads the world in per capita electricity consumption and CO_2 emissions.[6] But long-term environmental damage is not perceived by the average Qatari as a catastrophe in the making or even a point of concern. And questions about the prudence of all the buildings going up in Doha and its environs, about whether they will become white elephants or sources of national progress and pride, have taken a backseat to the hype and excitement of real estate speculation and the glitz of gleaming buildings. The wholesale importation of Western and especially US educational establishments, and the rapid implementation of profound changes to the country's educational system, is similarly done with little or no study of their long-term impacts. Qatar's high modernism may be a product of bad or shortsighted public policy. But unpopular, or negatively perceived, it is not.

At least for the foreseeable future, Qatar's prospects for continued growth, especially compared to its regional neighbors, appear quite positive. Across the Arabian Peninsula, despite phenomenal transformations and development in recent decades, vulnerabilities remain. Given their overreliance on hydrocarbon exports, the states of the Gulf Cooperation Council (GCC) have been vulnerable to cycles of boom and bust.[7] The one thing certain about oil is the uncertainty of its prices.[8] States with a fragile resource base in particular—most notably Bahrain, Yemen, and Saudi Arabia—can face serious challenges in times of economic downturns. The existence of numerous "fault-lines" and "fissures," along sectarian lines for example, can "heighten regime vulnerability to future politicization and contestation if resource scarcities develop and persist."[9]

But this is not the case with Qatar. The state has inordinate resources at its disposal in proportion to its national population. Throughout the 2000s, when the price of oil hovered around or above $100 a barrel, Qatari authorities based the country's national budget and their spending estimates on oil prices far below oil's actual market price, sometimes nearly by half.[10] Even when oil and gas prices dipped, and in times when the private sector suffered, as it did in the immediate aftermath of the 2008 global financial meltdown, the state's resources remained robust enough for it to maintain previous levels of spending and, more important, patronage and social welfare. Unless the world suddenly stops its reliance on hydrocarbons altogether, Qatar's comparative financial health appears secured.

The bigger question marks remain in relation to Qatar's diplomacy and international relations. With its proactive diplomacy and its attempts to exercise subtle power, is Qatar biting off more than it can chew? Is Qatar running the risk of overreach? The country has taken a number of controversial stands on contentious issues without, it seems, having fully considered the consequences. For example, in 2011 Qatar played perhaps the most prominent and public role of all Arab states in helping Libyan rebels overthrow Colonel Qaddafi. Later that year and in the following year, Qatar similarly led the effort—this time through the Arab League—in expediting the demise of the Assad regime in Syria. In Libya, some of the estimated twenty thousand tons of Qatari weapons and equipment sent to support the anti-Qaddafi rebels—by one estimate amounting to $400 million[11]—ended up in the hands of Islamist groups with goals and objectives inimical to Qatar's stated policies.[12] Although there is a possibility that this may be part of a calculated strategy to pursue complex political objectives—in both instances, Qatar appears to be supporting comparatively moderate Islamist groups to prop them up against more extremist, Salafist elements[13]—it appears more a result of unintended consequences of decisions not fully thought out and carelessly implemented. Whether or not Qatari leaders have given due consideration to the consequences of their actions in relation to Syria is similarly open to question.

There does appear to be a somewhat deeper logic at work here in guiding the foreign policy objectives of Qatari leaders. This is particularly evident with regard to the initial decision to become involved in Libya and Syria. In fact, it is here where we see the most direct manifestations of Qatari subtle power at work, when the country begins cashing in on the power and influence it had accumulated over time. Aware of their growing stature and influence regionally and beyond, Qatari leaders had begun their deliberate maneuvers for regional influence a number of years ago. An example occurred in 2008–2009, when through its mediation and investments Qatar sought to position itself favorably among Lebanon's contentious factions and to slowly replace Saudi Arabia's influence with its own. Ultimately, however, Saudi influence in Lebanon proved too pervasive to be easily dislodged. Similar efforts in Yemen and the Sudan met with equally ephemeral success. Throughout the 2000s, Qatari leaders continued to amass subtle power through deepening the combination of resources at their disposal, aggressively expanding their investments, fine-tuning their branding efforts and their national narrative, securing their image of indispensability to regional peace and stability, and steadily positioning themselves as one of the region's most consequential agenda-setters. At around the same time, those who were their primary competitors—most notably Saudi Arabia, Egypt, and Iran—were in deep morass or, worse yet, about to be engulfed in revolution. When the Arab Spring erupted in late 2010, Qatar was perfectly positioned to deploy the powers it had steadily accumulated over the previous decade and a half.

With the flare-up of the Arab Spring, Qatar and Saudi Arabia quickly set aside their differences and began cooperating, each guided by a different motivation. Saudi Arabia's octogenarian rulers were motivated by the imperative of regime survival, worried that the upheavals in Bahrain would stoke tensions in their own Eastern Province and may eventually even reach Riyadh. They hurriedly sent troops to Manama, pledged financial assistance to the stressed monarchy, and saw to it that the more accommodating elements within the Bahraini establishment, the most notable of whom was the Crown Prince Salman bin Hamad, were marginalized and lost their influence.

Domestically secure, Qatar saw the Arab Spring not as a threat but instead as an opportunity to expand its influence to those states crumbling under the weight of popular uprisings. But Doha's leaders were savvy enough to realize that they could not do so without Saudi acquiescence. Through first the GCC and then the Arab League, the two countries coordinated their efforts in setting a series of common regional agendas: the monarchies had to be saved at all costs; Qaddafi had to go; and, later on, so did Assad. This presented Qatar with a host of opportunities, from expansive investments to more direct forms of influence. Most important, the removal of strongmen such as Qaddafi and Assad would literally change the political face of the Middle East, bringing even more directly to the fore polities and politicians like those of Qatar and the vision of the future they represented. Qatar, meanwhile, busily set out to turn Libya into its own sphere of influence. In so doing, it hardly encountered the resistance of any other Arab state. Similar dynamics unfolded in Syria, with Qatar once again on the forefront of the effort to topple its former ally Bashar Assad. In the meanwhile, Al Jazeera all but forgot there was a country called Bahrain.

Power accumulation has its risks for all international players, and Qatar is no exception. Giulio Gallarotti has identified several symptoms of what he calls "power illusion" and "power curse," among the most notable of which are possibilities of overstretch, moral hazard arising from reckless- ness and a sense of limited vulnerability, and the trap of unilateralism.[14] Gallarotti warns of "hard disempowerment," which occurs when "nations can become weaker by attempting to augment national influence with strategies that rely excessively on hard power."[15] Power curse and power illusion can pertain to all nations intent on accumulating power, be they weak, aspiring, or dominant powers.[16] With Qatar throwing its weight around with increasing frequency, and in places where the mighty have fallen, craftiness and care will be needed more than ever before.

Ultimately, the issue of inadequate attention to the consequences of major state undertakings, both domestically and internationally, can be traced to the personalist character of the system. With national policymak- ing ultimately the preserve of the emir, based at most on advice from no more than a handful of individuals, and with a serious dearth of technical experts across the state machinery to provide input and advice upward, decisions are made without detailed study of their consequences. Instead, decisions are made based on their apparent prudence at the time they are taken. The same logic that led the state to get involved in the Libyan and Syrian civil wars—because it seemed like the right thing to do and at the urging of Western friends—had some years earlier resulted in US univer- sities being invited to set up branch campuses in Doha. Neither decision appears to have been taken with much advanced planning and study. Will Qatar's involvement in Libya and Syria turn out to be the right decision? Will Education City, home to American university campuses, turn out graduates who will begin questioning the legitimacy of the sociopolitical order that gave rise to them?

Paradoxically, the biggest challenge facing the Qatari system in the com- ing years has also been one of its biggest assets in the recent past, namely its personalist nature. The regime's focused decision making has given it agil- ity and flexibility. Sheikh Hamad, the balancer, has been a great navigator of his region's troubled waters and his own family's fractious past. Tamim has had on the job training for a number of years, since 2009–2010 assuming an increasingly more visible and active profile in decision making and diplomacy. But whether and how he and future generations of Qatari rulers will deal with the same challenges remains an open question.

Let us make no mistake about it. Regardless of its stewards and their vision and capabilities, Qatar's power is underwritten by its wealth. And as long as that wealth continues, so is the likelihood that the sheikhdom will project a much larger image of itself than its size and abilities warrant. The length of the country's current moment in history, and how long it can project a form of power that is by all accounts incommensurate with its size, history, infrastructure, and industrial and scientific resources, depend directly on how long and in what ways its wealth lasts and can be prolonged. The real challenge is for Qatar to carry on business as usual in the post-oil era. Until then, the country can rest reasonably assured of its place in the limelight of history.

NOTES

Preface to the Paperback Edition

1. Roger Owen, *The Rise and Fall of Arab Presidents for Life* (Cambridge, 2012), 172.

2. See the collection of articles in Robert O. Keohane and Hellen V. Milner, eds., *Internationalization and Domestic Politics* (Cambridge, 1996).

3. Simon Henderson, "Qatar's Gaza Motives," Policy Watch 2296, 29 July 2014, http://www.washingtoninstitute.org/policy-analysis/view/qatars-gaza-motives.

4. Andrew Hammond, "Qatar's Leadership Transition: Like Father, Like Son," *European Council on Foreign Relations, Policy Brief*, no. 95 (February 2014), 8.

5. Shabina Khatri and Peter Kovessy, "Emir's Accession, One Year On: What's Changed and What's Stayed the Same," Doha News, 25 June 2014, http://dohanews.co/emirs-accession-one-year-whats-changed-whats-stayed/.

6. Quoted in "HH the Emir Patronizes Opening of Advisory Council's 43rd Ordinary Session," Qatar News Agency, 11 November 2014, http://www.qna.org.qa/en-us/News/14111109530027/HH-the-Emir-Patronizes-Opening-of-Advisory-Councils-43rd-Ordinary-Session.

7. Hammond, "Qatar's Leadership Transition," 4–5.

8. Ibid., 2, 8.

9. The original Arabic draft of *The People Want Reform . . . In Qatar Too* is available online through http://www.dr-alkuwari.net.

10. Jenan Amin, "Interview with Dr. Ali Khalifa Al Kuwari, Author of *The People Want Reform . . . In Qatar, Too,*" Heinrich Boll Stiftung, 23 January 2013, p. 2.

11. Ibid. 3–6.

12. Justin Gengler, "Collective Frustration, But No Collective Action, in Qatar," *Middle East Research and Information Project,* 7 December 2013, http://www.merip.org/mero/mero120713.

13. "Huge Rise in Qatari Household Spending," 15 June 2014, http://www.zawya.com.

14. "Qatar Residents to Get Free Internet Access," 3 February 2014, http://www.zawya.com.

15. SpyFiles 4, FinFisher Customers, https://wikileaks.org/spyfiles4/customers.html#customer_21.

16. According to a former cabinet minister, the law was passed only to comply with a GCC Security Pact. Peter Kovessy, "Former Minister: Qatar's Cybercrime Law Result of GCC Security Pact," Doha News, 5 October 2014, http://dohanews.co/former-minister-qatars-cybercrime-law-stems-gcc-security-pact/.

17. SESRI, *Annual Omnibus Survey: A Survey of Life in Qatar, 2011* and *2012,* Qatar University, 2011 and 2012, pp. 4 and 7 respectively.

18. Shabina Khatri, "Qatar, US Sign 10-Year Military Cooperation Pact during Official Visit," 11 December 2013, http://dohanews.co/qatar-us-sign-10-year-military-cooperation-pact-during-official-visit/.

19. "Qatar to Buy Patriot Missiles in $11bn Deal," *Gulf Times* (Doha), July 15, 2014, p. 1.

20. Quoted in Rajiv Chandrasekaran, "Qatar's Take on Foreign Policy: Let's Be Friends," *Washington Post,* October 5, 2014, p. 1.

21. Amena Bakr, "Qatar Seeks Role as Gaza Mediator, Israel Wary," 17 July 2014, www.zawya.com. Qatar's offer of mediation was vehemently rejected by the Israeli government, which accused it of supporting alleged terrorism by Hamas.

22. Kristian Coates Ulrichsen, "Qatar and the Arab Spring: Policy Drivers and Regional Implications," Carnegie Endowment for International Peace, September 2014, p. 1.

23. Sigurd Neubauer, "Qatar's Changing Foreign Policy," *Sada: Analysis on Arab Reform,* 8 April 2014, http://carnegieendowment.org/sada/2014/04/08/qatar-s-changing-foreign-policy/h7gf.

24. Ulrichsen, "Qatar and the Arab Spring," 23.

25. Hammond, "Qatar's Leadership Transition," 6.

26. Ibid., 3.

27. "UAE, Saudi Arabia and Bahrain Issue Joint Statement on Qatar," *Gulf News,* 5 March 2014, p. 1.

28. Glenn Greenwald. "How Former Treasury Officials and the UAE Are Manipulating American Journalists," *The Intercept,* 25 September 2014, https://firstlook.org/theintercept/2014/09/25/uae-qatar-camstoll-group/.

29. Bilal Y. Saab, "The Dishonest Broker: Why Qatar's Peacemaking Shouldn't Be Trusted," *Foreign Affairs,* 30 July 2014, http://www.foreignaffairs.com/articles/141667/bilal-y-saab/the-dishonest-broker; Jeremy Shapiro, "The Qatar Problem," *Foreign Policy,* 29 August 2013, http://foreignpolicy.com/2013/08/28/the-qatar-problem/. See also Elizabeth Dickinson, "The Case against Qatar," *Foreign Policy,* 30 September 2014, http://foreignpolicy.com/2014/09/30/the-case-against-qatar/.

30. Ulrichsen, "Qatar and the Arab Spring," 19.

31. Quoted in Lesley Walker, "Qatar Emir Acknowledges 'Errors and Problems' over Human Rights," Doha News, 8 September 2014, http://dohanews.co/emir-admits-qatars-errors-problems-human-rights/.

32. US State Department, *Country Reports on Terrorism 2013—Qatar,* http://www.state.gov/j/ct/rls/crt/2013/224823.htm.

33. Peter Kovessy, "Qatar Clamps Down on Charities that Send Funds Abroad," Doha News, 20 September 2014, http://dohanews.co/qatar-clamps-charities-send-funds-abroad/.

34. Mahmoud Mourad, "Prominent Muslim Brotherhood Figures to Leave Qatar," 13 September 2014, http://www.zawya.com.

35. Peter Kovessy, "Despite Senior Members' Departure, Brotherhood Retains Presence in Qatar," Doha News, 14 September 2014, http://dohanews.co/despite-senior-members-departure-qatar-remains-base-brotherhood/.

36. Basma Atassi, "GCC Announces Steps to Bolster Security," *Al Jazeera*, 9 December 2014, http://www.aljazeera.com/news/middleeast/2014/12/gcc-announces-steps-bolster-security-201412918365534382.html.

37. "Qatar Reaches Out beyond the Gulf," *Gulf States Newsletter* 38, no. 966 (20 March 2014), 1.

38. "Qatar State Spending up 13 Pct last FY, Slowest in 11 Yrs," 27 July 2014, http://www.zawya.com.

39. "Qatar Seen Headed for Slowdown this Year," 22 August 2013, www.zawya.com; and, "Qatar Set to Sustain Solid Growth on Mega Projects, Population Expansion," 27 February 2014, http://www.zawya.com.

40. Andy Sambridge, "Qatar Building Costs Ranked Highest in the Middle East," 14 September 2013, http://www.arabianbusiness.com.

41. "Qatar Boosts Project Spending to USD200 bn," 23 December 2013, http://www.zawya.com.

42. "Hiring Spree over Mega Infrastructure Projects," 21 August 2013, http://www.zawya.com.

43. Shane McGinley, "Qatar Ranked Top Financial Center in the Region," 1 October 2013, http://www.arabianbusiness.com.

44. "Qatar Seeking Growth through Fertilisers," 17 July 2014, http://www.zawya.com.

45. Link Qatar Weekly Update, 20 September 2013, http://www.linkmeqatar.com.

46. "Qatar's GDP to Touch USD220.6bn by 2015," 23 June 2014, http://www.zawya.com; and, "Qatar GDP Projected to Hit USD230bn," 20 August 2014, http://www.zawya.com.

47. Behrendt, "Revisiting the Investment Policy of the Qatar Investment Authority," 1.

48. Qatar National Bank, "Monthly Monitor," *QNB Economics,* June 4, 2014, p. 1.

49. In her pioneering study on the topic, Babar argues that the extensive welfare and entitlement system offered by the state serves as a strong incentive for state actors to keep the number of nationals down and to impose stringent restrictions on possible avenues for naturalization. See Zahra Babar, "The Cost of Belonging: Citizenship Construction in the State of Qatar," *Middle East Journal* 68, no. 3 (Summer 2014), 403–420.

50. "Rising Population 'to Spur Non-Oil Growth' in Qatar," *Gulf Times* (Doha), 15 September 2013, p. 1.

51. Reuters, "Qatar Beefs Up SWF Team to Diversify Portfolio," 2 September 2013, http://www.arabianbusiness.com.

52. Sven Behrendt, "Revisiting the Investment Policy of the Qatar Investment Authority," *Geoeconomica* (May 2014), 1.

53. Reuters, "Qatar Beefs Up SWF Team to Diversify Portfolio."

54. Behrendt, "Revisiting the Investment Policy of the Qatar Investment Authority," 3.

55. See, for example, Robert Booth, Owen Gibson, and Pete Pattisson, "Qatar under Pressure over Migrant Labour Abuse," *Guardian*, 27 September 2013, p. 1; Abigail Hauslohner, "Behind Qatar's Glitter, a Harsh Labor," *Washington Post,* 21 November 2013, p. 10; and, "Amnesty Criticizes Exit Permit System," 2 May 2014, http://www.zawya.com.

56. Brian Homewood, "Soccer—FIFA Judges Give All-Clear to 2018/2022 Bids," 13 November 2014, http://www.zawya.com.

57. Supreme Committee for Delivery and Legacy, *SC Workers' Welfare Standards, Edition 1* (Doha, 2014).

58. "Businessmen Seek 'Balanced' Sponsorship Law," 23 May 2014, http://www.zawya.com.

59. Quoted in Lesley Walker, "Qatar Emir Acknowledges 'Errors and Problems' over Human Rights," Doha News, 8 September 2014, http://dohanews.co/emir-admits-qatars-errors-problems-human-rights/.

60. Hammond, "Qatar's Leadership Transition," 10.

61. Ibid., 9–10.

Introduction

1. Nazih N. Ayubi, *Over-Stating the Arab State* (London, 1999), 133.

2. The most notable of these included Rosemarie Said Zahlan's *The Creation of Qatar* (London, 1978).

3. See, for example, Allen J. Fromherz, *Qatar* (London, 2012); Steven Wright, "Qatar," in Davidson, ed., *Power and Politics in the Persian Gulf Monarchies* (New York, 2011), 113–133; and my own articles on the country, "Royal Factionalism and Political Liberalization in Qatar," *Middle East Journal* 63, no. 3 (Summer 2009), and "Mediation and Qatari Foreign Policy," *Middle East Journal* 65, no. 4 (Fall 2011).

4. Alanound Alsharekh, "Introduction," in Alanound Alsharekh, ed., *The Gulf Family* (London, 2007), 11.

5. Qatar Statistics Authority, *Qatar, Social Trends 1998–2010* (Doha, 2011), 5.

6. Jeremy Jones, *Negotiating Change* (London, 2008), 107.

7. Aryn Baker, "Magic Kingdom: Is Qatar Too Good To Be True?" *Time*, 2 November 2011.

8. Gulf Cooperation Council, *GCC, A Statistical Glance Volume II* (Riyadh, 2010), 44.

9. The location of every speed camera is well known to all drivers, who slow down for the minimum required length of time and then resume their normal, and normally unsafe, speed.

10. In November 2010, Crown Prince Tamim bin Hamad Al Thani signed Law No. 15, which bans groups of laborers from living in "family-designated areas." The law, which took effect on November 1, 2011, binds all employers of "laborers" to move their workers out of their current residences and into "allowed areas." The Ministry of Municipalities and Urban Planning has published a number of maps indicating the family-designated areas in Doha and Qatar's other towns. See "Municipality Designates Areas for Bachelor Living," *Alraya* (Doha), October 3, 2011, p. 24.

11. There are more journalistic accounts of the conditions of migrant workers in Qatar (and in the rest of the Persian Gulf) than there are academic ones. For a multidisciplinary treatment of the topic, including studies of migrant workers in Qatar, see the collection of essays in Mehran Kamrava and Zahra Babar, eds., *Migrant Labor in the Persian Gulf* (New York, 2012).

12. Shahram Chubin's analysis in this regard is worth quoting at length: "Iran is not a marginal state like Libya or Syria, but neither is it a great power. It has few friends and fewer allies. By alienating the United States and Europe, Iran has increased its dependence on Russia for diplomatic support, nuclear and other technology and conventional arms. It has thus compromised its vaunted 'independence,' inhibiting the pursuit of its interests in the Caspian and Caucasus. Iran has neither hard nor soft power. It has leveraged US mistakes in the last few years as its principal source of influence in the region. Playing on regional frustrations and anger, Iran has positioned itself as a spoiler and given rejectionism a new fillip in the Arab street. But these are limited and wasting assets, dependent on continued US errors and the failure of peaceful alternatives for Palestine. Iran can offer a rejectionist 'war option' but not a solution; for that the Arabs must turn to others. Iran's conventional military capabilities, especially its power-projection capabilities, are limited, even with respect to, or in comparison with, its immediate neighbours." Shahram Chubin, "Iran's Power in Context," *Survival* 51, no. 1 (February–March 2009), 179–180.

1. Setting the Stage

1. Some of these arguments have been fleshed out in Mehran Kamrava, "Iran and Regional Security Dynamics."

2. Tammen et al., *Power Transitions*, 193.

3. Ibid., 22.

4. David Lake, *Hierarchy in International Relations*. (Ithaca, 2009), 9–10.

5. Hedley Bull, *The Anarchical Society* (New York, 2002), 71.

6. Lake, *Hierarchy in International Relations,* 62.
7. Tammen et al., *Power Transitions,*. 20.
8. Ibid., 131, 58, 107.
9. Ibid., 44.
10. Lake, *Hierarchy in International Relations,* 13–15, 36, 41, 30
11. Ibid., 68–72.
12. Ibid., 82–83.
13. Tareq Y. Ismael, *International Relations of the Contemporary Middle East* (Syracuse, NY, 1986), 12.
14. Louis Fawcett, "Alliances, Cooperation, and Regionalism in the Middle East," in Louis Fawcett, ed. *International Relations of the Middle East.* 2nd ed. (Oxford, 2009), 191.
15. Ibid.
16. Michael N. Barnett, *Dialogue in Arab Politics,* x.
17. Ibid., 25.
18. Raymond Hinnebusch, "The Middle East Regional System," in Raymond Hinnebusch and Anoushiravan Ehteshami, eds., *The Foreign Policies of Middle East States* (Boulder, CO, 2002), 41.
19. Ibid., 49.
20. Raymond Hinnebusch. "Introduction," in Raymond Hinnebusch and Anoushiravan Ehteshami, eds., *The Foreign Policies of Middle East States* (Boulder, 2002), 6.
21. Hinnebusch, "The Middle East Regional System," 50.
22. George Lenczowski, *The Middle East in World Affairs.* 2nd ed. (Ithaca, 1956), 417.
23. Hamied Ansari, *Egypt* (Albany, NY, 1986), 236–239.
24. Gregory L. Aftandilian, *Egypt's Bid for Arab Leadership* (New York, 1993), 44.
25. Mehran Kamrava, "The Arab Spring and the Saudi-Led Counterrevolution," *Orbis* 56, no. 1 (Winter 2012), 96–104.
26. Vali Nasr, *Meccanomics* (Oxford, 2010), 5.
27. Fawcett, "Alliances, Cooperation, and Regionalism in the Middle East," 192.
28. Anoushiravan Ehteshami and Raymond Hinnebusch, "Conclusion," in Raymond Hinnebusch and Anoushiravan Ehteshami, eds. *The Foreign Policies of Middle East States.* (Boulder, CO, 2002), 346.
29. David Held and Kristian Ulrichsen, "The Transformation of the Gulf," in David Held and Kristian Ulrichsen, eds. *The Transformation of the Gulf* (London, 2012), 8.
30. Clement M. Moore, "The Clash of Globalizations in the Middle East," in Fawcett, ed., *International Relations of the Middle East.* 2nd ed. (Oxford, 2009), 109.
31. Held and Ulrichsen, "The Transformation of the Gulf," 22.
32. Giacomo Luciani, "Oil and Political Economy in the International Relations of the Middle East," in Louis Fawcett, ed., *International Relations of the Middle East* (Oxford, 2009), 99.
33. Samer N. Abboud, "Oil and Financialization in the Gulf Cooperation Council," in Bessama Momani and Matteo Legrenzi, eds., *Shifting Geo-Economic Power of the Gulf* (Burlington, VT, 2011), 92.
34. Bessama Momani and Matteo Legrenzi, "Introduction," in *Shifting Geo-Economic Power of the Gulf,* 6.
35. Kristian Coates Ulrichsen, *Insecure Gulf* (New York, 2011), 69.
36. Luciani, "Oil and Political Economy in the International Relations of the Middle East," 97.
37. According to http://www.globalfirepower.com, based on some forty-five different factors, in 2011 Iran's military strength ranked twelfth in the world. In a statement before the US Senate, the director of the US Defense Intelligence Agency maintained that "Iran's military strategy is designed to defend against external threats, particularly from the United States and Israel. Its principles of military strategy include deterrence, asymmetrical retaliation, and attrition warfare." The text of the statement, titled "Iran's Military Power," is available at http://armed-services.senate.gov/statemnt/2010/04%20April/Burgess%2004-14-10.pdf.

38. Robert E. Hunter, *Building Security in the Persian Gulf* (Santa Monica, CA, 2010), xiii.

39. Joseph S. Nye, *The Future of Power* (New York, 2011), xv.

40. Ulrichsen, *Insecure Gulf*, 68.

41. Held and Ulrichsen, "The Transformation of the Gulf," 9.

42. For an excellent historical account of the region, see Svet Soucek, *The Persian Gulf* (Costa Mesa, CA, 2008). See also Lawrence Potter, ed., *The Persian Gulf in History* (New York, 2009).

43. Ulrichsen, *Insecure Gulf*, 16.

44. Luciani, "Oil and Political Economy in the International Relations of the Middle East," 87.

45. F. Gregory Gause, III. *The International Relations of the Persian Gulf* (Cambridge, 2010), 246.

46. Ulrichsen, *Insecure Gulf*. 22.

47. Hinnebusch, "Introduction," 15.

48. Gause, *The International Relations of the Persian Gulf,* 9, 241, 86, 12.

49. Ulrichsen, *Insecure Gulf,* 25.

50. Ibid., 78–79.

51. Joseph Kostiner, "GCC Perceptions of Collective Security in the Post-Saddam Era," in Mehran Kamrava, ed., *International Politics of the Persian Gulf* (Syracuse, NY, 2011), 117.

52. N. Janardhan, *Boom amid Gloom* (Reading, UK, 2011), 151.

53. Ibid., 97.

54. Steve A. Yetiv, *The Absence of Grand Strategy* (Baltimore, MD, 2008), 2–3.

55. Ibid., 168.

56. Kostiner, "GCC Perceptions of Collective Security in the Post-Saddam Era," 108.

57. Gause, *The International Relations of the Persian Gulf*, 6.

58. Ulrichsen, *Insecure Gulf*, 26.

59. Anoushiravan Ehteshami, "Security and Strategic Trends in the Middle East," in David Held and Kristian Ulrichsen, eds., *The Transformation of the Gulf* (London, 2012), 275.

60. According to a 2009 cable sent from the US embassy in Cairo to Washington, DC, for example, former Egyptian president Hosni Mubarak not only had "a visceral hatred" for Iran and repeatedly referred to its leaders as "liars," but he also saw Syrians and Qataris "as sycophants and as liars themselves." Wikileaks, "Scenesetter for Requested Egyptian FM Aboul Gheit Meeting with the Secretary," 9 February 2009, 09CAIRO231.

61. N. Janardhan, *Boom amid Gloom* (Reading, UK, 2011), 148.

62. Henry R. Nau, *Perspectives on International Relations,* 2nd ed. (Washington, DC, 2006), 23.

63. Tammen et al., *Power Transition*, 6–7, 182.

64. Ibid., 10.

65. Ibid., 79.

66. Gause, "The International Politics of the Gulf," in Louis Fawcett, ed. *International Relations of the Middle East,* 2nd ed. (Oxford, 2009), 282.

67. Hunter, *Building Security in the Persian Gulf,* 18.

68. Yetiv, *The Absence of Grand Strategy*, 193–94.

69. Gause, *The International Relations of the Persian Gulf,* 86.

70. Quoted in Hunter, *Building Security in the Persian Gulf,* 16–17.

71. Ibid., xi.

72. Yetiv, *The Absence of Grand Strategy*, 147.

73. Gause, *The International Relations of the Persian Gulf,* 2. Gause is adamant that what drove America into Iraq was not, contrary to popular assumptions, oil. It was, rather, perceptions of threats to the United States emanating from the region, with Iraq, and Iran—two of the pillars of the "Axis of Evil"—as epicenters of threat. "This was not a 'war for oil' in any direct way," he writes, and "it is remarkable how little the oil factor appears in the accounts of the Bush administration policy-making on the Iraq War" (238–239).

74. Ulrichsen, *Insecure Gulf*, 28.

75. United States Senate Committee on Foreign Relations, "The Gulf Security Architecture," 2.

76. Ibid., 4.

77. Ibid., 3. The report goes on to recommend that the United States "should preserve the model of 'lily pad' bases throughout the Gulf, which permit rapid escalation of military force in case of emergency" (25).

78. Ulrichsen, *Insecure Gulf*, 183.

79. Michael C. Hudson, "The United States in the Middle East," in Louis Fawcett, ed., *International Relations of the Middle East.* 2nd ed. (Oxford, 2009), 326.

80. Davidson, *The Persian Gulf and Pacific Asia*, 1, 24, 21, 34, 40–41.

81. Ibid., 9.

82. Ibid., 13.

83. Abboud, "Oil and Financialization in the Gulf Cooperation Council," 97.

84. Davidson, *The Persian Gulf and Pacific Asia*, 64–65.

85. Ibid., 33.

86. Janardhan, *Boom amid Gloom*, 159.

87. Ulrichsen goes as far as to warn of "an emerging disconnect" between the Persian Gulf's deepening economic linkages with the East and its political and security ties with the West. Ulrichsen, *Insecure Gulf*, 70–71.

88. Davidson, *The Persian Gulf and Pacific Asia*, 30.

89. Ibid., 28.

90. Ibid., 18.

91. Janardhan, *Boom amid Gloom*, 160.

92. Vanessa Rossi, "Global Financial Markets," in John Nugee and Paola Subacchi, eds., *The Gulf Region* (London, 2008), 12.

93. Daniel Hanna, "The Gulf's Changing Financial Landscape," in ibid., 109.

94. Hanna insists that if there were greater cooperation and coordination among GCC policymakers, the region would have already become a major, thriving international financial hub. Ibid., 116.

95. Ahmet Akarli, "The GCC," in John Nugee and Paola Subacchi, eds., *The Gulf Region* (London, 2008), 49.

96. Ibid., 50.

97. British Petroleum, *BP Statistical Review of World Energy, June 2011*, 6, 20.

98. Akarli, "The GCC," 51.

99. Ibid.

100. Ibid. 52.

101. Mina Toksoz, "The GCC," in John Nugee and Paola Subacchi, eds., *The Gulf Region* (London, 2008), 81.

102. Abboud, "Oil and Financialization in the Gulf Cooperation Council," 96–97.

103. Equally important has been the establishment of a number of independent regulatory agencies across a variety of sectors, especially in telecommunications, to better attract foreign investments. Mark Thatcher, "Governing Markets in the Gulf States," in David Held and Kristian Ulrichsen, eds., *The Transformation of the Gulf* (London, 2012), 140.

104. Abboud, "Oil and Financialization in the Gulf Cooperation Council," 101.

105. Rachel Ziemba and Anton Malkin, "The GCC's International Investment Dynamics," in Bessama Momani and Matteo Legrenzi, eds., *Shifting Geo-Economic Power of the Gulf* (Burlington, VT, 2011), 119.

106. Martin Hvidt, "Economic Diversification in the Gulf Arab States," in ibid., 43.

107. Andrea Goldstein and Fabop Scacciavillani, "Financial Markets under Attack?" in ibid., 181.

108. Abboud, "Oil and Financialization in the Gulf Cooperation Council," 99.

109. Diana Farrell and Susan Lund, "The World's New Financial Power Brokers," *The McKinsey Quarterly*. (December 2007), 4.

110. Kristen Coats Ulrichsen, "The GCC States and the Shifting Balance of Global Power," Center for International and Regional Studies, Georgetown University School of Foreign Service in Qatar, *Occasional Paper*, no. 6 (2010), 9.

111. Ibid., 1.

112. Ibid., 8.

113. Held and Ulrichsen, "The Transformation of the Gulf," 10.

114. Martin Rivers, "Flying into the Unknown," *The Gulf*, November 2011, 43.

115. Hvidt, "Economic Diversification in the Gulf Arab States," 52.

116. FDI Intelligence, *FDI Global Outlook Report 2011* (London, 2011), 18, 20.

117. Mary Ann Tetrault, "Gulf Arab States' Investment of Oil Revenues," in Bessama Momani and Matteo Legrenzi, eds., *Shifting Geo-Economic Power of the Gulf* (Burlington, VT, 2011), 20.

118. Ibid., 14.

119. Bessma Momani, "Shifting Gulf Arab Investments in the Mashreq: Underlying Political Economy Rationals?" in Bessama Momani and Matteo Legrenzi, eds., *Shifting Geo-Economic Power of the Gulf* (Burlington, VT, 2011), 161.

120. Florence Eid, "The New Face of Arab Investment," in John Nugee and Paola Subacchi, eds., *The Gulf Region* (London, 2008), 73–75.

121. "Qatar to Pay $1.25bn to Jordan through GCC Fund," 10 June 2012, http://www.zawya.com.

122. Luciani, "Oil and Political Economy in the International Relations of the Middle East," 98.

123. Momani, "Shifting Gulf Arab Investments in the Mashreq," 167.

124. For a series of empirically based treatments of the topic, see Mehran Kamrava and Zahra Babar, eds., *Migrant Labor in the Persian Gulf* (New York, 2012).

125. John Chalcraft, "Migration Politics in the Arabian Peninsula," in David Held and Kristian Ulrichsen, eds., *The Transformation of the Gulf* (London, 2012), 80.

126. Ulrichsen, "The GCC States and the Shifting Balance of Global Power," 6.

127. Luciani, "Oil and Political Economy in the International Relations of the Middle East," 100.

128. Fred Lawson, "Security Dilemmas in the Contemporary Persian Gulf," in Mehran Kamrava, ed., *International Politics of the Persian Gulf* (Syracuse, NY, 2011), 51.

129. Ulrichsen, *Insecure Gulf*, 6.

130. Ibid., 4.

131. Ibid., 34–35.

132. Sean Foley, *The Arab Gulf States* (Boulder, CO, 2010), 152.

133. Held and Ulrichsen, "The Transformation of the Gulf," 23.

134. Ulrichsen, *Insecure Gulf*, 173.

135. Ibid., 3.

136. Ibid., 59.

137. Toksoz, "The GCC," 94.

138. Ulrichsen, *Insecure Gulf*, 181, 173, 91, 77.

139. Ibid., 76.

140. Foley, *The Arab Gulf States*, 148.

141. Two examples include the purpose-built cities of Masdar in Abu Dhabi and Lusail in Qatar. Lusail will be discussed in chapter 5. On Masdar, see http://www.masdarcity.ae.

142. "Abu Dhabi Property Market Continues to Soften," 5 July 2011, http://www.zawya.com.

143. "Rent-Free Periods to Continue in 2012; Expect Further Declines," 8 January 2012, http://www.zawya.com.

144. Kenneth Waltz, *Theory of International Politics* (Long Grove, IL1979), 65–66.

145. Hunter, *Building Security in the Persian Gulf*, 19.

146. Hinnebusch, "Introduction," 15.

147. Barnett, *Dialogue in Arab Politics*, ix.

148. Ibid., 39.

149. Foley, *The Arab Gulf States*, 144.

150. Fred Halliday, *The Middle East in International Relations* (Cambridge, 2005), 5.

151. Ulrichsen, *Insecure Gulf*, 126.

152. For a good, if by now outdated, background summary of Qatar's LNG production and exports, see Justin Dargin, "Qatar's Natural Gas" *Middle East Policy* 14, no. 3 (Fall 2007), 136–142.

153. "Iran Starts Drilling in Largest Joint Oil Field with Qatar," 16 July 2012, http://www.zawya.com.

154. British Petroleum, *BP Statistical Review of World Energy, June 2011*, 22.

155. James C. Scott, *Seeing Like a State* (New Haven, CT, 1998), 87–90.

156. Ulrichsen, *Insecure Gulf*, 102.

157. Robert O. Keohane, *After Hegemony* (Princeton, NJ, 1984), 107.

158. Ibid., 84.

159. Keohane argues that international regimes are established by hegemons, rather than by less powerful actors, though the successful articulation of a vision of mutual benefits. Ibid., 137.

2. The Subtle Powers of a Small State

1. John J. Mearsheimer, *The Tragedy of Great Power Politics* (New York, 2001), 5.

2. Kenneth Waltz, *Theory of International Politics* (Long Grove, IL, 1979), 72.

3. Ibid., 73.

4. Miriam Fendius Elman, "The Foreign Policies of Small States," *British Journal of Political Science* 25, no. 2 (April 1995), 175.

5. Anthony Payne, "Small States in the Global Politics of Development," *Round Table* 93, no. 376 (2004), 634.

6. Two essays, both in the same volume, best represent this trend: Andrew F. Cooper and Timothy W. Shaw, "The Diplomacies of Small States at the Start of the Twenty-First Century: How Vulnerable? How Resilient?" and Anthony Payne, "Vulnerability as a Condition, Resilience as a Strategy," in Andrew F. Cooper and Timothy W. Shaw, eds., *The Diplomacies of Small States: Between Vulnerability and Resilience* (New York, 2009), 1–18 and 279–285, respectively.

7. Neil Ford, "Qatar Punches above Its Weight," *Middle East* (March 2004), 49–54.

8. Robert Keohane, "The Big Influence of Small Allies," *Foreign Policy*, no. 2 (Spring 1971), 162–163.

9. Cooper and Shaw, "The Diplomacies of Small States at the Start of the Twenty-First Century," 4.

10. Richard L. Armitage and Joseph S. Nye, Jr., "How America Can Become a Smarter Power," in Richard Armitage and Joseph Nye, eds. *CSIS Commission on Smart Power* (Washington, DC, 2007), 7.

11. Despite a number of groundbreaking works on the topic, the definition of a small state remains essentially contested. See, for example, Jeanne A. K. Hey, "Introducing Small State Foreign Policy," in Jeanne A. K. Hey, ed. *Small States in World Politics* (Boulder, CO, 2003), 2–4; Christos Kassimeris, "The Foreign Policy of Small Powers," *International Politics* 46, no. 1 (2009), 88–89; Matthias Maas, "The Elusive Definition of the Small States," *International Politics* 46, no. 1 (2009), 65–83; Iver B. Neumann and Sieglinde Gstohl, "Introduction?" in Christine Ingebritsen et al., eds., *Small States in International Relations* (Seattle, WA), 4–7; and Payne, "Small States in the Global Politics of Development," 626. Much of the difference in the conception of small state can

be traced to the criterion used to measure smallness—that is geographic or population size, leaders' perceptions, etc. Sutton goes so far as to say that it is difficult to classify small states as a "distinct category" and instead "we are dealing with degrees, not kind." Paul Sutton, "What Are the Priorities for Small States in the International System?" *Round Table,* no. 351 (1999), 399. In specific relation to Qatar, the country is small regardless of the yardstick against which it is measured. The country's total population numbers approximately 1.6 million, of whom only about 15 percent are citizens, with the rest tightly controlled and segregated. The country's landmass, meanwhile, measures only 11,500 sq. km., as compared to the neighboring states of Saudi Arabia (approximately 2,000,000 sq. km.), the United Arab Emirates (77,700 sq. km.), and Iran (1,640,000 sq. km.), with only Bahrain being smaller (691 sq. km.).

12. Christopher Easter, "Small States Development: A Commonwealth Vulnerability Index," *Round Table*, no. 351 (1999), 403–422; Anthony Payne, "Small States in the Global Politics of Development" *Round Table, 93*, no. 376 (2004), 623–635; Barbara Von Tigerstrom, "Small Island Developing States and International Trade" *Melbourne Journal of International Law* 6 (2005), 402–407; Ganesh Wignaraja, Marlon Lezama, and David Joiner, *Small States Transition from Vulnerability to Competitiveness* (London, 2004), 4; and World Bank, *Small States* (Washington, DC, 2006), 2–3.

13. Christos Kassimeris, "The Foreign Policy of Small Powers," *International Politics* 46, no. 1 (2009), 90.

14. Stephen Walt, "Alliance Formation and the Balance of World Power," *International Security* 9, no. 4 (1985), 33.

15. Heinz Gartner defines alliances as "formal associations of states bound by mutual commitment to use military force against non-member states to defend member states' integrity" (Heinz Gartner, "Small States and Alliances," in Erich Reiter and Heinz Gartner, eds., *Small States and Alliances* (New York, 2001), 2). My usage of "alliance" here is less restrictive in that it may involve a formal security pact or, alternatively, a less formalized but no less solid arrangement or understanding whereby the small state endorses the general policy objective of the great power in exchange for overall support in international relations, as well as guarantees of security and protection against outside threats.

16. Robert O. Keohane, "The Big Influence of Small Allies," *Foreign Policy* 2 (1971), 166.

17. Gartner, "Small States and Alliances," 3.

18. Charles-Michel Geurts, "The European Commission," in Laurent Goetschel, ed., *Small States Inside and Outside the European Union* (London, 1998), 49–64; Antti Kuosmanen, "Decision-Making in the Council of the European Union," in ibid., 65–78.

19. Mark Hong, "Small States in the United Nations," *International Social Science Journal* 47, no. 2 (1995), 278.

20. Laurent Goestschel, "The Foreign and Security Policy Interests of Small States in Today's Europe," in Laurent Goestschel, ed. *Small States Inside and Outside the European Union* (London, 1998), 17. For a full treatment of alliance behavior, see Glenn Snyder, "The Security Dilemma in Alliance Politics," *World Politics* 36, no. 4 (1984), 461–495.

21. Volker Kraus and J. David Singer, "Minor Powers, Alliances, and Armed Conflict: Some Preliminary Patterns," in Erich Reiter and Heinz Gartner, eds., *Small States and Alliances* (New York, 2001), 19.

22. Svend Aage Christensen, "The Danish Experience—Denmark in NATO, 1949–1999," in ibid., 93.

23. Gartner, "Small States and Alliances," 2.

24. Neumann and Gstohl, "Introduction?" 11.

25. J. W. Kingdon, *Agendas, Alternatives, and Public Policy* (Boston, MA, 1984), 189.

26. Peter Viggo Jakobsen, "Small States, Big Influence," *Journal of Common Market Studies* 47, no. 1 (2009), 86–87.

27. Ibid., 87.

28. Hong, "Small States in the United Nations," 279.

29. Kuik Cheng-Chwee, "The Essence of Hedging," *Contemporary Southeast Asia* 30, no. 2 (2008), 163.

30. Evan Medeiros, "Strategic Hedging and the Future of Asia-Pacific Security," *Washington Quarterly* 29, no. 1 (2005–06), 145.

31. Evelyn Goh, *Meeting the China Challenge* (Washington, DC, 2005), viii.

32. Balancing and bandwagoning need not be viewed as opposites. Walt sees both strategies as responses to threats as "states will ally with or against the most *threatening* power" (Walt, "Alliance Formation and the Balance of World Power," 8–9). Schweller agrees, to a point. "The aim of balancing," he argues, "is self-preservation and the protection of values already possessed, while the goal of bandwagoning is usually self-extension: to obtain values coveted. Simply put, balancing is driven by the desire to avoid losses; bandwagoning by the opportunity for gain." He goes on to argue that "the presence of a significant external threat, while required for effective balancing, is unnecessary for states to bandwagon." Randall Schweller, "Bandwagoning for Profit," *International Security* 19, no. 1 (1994), 74.

33. Cheng-Chwee, "The Essence of Hedging," 164.

34. Ibid., 164–165.

35. Ibid., 171.

36. Joseph S. Nye, *The Future of Power* (New York, 2011), 5.

37. Robert A Dahl, "The Concept of Power," *Behavioral Sciences* 2, no. 3 (July 1957), 202–203.

38. Waltz, *Theory of International Politics*, 194–195.

39. Henry R. Nau, *Perspectives on International Relations* (Washington, DC, 2007), 22.

40. Barnett and Duvall, "Power in International Politics," 42.

41. Waltz, *Theory of International Politics*, 131.

42. Tammen et al., *Power Transitions*, 15, 44.

43. Ibid., 18.

44. Mearsheimer, *The Tragedy of Great Power Politics,* 43, 61, 57, 21, 45, 67, 55, 56.

45. Paul Kennedy, *The Rise and Fall of the Great Powers* (New York, 1989), xxiv.

46. Keohane, *After Hegemony*, 18, 32, 33–34, 40.

47. Nye, *The Future of Power*. 21.

48. Joseph S. Nye, *Soft Power* (New York, 2004), 5.

49. Ibid., 7, 15, 8.

50. Nye, *The Future of Power*, 8.

51. Joseph S. Nye, *Bound to Lead* (New York, 1990), 27.

52. Ibid., 198.

53. Ibid., 27.

54. Ibid., 7.

55. Ibid., 179.

56. Nye, *The Future of Power*, xiii.

57. Nye, *Bound to Lead*, 187.

58. Nye, *The Future of Power*, 5.

59. Nye, *Bound to Lead*, 32.

60. Nye, *The Future of Power*, 10.

61. Nye, *Bound to Lead*, 31.

62. Nye, *The Future of Power*, 61.

63. Nye, *Soft Power*, 16.

64. Nye, *Bound to Lead*, 182.

65. Nye, *The Future of Power*, 114–115. The concept of soft power is not without its critics. Colin Gray, for example, maintains that there are "serious limitations" to the concept since "it

utterly depends upon the uncoerced choices of foreigners." Colin S. Gray, *Hard Power and Soft Power* (Carlisle, PA, 2011), viii. Gray states that soft power is "a historically imprecise concept" and "potentially a dangerous idea" (28–29).

66. Nye, *Soft Power*, 18–19.

67. Nye, *Bound to Lead*, 30–31.

68. Nye, *The Future of Power*, xiii.

69. Ibid., 22–23. There is a complex relationship between soft and hard power, with some hard power resources increasing the effectiveness of soft power, and vice versa. See Gallarotti, *Cosmopolitan Power in International Relations*, 33. Also, as Nye points out, "no country likes to feel manipulated, even by soft power. At the same time, . . . hard power can create myths of invincibility or inevitability that attract others." Nye, *Soft Power*, 25.

70. Nye, *The Future of Power*, 208–209.

71. Ibid., 210.

72. Giulio M. Gallarotti. *Cosmopolitan Power in International Relations* (Cambridge, 2010), 35.

73. Ibid.

74. Nye. *The Future of Power.* 80.

75. Ibid., 55, 70, 60.

76. Gallarotti, *Cosmopolitan Power in International Relations*, 5, 16–17, 268, 42–48.

77. Michael Barnett and Raymond Duvall, "Power in International Politics," *International Organizations* 59, no. 1 (Winter 2005), 39–40.

78. Gallarotti, *Cosmopolitan Power in International Relations*, 37.

79. Nye, *The Future of Power*, xvii.

80. Ibid., 119.

81. Nye, *Bound to Lead*, 196.

82. Nye, *The Future of Power*, 8.

83. Keohane, *After Hegemony*, 26.

84. Barkin defines agency as the "behaviors that individuals purposively choose to undertake . . . that are affected but not determined by the structures, social or biological, within which actors find themselves." J. Samuel Barkin, *Realist Constructivism* (Cambridge, 2010), 102.

85. Richard Ned Lebow, *A Cultural Theory of International Relations* (Cambridge, 2008), 18–19.

86. Ibid., 28–29. Lebow argues that spirit and appetite lead to risk-taking while reason leads to caution and restraint. There are, according to Lebow, different patterns of risk acceptance by actors motivated by either fear or honor. An actor motivated by honor and standing tends to be especially risk-accepting with respect to both perceived losses and gains (31).

87. Ibid., 470.

88. Ibid., 492.

89. Barnett and Duvall, "Power in International Politics," 48.

90. van Ham calls this "social power," which he defines "as the ability to set standards, and create norms and values that are deemed legitimate and desirable, without resorting to coercion or payment. . . . [It] involves discursive power, drawing attention to the impact of framing, norm-advocacy, agenda-setting, the impact of media and communications, as well as lesser-known practices like place branding and public diplomacy." Peter van Ham, *Social Power in International Politics* (London, 2010), 8.

91. Nye, *The Future of Power*, xvii.

92. See Hanna Newcombe, Michael Ross, and Alan G. Newcombe, "United Nations Voting Patterns," *International Organization* 24, no. 1 (Winter 1970), 100–121, especially 102–110.

93. After the US subtle participation in the NATO campaign to oust Moammar Qaddafi from power in 2011, through the organization's imposition of a no-fly zone over Libyan airspace in support of rebel forces operating on the ground, the phrase "leading from behind" was used to describe an emerging "Obama doctrine." "It's a different definition of leadership than America

is known for. Pursuing our interests and spreading our ideals . . . requires stealth and modesty as well as military strength." Ryan Lizza, "The Consequentialist," *The New Yorker*, May 2, 2011, 55.

94. Waltz, *Theory of International Politics*, 102.

95. Referring to two highly popular American TV shows, van Ham makes the following observation: "As long as America presents the world with its *Desperate Housewives* and *Mad Men*, it seems to get away with policy failures like Iraq." van Ham, *Social Power in International Politics*, 164.

96. Consumers are shown to form attitudes toward products based on perceptions about the products' country of origin and vice versa. There are "structural interrelationships between country image, beliefs about product attitudes, and brand attitudes." C. Min Han, "Country Image," *Journal of Marketing Research* 26 (May 1989), 228.

97. See Mehran Kamrava. "Mediation and Qatari Foreign Policy," *Middle East Journal* 65, no. 4 (Autumn 2011), 1–18.

98. Peter Beaumont, "Qatar Accused of Interfering in Libyan Affairs," *Guardian*, 4 October 2011, 22.

99. Reuters, "Qatar's Big Libya Adventure," Arabianbusiness.com, 13 June 2011; Andrew Hammond and Regan Doherty, "Qatar Hopes for Returns after Backing Libyan Winners," http://af.reuters.com, 24 August 2011.

100. Sheikh Jabor bin Yusef bin Jassim al-Thani, former chief of staff in the offices of the prime minister and foreign minister, quoted in Clifford Krauss, "For Qatar, Libyan Intervention May Be a Turning Point," *New York Times*, 4 April 2011, p. 9.

101. A number of studies have empirically demonstrated that the size of SWFs have often been grossly exaggerated. See, for example, Jean-Francois Seznec, "The Gulf Sovereign Wealth Funds," *Middle East Policy* 15, no. 2 (Summer 2008), 97–110; Jean-Francois Seznec. "The Sovereign Wealth Funds of the Persian Gulf," in Mehran Kamrava, ed., *The Political Economy of the Persian Gulf* (New York, 2012), 69–93; and Christopher Balding, "A Portfolio Analysis of Sovereign Wealth Funds," in Renee Fry, Warwick J. McKibbin, and Justin O'Brien, eds., *Sovereign Wealth* (London, 2011), 43–70.

102. In the aftermath of the global economic recession of 2008–2009, in fact, most SWFs were estimated to have lost substantial sums of money—according to one estimate, altogether in excess of $66 billion by 2009—thus lessening their luster as lucrative investment instruments and as potential sources of power and influence. Bernardo Bertolotti, et al., "Sovereign Wealth Fund Investment Patterns and Performance," 1. I am grateful to William Megginson for sharing a draft of this unpublished paper with me.

103. Nye, *The Future of Power*, 212.

104. Cheng-Chwee, "The Essence of Hedging," 172–179.

105. The sponsorship of major football teams is a favorite branding tool for these three Persian Gulf emirates. Arsenal and Manchester City Football Clubs are sponsored by Emirates and Etihad Airlines, respectively, while Barcelona FC is sponsored by the Qatar Foundation.

106. Hugh Eakin, "The Strange Power of Qatar," *New York Review of Books*, 27 October 2011, 43–45.

107. Waltz, *Theory of International Politics*,111.

108. Because of economies of scale, according to Nye, larger countries will still benefit more from the information revolution for example, as they are better positioned to benefit from "network effects." Nye, *The Future of Power*, 116–117.

109. Fareed Zakaria, *The Post-American World* (New York, 2008).

110. Lebow, *A Cultural Theory of International Relations*, 442.

111. Nye, *Soft Power*, 14.

112. On quasi-democracies, see Mehran Kamrava, "Conceptualising Third World Politics," *Third World Quarterly* 14, no. 4 (November 1993), 710–711. On Kuwait's tug of war with democracy, see, Mehran Kamrava. "Preserving Non-Democracies: Leaders and Institutions in the Middle East," *Middle Eastern Studies* 46, no. 2 (March 2010), 251–270.

3. Foreign Policy and Power Projection

1. Christopher Davidson, "The United Arab Emirates," in Joshua Teitelbaum, ed., *Political Liberalization in the Persian Gulf* (New York, 2009), 223–248.

2. William Rugh, "The Foreign Policy of the United Arab Emirates," *Middle East Journal* 50, no. 1 (Winter 1996), 58.

3. In 2007 and 2008, for example, President Bush informed the Congress of over $19.4 billion in potential arm sales to the UAE, including what was at the time the most sophisticated air defense system in the US arsenal. This close security relationship culminated in the signing of a nuclear cooperation agreement between the two countries in December 2009. For background, see Christopher Blanchard and Paul Kerr, "The United Arab Emirates Nuclear Program and Proposed U.S. Nuclear Cooperation," *Congressional Research Service* (March 10, 2009), 1–14.

4. US diplomatic correspondences released by Wikileaks present insights into the innerworkings of American diplomacy on the ground, in this instance in relation to Bahrain and Qatar. For instance, in a confidential 2010 embassy cable drafted by the US ambassador to Bahrain Adam Ereli, King Hamad bin Isa Al Khalifa is said to have complained bitterly about Qatar's seemingly warm relations with both Iran and Al Qaeda, allegedly though Al Jazeera. According to the ambassador, the king was "looking to the United States, as Bahrain's most important ally, to help him manage (various) challenges, which [the US] should keep in mind as we plan our engagement with regional leaders in the coming months." The king is quoted as having told the ambassador that "as allies, we should deal with these issues together." (Wikileaks, "Bahrain's King Hamad Concerned about Qatar, GCC Unity," 18 January 2010, 10MANAMA26.) Both the tenor and substance of the exchange are in marked contrast to liaisons between American and Qatari diplomats.

5. "Kuwait Foreign Assets Soar to 277 Billion Dollars," 5 June 2010, www.zawya.com.

6. Majid Al-Khalili, *Oman's Foreign Policy* (Westport, CT, 2009); Jeffrey Lefebvre, "Oman's Foreign Policy in the Twenty-First Century." *Middle East Policy* 27, no. 1 (Spring 2010), 99–114.

7. Sultan Qaboos's vision for Oman is laid out in his annual state of the Sultanate speeches in which he covers an array of domestic and international issues. See Joseph Kechichian, "A Vision of Oman," *Middle East Policy* 15, no. 3 (Fall 2008), 112–133.

8. Jill Crystal, *Oil and Politics in the Gulf* (Cambridge, 1995), 164–165.

9. Al Udaid is one of the largest pre-positioned airbases in the world and in terms of war reserve material, but not actually largest in terms of active equipment or personnel. Both bases and the city of Doha are covered under the protection of US Patriot missile batteries that are meant to shoot down incoming Iranian missiles, cold comfort, no doubt, to Qatari policymakers weary that the animus between Washington and Tehran erupt into warfare.

10. Joe Bolger, "A War against Iran 'Could Drive Oil Price above $200 a Barrel,'" *Times*, 22 June 2006, 48.

11. F. Gregory Gause, III. *The International Relations of the Persian Gulf* (Cambridge, 2010), 9.

12. Vali Nasr, "Regional Implications of Shi'a Revival in Iraq," *Washington Quarterly* 27, no. 3 (Summer 2004), 17.

13. For the predicament of the Shi'a in Saudi Arabia and Bahrain see, Yitzhak Nakash. *Reaching for Power* (Princeton, NJ, 2006), ch. 2. Of all the GCC states, the situation of Qatari Shi'a most closely resembles that of the Shi'a in Oman. See Marc Valeri, "High Visibility, Low Profile," *International Journal of Middle East Studies* 42, no. 2 (May 2010), 257–261.

14. Laurence Louer, *Transnational Shia Politics* (New York, 2008), 10. For more on the Arab Shi'a see Graham Fuller and Rend Rahim Francke, *The Arab Shi'a* (New York, 1999).

15. Other notable Shi'a families in Qatar include the Darwish and the Fakhru.

16. This misperception about the Shi'a necessarily having Iranian roots is not unique to Qatar. As Fuller and Francke argue in *The Arab Shi'a*, "there is a widespread sense in the Arab world that

Arab culture is somehow 'inherently' Sunni, that Sunnism is the natural state of the Arabs. From this perspective, the Shi'a are by definition schismatic who have willingly taken themselves out of the Arab fold by espousing Shi'ism, perhaps even with some Persian connivance" (34).

17. Martin Walker, "The Revenge of the Shia," *Wilson Quarterly* 30, no. 4 (Autumn 2006), 16.

18. See, for example, Qatar Statistics Authority, *Qatar in Figures* (Doha, 2008).

19. According to the constitution, legislative authority is to be vested in a Consultative Assembly, thirty of whose forty-five members are to be elected through direct ballot (Articles 76–116). For additional reasons underlying the absence of parliamentary politics in Qatar so far, see Mehran Kamrava, "Royal Factionalism and Political Liberalization in Qatar," *Middle East Journal* 63, no. 3 (Summer 2009), 401–420.

20. According to a 2010 cable sent to Washington by US diplomats in Jerusalem, for example, the salaries of employees at Hamas's Ministry of Education in Gaza were all covered by Qatari donations. Wikileaks, "Does Hamas Have a Cash Flow Problem in Gaza," 12 February 2010, 10JERUSALEM276.

21. Anoushiravan Ehteshami, "The Middle East's New Power Dynamics," *Current History* (December 2009), 399–400.

22. Wikileaks, "The Move toward an Interagency Synchronization," n.d., 07DOHA677.

23. Ibid.

24. Wikileaks, "Crown Prince on Qatar's Relations with Iran," 15 July 2009, 09DOHA454. In the same meeting, the heir apparent insisted that President Obama "would benefit from the Amir's realistic point of view from our work on the ground with several parties."

25. On a trip to Jerusalem and Ramallah in June 2011, I discovered that one of the few issues on which both my Israeli and Palestinian informants agreed was their certainty that Al Jazeera was a tool of Qatari foreign policy. This sentiment was shared by Doha-based US diplomats, who in 2009 reported that Qatar used the network as a "bargaining tool to repair relationships with other countries." "We expect," the cable continued, "the trend in favor of using Al Jazeera as an informal tool of GOQ foreign policy to continue undiminished." Wikileaks, "The Move Toward an Interagency Synchronization." In another cable, the US ambassador to Qatar Joseph LeBaron calls Al Jazeera "one of Qatar's most valuable political and diplomatic tools." Wikileaks, 1 July 2009, 09DOHA225. This view is shared by many journalists. Referring to the network's coverage of Bahrain following its dispute with Qatar over Hawar Islands in the early 2000s, one UAE-based journalist and academic argued that "unable to vent its anger in any other form, Doha used Al Jazeera in retaliation." N. Janardhan, *Boom amid Gloom* (Reading, UK, 2011), 149.

26. Wikileaks, "Ambassador Untermeyer's 14 October 2005 Meeting with Foreign Minister Hamad Bin Jassim Al-Thani," 17 October 2005, 05DOHA1744.

27. Ibid.

28. Wikileaks, "PAO Meeting with Al Jazeera Managing Director," 20 October 2005, 05DOHA1765.

29. Sultan Sooud Al Qassemi, "How Saudi Arabia and Qatar Became Friends Again." 21 July 2011, http://www.foreignpolicy.com.

30. "Saudi Arabia/Qatar: Saudis Reportedly Bar Al-Jazeera TV from Covering Hajj," BBC Summary of World Broadcasts, 2 February 2004.

31. Worth, "Al Jazeera No Longer a Hammer to Saudis; Qatar Presses Network to Lighten Up," *International Herald Tribune*, 5 January 2008, p. 8.

32. Quoted in Ibid.

33. Quoted in Hammond, "Coverage of Revolts Varies on Al Jazeera," *International Herald Tribune*, 14 April 2011, p. M1.

34. Ibid.

35. Ibid.

36. Ibid.

37. Erdbrink, "For Al Jazeera, a Double Standard in Coverage?" *Washington Post*, May 15, 2011, p. 12.

38. Brian Stelter, "Al Jazeera Changes Plan to Rerun Documentary," *New York Times*, 10 August 2011, p. 8. The documentary, *Shouting in the Dark*, is available on Al Jazeera's English website at http://www.aljazeera.com/programmes/2011/08/201184144547798162.html.

39. Hayder al-Khoei, "Deadly Shootings in Saudi Arabia, but Arab Media Look the Other Way," *Guardian*, 28 November 2011, http://www.guardian.co.uk.

40. Ibid.

41. See Sultan Sooud Al Qassemi, "Morsi's Win Is Al Jazeera's Loss," Al-Monitor, 1 July 2012, http://www.al-monitor.com/pulse/originals/2012/al-monitor/morsys-win-is-al-jazeeras-loss.html. Al Qassemi cites specific examples of the network's questionable coverage of Morsi's campaign and election.

42. See, for example, Wikileaks, "Wadah Khanfar Loses Position as Member of Al Jazeera Board; May Also Lose Job Managing Al Jazeera Network," 16 May 2007, 07DOHA495; and Wikileaks, "Beginning of the End? Khanfar still at the Helm of Al Jazeera, but Stripped of Financial and Admin Power," 18 June 2007, 07DOHA641. Robert Fisk, the renowned British journalist, maintains that Khanfar "behaved with as much integrity as he did courage." Fisk, "Al Jazeera: 15 Years in the Headlines," *Independent* (London), 2 November 2011, p. 40.

43. Aref Hijjawi, "The Role of Al-Jazeera (Arabic) in the Arab Revolts of 2011," in Heinrich Böll Stiftung, *Perspectives,* no. 2 (May 2011), 69–70.

44. For more on this point, see Kamrava, "Royal Factionalism and Political Liberalization in Qatar," 409–411.

45. Peter Beaumont, "Qatar Accused of Interfering in Libyan Affairs," *Guardian*, 4 October 2011, 22.

46. An example includes Ahmed Azem, "Qatar's Ties with the Muslim Brotherhood Affect Entire Region," *National* (Abu Dhabi), 18 May 2012.

47. See, for example, Nour Abuzant, "It Is Genocide, Says Qaradawi," *Gulf Times* (Doha), 26 February 2011, p. 1; Nour Abuzant, "Qaradawi Condemns 'Atrocities' against Protestors in Syria," *Gulf Times*, 26 March 2011, p. 1; Ayman Adly, "Qaradawi in Call for Arab, Muslim Unity," *Gulf Times*, 24 December 2011, p. 3.

48. In March 2012, Al Jazeera reporter Ali Hashem resigned from his position in protest over the network's coverage of Bahrain and Syria. For Hashem's side of the story, see his interview with TheRealNews.com at http://therealnews.com/t2/index.php?option=com_content&task=view&id=31&Itemid=74&jumival=8108. See also, Thomas Erdbrink. "For al-Jazeera, a double standard in coverage?" *Washington Post,* 15 May 2011, p. 12.

49. David Lake, *Hierarchy in International Relations* (Ithaca, 2009), 138; see also chapter 2 of this volume.

50. Ibid., 113.

51. Wikileaks, "Terrorist Finance: Action Request for Senior Level Engagement on Terrorism Finance," 30 December 2009, 09STATE13801.

52. Wikileaks, "Crown Prince on Qatar's Relations with Iran," 15 July 2009, 09DOHA454.

53. Renowned for his outspoken and at times controversial views, Yousef Al-Qaradawi's biography and a summary of his views appear in Jakob Skovgaard-Petersen and Bettina Graf, eds., *The Global Mufti* (New York, 2006). See also Bettina Gräf, "Sheikh Yūsuf al-Qaradāwī in Cyberspace," *Die Welt des Islams* 47, nos. 3–4 (2007), 403–442.

54. Wikileaks, "Ambassador Discusses Qaradawi with MFA Minister of State Al-Mahmoud; GOQ to Provide Written Response to Treasury Letter," 25 November 2009, 09DOHA689.

55. In a 2006 meeting with the network's managing director, for example, the US embassy's Public Affairs officer conveyed the "continuing USG concerns with Al Jazeera programming."

Wikileaks, "Entering Its Tenth Year, Al Jazeera Covets Its Global Role," 23 January 2006, 06DOHA104.

56. Tahani Karrar, "Qatar Rethinks Dollar Peg amid Gulf-Wide Inflation," *Wall Street Journal*, 12 March 2008, p. 17; "Soaring Inflation Threatens Peg to $US," *Toronto Star*, 3 June 2008, p. B2; "Reports of Qatar Depegging from Dollar Not True," *Peninsula* (Doha), 28 May 2008, p. 1.

57. Unless otherwise noted, all data in this paragraph are drawn from the Office of the United States Trade Representative, http://www.ustr.gov/countries-regions/europe-middle-east/middle-east/north-africa/qatar.

58. Qatar Central Bank, *Thirty Second Annual Report 2008* (Doha, 2009), 131.

59. Wikileaks, "The Move toward an Interagency Synchronization."

60. Data collected from US Census Bureau, US Bureau of Economic Analysis, "U.S. International Trade in Goods and Services," 2001 and 2011, http://www.census.gov/foreign-trade.

61. "Qatar Eyes Stake in U.S. Banks," *Toronto Star*, 28 January 2008, p. B2.

62. Iran Ministry of Commerce, *Bazargani-e Khareji* (Foreign Trade) (Tehran, 1388/2009). Available at http://www.moc.gov.ir/system/upload/doc/r%20.pdf, accessed on May 13, 2010.

63. "Iran, Russia, Qatar Discuss Gas Cooperation," Islamic Republic News Agency, 21 October 2008.

64. See, for example, Lynn A. Karoly and Michael Mattock, *Qatar Supreme Council for Family Affairs Database of Social Indicators* (Santa Monica, CA, 2006); Catherine H. Augustine and Cathy Krop, *Aligning Post-Secondary Educational Choices to Societal Needs* (Santa Monica, CA, 2008); and Cassandra M. Guarino et al., *Developing a School Finance System for K-12 Reform in Qatar* (Santa Monica, CA, 2009).

65. Dominic Brewer et al., *Education for a New Era* (Santa Monica, CA, 2007); and Dominic Brewer, et al. *An Introduction to Qatar's Primary and Secondary Education Reform* (Santa Monica, CA, 2006), 14.

66. Joy S. Moini et al., *The Reform of Qatar University* (Santa Monica, CA, 2009).

67. General Secretariat for Development Planning, *Qatar National Vision 2030*, 2.

68. Ibid., 16.

69. Ibid., 29.

70. Alongside an especially commissioned piece by the Lebanese composer Marcel Khalife, the orchestra's inaugural performance included Beethoven's Symphony No. 5 and Maurice Ravel's Bolero.

71. http://www.dohatribecafilm.com/festival/leadership.htm.

72. Some of the luminaries at the 2010 US-Islamic World Forum included prominent Obama Administration and other U.S. officials, Turkish prime minister Recep Tayyip Erdoğan, US secretary of state Hillary Clinton, White House senior director for global engagement Pradeep Ramamurthy, US special representative for Afghanistan and Pakistan Richard Holbrooke, and US senator John Kerry.

73. General Secretariat for Development Planning. *Qatar National Vision 2030*, 4.

74. In addition to the Shi'a presence mentioned earlier, across the Gulf states there are scattered populations of Hawwalah, Persian-origin Sunnis who migrated to the northern shores of the Arabian Peninsula in the nineteenth century. See Lawrence G. Potter, "Introduction," in Lawrence G. Potter, ed,. *The Persian Gulf in History* (New York, 2009), 11.

75. Wikileaks, "Visit of Qatar's Prime Minister to Washington January 4–5," 21 December 2009, 09DOHA733.

76. Wikileaks, "Qatar's Prime Minister on Iran: 'They Lie to Us; we Lie to Them'," 20 December 2009, 09DOHA728.

77. Wikileaks, "Qatari MFS Official's Perspective of Heir Apparent's Visit to Tehran," 23 February 2010, 10DOHA69.

78. Robert O. Keohane, *After Hegemony* (Princeton, NJ, 1984), 137.

79. Ibid., 178–180.

80. Daniel W. Drezner, *Theories of International Politics and Zombie* (Princeton, NJ, 2011), 48.

81. There is always the potential that the South Pars-North Field gas deposits that Iran and Qatar share in the Persian Gulf become a source of friction between the two states. See, for example, Reyhaneh Mazaheri, "Gaz-e Iran dar Jib-e Qatar" (Iran's Gas in Qatar's Pocket), *E'temad-e Melli*, 18 November 2008, pp. 1, 10.

82. Wikileaks, "The Move toward an Interagency Synchronization."

83. Wikileaks, "Scensetter for U.S.-Qatari Military Consultative Commission," 7 January 2010, 10DOHA8.

84. Ibid.

85. Ibid.

86. The Pentagon does not release precise numbers about US forces stationed abroad, in 2009 listing a total of less than 500 troops in Qatar (US Department of Defense, "Active Duty Military Personnel Strengths by Regional Area and by Country (309A)," 31 December 2009). According to confidential sources within the Al Udaid US airbase, located outside of Doha, in 2010 there were an estimated 8,000 US military personnel stationed there, and the base could accommodate as many as 10,000 troops. This is consistent with the figure of 7,500 reported in 2012 by a US Congressional report (United States Senate Committee on Foreign Relations. "The Gulf Security Architecture," 15).

87. "Al Udeid Air Base, Qatar" and "Camp As Sayliyah," both at http://www.globalsecurityorg.

88. Christopher Blanchard, "Qatar," *Congressional Research Service,* May 16, 2011, pp. 9–10.

89. Adam Entous and Julian E. Barnes, "Pentagon Bulks up US Defenses in the Gulf," *Wall Street Journal*, 17 July 17, p. 1.

90. Wikileaks, "Scensetter for U.S.-Qatari Military Consultative Commission."

91. Wikileaks, "Crown Prince on Qatar's Relations with Iran," 15 July 2009, 09DOHA454.

92. Peterson, "Qatar and the World," 746.

93. Van Ham, "The Rise of the Branded State," 2–3.

94. Peterson, "Qatar and the World," 746–747. As Peterson observes (746), "few countries seem to have taken the lessons and importance of branding to heart more thoroughly than Qatar."

95. According to Qatar Foundation's director of public relations, the multimillion dollar, global "think campaign" is "designed to raise the profile of Qatar Foundation's vision, mission and objectives." Haya Khalifa Al Nassr, "Unlocking Inner Potential," *Foundation*, September 2009, p. 2.

96. Angela Shah, "Qatari Spearheads Effort to Education 61 Million Children," *International Herald Tribune*, 19 November 2012, p. 14.

97. Bahry, "The New Arab Media Phenomenon," *Middle East Policy* 3, no. 2 (June 2001), 89.

98. Ibid., 91.

99. Hugh Miles, *Al-Jazeera* (New York, 2005), 37–46.

100. Ibid., 63–65.

101. Alan Cowell, "Al Jazeera: From Network, to a Bush Target, to Courts," *New York Times*, 11 January 2006, 12.

102. Olivier Da Lage, "The Politics of Al Jazeera or the Diplomacy of Doha," in Mohamed Zayani, ed., *The Al Jazeera Phenomenon* (London, 2005), 49.

103. Shibley Telhami, *2010 Arab Public Opinion Poll* (Washington, DC, 2010), 77–78.

104. See, for example, Hugh Miles, "Al Jazeera." *Foreign Policy,* no. 155 (July-August 2006), 20–24.

105. "Al-Jazeera Live Chief Says Channel 'Experienced Rebirth' since Arab Spring," BBC Monitoring Middle East, 3 November 2011.

106. Asaf Siniver, "Power, Impartiality and Timing," *Political Studies* 54, no. 4 (2006), 808.

107. Alan Henrikson, "Niche Diplomacy in the World Public Arena," in Jan Melissen, ed., *The New Public Diplomacy* (New York, 2007), 1.

108. R. Green, "Solving the Darfur Crisis: The U.S. Prefers Qatar to Egypt as Mediator," MEMRI, 19 August 2009, http://www.memri.org/report/en/0/0/0/0/0/0/0/3572.htm.

109. For a firsthand account of the secret negotiations that led to the Oslo Accords, see Jan Egeland, "The Oslo Accords: Multiparty Facilitation through the Norwegian Channel," in Chester A. Croker, Fen Osler-Hampson, and Pamela Aall, eds., *Herding Cats* (Washington, DC, 1999), 529–546.

110. For Egyptian and Saudi foreign policies, see, respectively, Raymond Hinnebusch, "The Foreign Policy of Egypt," and F. Gregory Gause, III. "The Foreign Policy of Saudi Arabia," both in Raymond Hinnebusch and Anoushiravan Ehteshami, eds., *The Foreign Policies of Middle East States* (Boulder, CO, 2002), 91–114 and 193–211.

111. G. R. Berridge, *Diplomacy* (New York, 2010), 239.

112. R. P. Barston, *Modern Diplomacy* (London, 2006), 239.

113. Saadia Touval, "Mediation and Foreign Policy," *International Studies Review* 5, no. 4 (2003), 92.

114. Barston, *Modern Diplomacy,* 240.

115. See, for example, Reuters, "Qatar Pulls Off Mediation Coup in Lebanon Crisis," 22 May 2008, http://uk.reuters.com/article/idUKL2274043520080522.

116. Paul Wilkinson, *International Relations* (London, 2010), 13.

117. For a fuller discussion of Qatari mediation efforts in Lebanon and elsewhere, see Mehran Kamrava, "Mediation and Qatari Foreign Policy," *Middle East Journal* 65, no. 4 (Autumn 2011), 539–556.

118. Christopher Portman, "The Economic Significance of Sovereign Wealth Funds," *Economic Outlook* 32, no. 1 (January 2008), 26.

119. In the words of an international banker, "from the time kings invested in building pyramids, raising armies and bankrolling explorers, sovereign wealth attracted political controversy." Gordon Platt, "Sovereign Wealth Funds Prepare to Take More Active Role in M&A," *Global Finance* (October 2009), 107.

120. Jean-Francois Seznec, "The Sovereign Wealth Funds of the Persian Gulf," in Mehran Kamrava, ed., *The Political Economy of the Persian Gulf* (New York, 2012), 69–70.

121. Balding, "A Portfolio Analysis of Sovereign Wealth Funds," in Renee S. Fry, Warwick J. McKibbin, and Justin O'Brien, eds. *Sovereign Wealth* (London, 2011), 61.

122. Seznec, "The Sovereign Wealth Funds of the Persian Gulf," 72. In April 2012, a QIA official put the size of the fund at "much more" than $100 billion. "Qatar Sovereign Fund Exceeds $100 Billion: Top Official," 22 April 2012, http://www.zawya.com.

123. Balding, "A Portfolio Analysis of Sovereign Wealth Funds," 66.

124. Quoted in Platt, "Sovereign Wealth Funds Prepare to Take More Active Role in M&A," 107.

125. Ibid., 108.

126. Hamdan, "Qatar Shows Its Faith in Europe," *International Herald Tribune*, 15 September 2011, p. M2.

127. Qatar is estimated to have supplied the Libyan rebels with $400 million worth of arms and military training. See United States Senate Committee on Foreign Relations, "The Gulf Security Architecture" Majority Staff Report, June 19, 2012, p. 16. See below, chapter 6.

128. Anonymous, "Qatar to Buy Tunisia's backing for NTC?" *Maghreb Confidential*, 7 July 2011.

129. "Qatari Investment in Libya Accounting for around USD 10 Billion," 4 December 2011, http://www.zawya.com.

130. Omar Al-Halabi, "Lebanon, Qatar to Announce Joint Committee, Agreements—Qassar," Kuwait News Agency, 28 April 2010.

131. Anwar Elshamy, "Qatari Diar Launches $350mn Project in Syria," *Gulf Times*, 28 February 2008, p. 1.

132. Hamdan, "Qatar Shows Its Faith in Europe," p. M2.
133. Patrick Hosking, "Qatar Wealth Fund Moves to Bolster Stake in Brazil Bank," *Times*, 19 October 2010, p. 45.
134. Santhous V. Perumal, "QIA Has $30bn to Invest This Year," *Gulf Times*, 23 April 2012, p. 1.
135. Cahal Milmo, "Qatar, the Tiny Gulf State That Bought the World," *Independent*, 11 May 2010, p. 22.
136. "Qatar's European Investments Yield QR2.3bn," 8 May 2011, http://www.zawya.com; Martin Flanagan, "Qatar on Pole Position as It Plans Swoop Fir Stake in Second Major UK Bank," *Scotsman*, 20 June 2011, p. 34.
137. Dominic O'Neill, "Sovereign Funds: Qatar Invests in Indonesia," *Euromoney*, January 2008, 52.
138. Sven Behrendt, "When Money Talks: Arab Sovereign Wealth Funds in the Global Policy Discourse," *Carnegie Papers*, October 2008, 13.
139. Christian Hetzner and John Irish, "Qatar Tops Up War Chest by Selling VW Pref Shares," Thomson Reuters, 10 November 2009, http://thomsonreuters.com.
140. Wikileaks, "Qatar Investment Authority's 2010 Investment Strategy Outlined," 25 November 2009, 09DOHA691.
141. Dominic O'Neill, "Qatar: Minister Says Sovereign Funds Are Transparent," *Euromoney*, November 2007, 58.
142. O'Neill, "Sovereign Funds," 52.
143. "Qatari Diar Committed to Halted Projs in Troubled Syria," 5 May 2011, http://www.zawya.com; Julia Kollewe. "Qatari Power: Emirate Enjoys Rich Pickings in London Property," *Guardian*, 15 June 2010, p. 6.
144. Platt, "Sovereign Wealth Funds Prepare to Take More Active Role in M&A," 107.
145. Kollewe, "Qatari Power," 6.
146. David Jackson, "Less Noise from Leveraged Wealth Funds," *Euromoney*, November 2008, 50.
147. Anonymous, "Sovereign Wealth Funds," *Euromoney*, February 2008, 30.
148. Ben Chu, "Qatar Swoops for Greek Assets as Europe Looks Abroad for Help," *Independent*, 3 October 2011, p. 30; Matthew Saltmarsh, "Greece in a Deal for Investment from Qatar," *New York Times*, 25 September 2010, p. 2.
149. "Qatar Acquires 5.2% Stake in US Jewelry Giant," 20 April 2012, http://www.zawya.com.
150. "Qatar Top Sovereign Europe Property Buyer with 6 Weeks Gas Cash," 17 August 2012, http://www.zawya.com.
151. "Qatar's European Investments Yield QR2.3bn."
152. "Qatari Diar $543.8m Investment Set to Create 4000 Jobs for Egyptians," 23 October 2011, http://www.zawya.com.
153. "Qatar Ready to Provide More Finance to Egypt," 13 November 2011, http://www.zawya.com.
154. "Qatar Deposits $2 Billion to Support Egyptian Economy," 11 August 2012, http://www.zawya.com.
155. "Qatari Investments in Libya Accounting for around USD 10 Billion."
156. Valentine Low, "Full Pomp and Pageantry as Qatari Royals Are Welcomed," *Times*, 27 October 2010, p. 15.
157. "Qatar Top Sovereign Europe Property Buyer with 6 Weeks Gas Cash."
158. Will Pavia et al., "Why the Wealth of Qatar Was No Match for Camilla's Ear," *Times*, 17 June 2010, p. 18.
159. Seznec, "The Sovereign Wealth Funds of the Persian Gulf," 75.
160. Quoted in Pavia et al., "Why the Wealth of Qatar Was no Match for Camilla's Ear," 18.

161. Una Galani, "Qatar Headed Down a Risky Path," *Globe and Mail* (Toronto), 20 September 2011, p. B15.

162. Perumal, "QIA Has $30bn to Invest This Year," 1.

163. Benjamin Shepherd, *GCC Land Purchases Abroad,* Center for International and Regional Studies, Georgetown University School of Foreign Service in Qatar, *Summary Report.* No. 5, 2012. pp. 3, 17.

164. Matthew Cranston, "Hassad Fills Its Portfolio," *Australian Financial Review*, 7 May 2012, p. 48.

165. Bonnie James, "Hassad Food Plans to Invest $700mn in Global Projects," *Gulf Time*, 1 June 2010, p. 4.

166. For purposes of guaranteeing the country's food security, in 2008 the government, under the Office of Heir Apparent, set up the Qatar National Food Security Program, more on which is available at http://www.qnfsp.gov.qa.

167. Allen J. Fromherz, *Qatar* (London, 2012), 2.

168. See, for example, "Yemen Shia Rebels Hail Qatar Offer," *Gulf Times*, 21 July 2010, p. 7.

169. Hugh Tomlinson, "Power Broker Never Loses Sight of Goals," *Times*, 25 June 2011, p. 25.

4. The Stability of Royal Autocracy

1. One of the most important example of this strategy was the creation of the Supreme Council of Education (SEC) in 2002, with its own separate and "modernizing agenda," which for seven years operated alongside the Ministry of Education. Then in 2009–2010, the Ministry and its personnel were formally incorporated into the SEC.

2. Jill Crystal, *Oil and Politics in the Gulf* (Cambridge, 1990), 28.

3. Frederick F. Anscombe, *The Ottoman Gulf* (New York, 1997), 144.

4. Ibid., 90.

5. Ibid., 143.

6. As one British observer commented at the time, "The ruler of Doha should at once be both a soldier and a statesman, able to beat out the tribes at to march long distances whenever necessary, and while in Doha to keep order in the town, to remain conciliatory with the different tribes and to keep himself out of playing in the hands of the Turks. The Turks according to Sheikh Jasim are powerless to do any harm when kept at a distance, but when close are difficult to manage." Quoted in Habibur Rahman, *The Emergence of Qatar* (London, 2005), 178.

7. Ibid., 20–21.

8. Ibid., 15.

9. Anscombe, *The Ottoman Gulf*, 33.

10. Quoted in Rahman, *The Emergence of Qatar*, 8.

11. Quoted in ibid., 78.

12. Nazih N. Ayubi, *Over-Stating the Arab State* (London, 1999), 133.

13. Rosemarie Said Zahlan, *The Creation of Qatar* (London, 1979), 60.

14. Crystal, *Oil and Politics in the Gulf*, 169.

15. Quoted in ibid., 128.

16. Anscombe, *The Ottoman Gulf*, 56.

17. Crystal, *Oil and Politics in the Gulf*, 140–141.

18. Ibid., 122, 128–129.

19. Ibid., 129.

20. Alanound Alsharekh, "Introduction," in Alanound Alsharekh, ed., *The Gulf Family* (London, 2007), 9.

21. Allen J. Fromherz, *Qatar* (London, 2012), 7.

22. Ayubi, *Over-Stating the Arab State*, 241.

23. Ibid., 245.

24. Given the fact that nine years had elapsed before this punitive action, there were speculations at the time that perhaps the Al Murrah had again been implicated in some more recent political action. Rumors began circulating that in 2002 another undisclosed coup was attempted. As with many similar rumors, the veracity of this one is open to question.

25. Joel Migdal, *State in Society* (Cambridge, 2001), 15.

26. Ibid., 56, 92–93, 100.

27. S. N. Sangmpan, *Comparing Apples and Mangoes* (Albany, NY, 2007), 197.

28. Michael Herb, *All in the Family* (Albany, NY, 1999), 111–113.

29. Fromherz, *Qatar*, 80.

30. Crystal, *Oil and Politics in the Gulf*, 159.

31. Herb, *All in the Family*, 114.

32. Ayubi, *Over-Stating the Arab State*, 133.

33. Crystal, *Oil and Politics in the Gulf*, 7.

34. Gerd Nonneman, "Political Reform in the Gulf Monarchies," in Anoushiravan Ehteshami and Steven Wright, eds., *Reform in the Middle East Oil Monarchies* (Reading, UK, 2008), 8.

35. Herb, *All in the Family*, 30.

36. Hisham Sharabi, *Neopatriarchy* (Oxford, 1988), 8. Sharabi uses the concept of neopatriarchy to describe a social phenomenon, "a duality [that] manifests itself most clearly in the petty bourgeoisie."

37. Nonneman, "Political Reform in the Gulf Monarchies," 5.

38. Raymond Hinnebusch, "Toward a Historical Sociology of State Formation in the Middle East," *Middle East Critique,* 19, no. 3 (Fall 2010), 205–206.

39. Fromherz, *Qatar*, 81.

40. Ibid., 84–85.

41. Herb, *All in the Family*, 119.

42. Quoted in Patrick Cockburn, "Emir of Qatar Deposed by His Son," *Independent*, 28 June 1995.

43. Herb, *All in the Family*, 119.

44. Wikileaks, "The Move toward an Interagency Synchronization," n.d., 07DOHA677.

45. Ayubi, *Over-Stating the Arab State,* 230.

46. http://www.al3nabi.com/vb/f10/t126756.html.

47. Herb, *All in the Family*, 41. Held at all levels in society, the *majlis* is an informal social gathering of men, held usually on weekly basis in a special tent-like room built for the purpose.

48. Ibid., 45.

49. Much has been written on Sheikha Moza and all that she represents for Qatar in general and Qatari women in particular. See, for example, Louay Bahry and Phebe Marr, "Qatari Women," *Middle East Policy* 12, no. 2 (Summer 2005), 104–119.

50. http://www.mozahbintnasser.qa/output/page6.asp.

51. Others in this short list include Queen Rania of Jordan and the Syrian first lady Asma Al-Assad. Princess Haya bint Hussein, the junior wife of the ruler of Dubai, Sheikh Mohammed bin Rashid Al Maktoum, also has a highly visible public profile, though she is known as much for controversies as she is for her charity works and her involvement in international sports, having served as the president of the International Equestrian Federation.

52. Justin Dargin, "Qatar's Natural Gas," *Middle East Policy* 14, no. 3 (Fall 2007), 140.

53. Nathalie Thomas, "The Qatari That Got the Cream," *Scotland on Sunday*, 29 June 2008, 5. For more on Qatar's hyperactive diplomacy see chapters 3 and 4 in this volume.

54. Conversely, the depth and efficacy of institutions are key to the success of so-called developmental states. See Ziya Öniş. "The Logic of the Developmental State," *Comparative Politics* 24, no. 1 (October 1991), 110.

55. Abdullah Juma Alhaj, "The Political Elite and the Introduction of Political Participation in Oman." *Middle East Policy* 7, no. 3 (June 2000), 103–106.

56. Thomas Fuller, "Rallies in Oman Steer Clear Of Criticism of Its Leader," *New York Times*, 2 March 2011, p. 8.

57. See Mehran Kamrava, "Royal Factionalism and Political Liberalization in Qatar." *Middle East Journal* 63, no. 3 (Summer 2009), 401–420.

58. Crystal, *Oil and Politics in the Gulf*, 162.

59. Independence Day, 3 September—the date of Qatar's formal independence from Britain in 1971—has now been eclipsed by the National Day.

60. Ahmed Abdelkareem Saif, "Deconstructing before Building," in Anoushiravan Ehteshami and Steven Wright, eds., *Reform in the Middle East Oil Monarchies* (Reading, UK, 2008), 110.

61. "43 Percent Cast Ballot in CMC Poll," *Peninsula* (Doha), 11 May 2011, p. 1.

62. "On Hold: Parliament Polls Not Likely in '08," *Peninsula*, 28 February 2008, p. 1.

63. "Emir Opens Advisory Council Session," *Gulf Times*, 2 November 2011, p. 11.

64. Michael Herb, "Princes, Parliaments, and the Prospects for Democracy in the Gulf," in Marsha Pripstein Posusney and Michele Penner Angrist, eds., *Authoritarianism in the Middle East* (Boulder, CO, 2005), 180.

65. Max Weber, *On Charisma and Institution Building* (Chicago, IL, 1968), 46.

66. Juan J. Linz, *Totalitarian and Authoritarian Regimes* (Boulder, CO, 2000), 159.

67. Ibid., 162.

68. Ibid., 152.

69. Daniel Brumberg, "The Trap of Liberalized Autocracy," *Journal of Democracy* 13, no. 4 (October 2002), 57–58.

70. Ibid., 61.

71. For an elaboration of this line of argument, see Mehran Kamrava, "Non-Democratic States and Political Liberalisation in the Middle East," *Third World Quarterly* 19, no. 1 (March 1998), especially 76–82.

72. Lisa Anderson, "Absolutism and the Resilience of Monarchy in the Middle East," *Political Science Quarterly* 106, no. 1 (Spring 1991), 13.

73. Ibid., 12.

74. Nonneman, "Political Reform in the Gulf Monarchies," 22.

75. Hinnebusch, "Toward a Historical Sociology of State Formation in the Middle East," 208.

76. Adam Hanieh, *Capitalism and Class in the Arab Gulf States* (New York, 2011), 60–66.

77. Miriam R. Lowi, *Oil Wealth and the Poverty of Politics* (Cambridge, 2009), 43.

78. Stephen J. King, *The New Authoritarianism in the Middle East and North Africa* (Bloomington, IN, 2009), 192.

79. Herb, *All in the Family*, 10.

80. Ibid., 49–50.

81. Crystal, *Oil and Politics in the Gulf*, 167.

82. Michael Mann, *The Sources of Social Power* (Cambridge, 1993), 9–10.

83. Alsharekh, "Introduction," 15.

84. Ayubi, *Over-Stating the Arab State*, 242.

85. For more on differences between different kinds of rentier states in the Persian Gulf, see Mehran Kamrava, "The Political Economy of Rentierism in the Persian Gulf," in Mehran Kamrava, ed., *The Political Economy of the Persian Gulf* (New York, 2012), 39–68.

86. This is the highest per capita GDP in the Persian Gulf and indeed in the world. For a comparative analysis, see ibid., 59.

87. Steffan Hertog and Giacomo Luciani, "Energy and Sustainability Policies in the GCC," (Kuwait Programme in Development, Governance and Globalisation in the Gulf States: Center for the Study of Global Governance, 2009), 4.

88. World Wildlife Fund, *Living Planet Report 2012* (Gland, Switzerland, 2012), 43, 47.

89. The interview is available at http://www.cbsnews.com/video/watch/?id=7395216n.

90. General Secretariat of Development Planning, *Building an Effective Social Protection System* (Doha, 2011), 3.

91. Ibid., 15.

92. Matthew Gray, "A Theory of 'Late Rentierism'," Center for International and Regional Studies, Georgetown University School of Foreign Service in Qatar, *Occasional Paper.* No. 7, 2011, p. 19.

93. Ibid., 33.

94. Ibid., 23.

95. Seznec, "Changing Circumstances," in Alanound Alsharekh, ed., *The Gulf Family* (London, 2007), 80–81.

96. J. E. Peterson, "Rulers, Merchants and Shaikhs in Gulf Politics," in ibid., 30.

97. Laurence Louer, *Transitional Shia Politics* (New York, 2008), 10.

98. For the efforts of one of the country's largest employers, Qatar Petroleum, to spearhead Qatarization, see http://www.qatarization.com.qa.

99. General Secretariat of Development Planning, *Qatar National Vision 2030* (Doha, 2008), 4.

100. "HH the Emir Inaugurates Imam Muhammad Ibn Abdul Wahhab Mosque," Qatar News Agency, 16 December 2011.

101. Royal palaces are also discreetly situated outside of the city, again unlike most other regional capitals, and royal displays of ostentatious wealth are often carefully avoided.

102. See James C. Scott, *Seeing Like a State* (New Haven, CT, 1998); and Charles Tilly, "War Making and State Making as Organized Crime," in Peter R. Evans, Dietrich Rueschemeyer, and Theda Skocpol, eds., *Brining the State Back In* (Cambridge, 1985), 169–191. I am grateful to Robert Wirsing for his thoughts on this particular topic and for bringing these references to my attention.

103. Wikileaks, "The Move toward an Interagency Synchronization."

104. An exception was Sultan Al-Khalaifi, a blogger and former secretary general of Al-karama, an Arab human rights organization based in Geneva. Al-Khalaifi was arrested in early March 2011, presumably for his blogs, which were soon deleted from the Internet. He was released after spending a month in prison.

105. See the chapters on Iran, Turkey, and the Arab world in Ali Farazmand, ed., *Administrative Reform in Developing Nations* (Westport, CT, 2001), respectively chapters 8, 9, and 10.

106. Herb, *All in the Family*, 55–56.

5. State Capacity and High Modernism

1. Theda Skocpol, "Bringing the State Back In," in Peter B. Evans, Dietrich Rueschemeyer, and Theda Skocpol, eds., *Bringing the State Back In* (Cambridge, 1985), 9. For a more thorough definition of state capacity, see Kjeld Erik Brodsgaard and Susan Young, "Introduction," in Kjeld Erik Brodsgaard and Susan Young, eds. *State Capacity in East Asia* (Oxford, 2000), 1–16.

2. British Petroleum, *BP Statistical Review of World Energy, June 2011*, 8.

3. Ibid., 22.

4. Pratap John, "Qatar GDP Hits Record QR628bn," *Gulf Times* (Doha), 26 February 2012, 1.

5. Jean-François Seznec, "The Gulf Sovereign Wealth Funds," *Middle East Policy* 15, no. 2 (Summer 2008), 103.

6. Sovereign Wealth Fund Institute, "Qatar Investment Authority," http://www.swfinstitute.org/swfs/qatar-investment-authority/.

7. Qatar Investment Authority, http://www.qia.qa/qia/index.html.

8. "Qatar Economy to Soar 18%," 21 May 2011, http:// www.zawya.com. In 2011, one local economist went as far as to put the rate of economic growth at 33.8 percent. See "Qatar Growth Expected to Be 33.8pc," 18 July 2011, http://www.zawya.com.

9. "Qatar to Spend $150bn on Infrastructure, Spanish Businessmen Told," 26 October 2011, http://www.zawya.com; and "$225B Bonanza," 29 March 2011, http://www.zawya.com.

10. "Qatar: Budget Surplus for First Half to Be QR50bn," 5 July 2011, http://www.zawya.com.

11. "Qatar Exchange Index up 20pc in First Half This Year," 21 July 2011, http://www.zawya.com.

12. "Dubai Loses Financial Center Crown to Doha," 27 September 2011, http://www.zawya.com.

13. Soumitra Dutta, ed., *The Global Innovation Index 2012* (Fontainebleau, 2012), 8.

14. "Qatar Plans to Build World's Tallest Tower," 22 April 2011, http://www.zawya.com.

15. On the state's welfare policies aimed at the citizen population, see Mehran Kamrava, "Royal Factionalism and Political Liberalization in Qatar," *Middle East Journal* 63, no. 3 (Summer 2009), 406–407.

16. For example, in 2010 the state-owned real estate development company Qatari Diar was estimated to have $42 billion in assets under management, with investments in Qatar, the United Kingdom, Italy, Oman, Morocco, Egypt, Syria, Sudan, and Seychelles. Sovereign Wealth Fund Institute, "Qatar Investment Authority."

17. Qatar National Bank, *Qatar Economic Review, October 2009* (Doha, 2009), 28.

18. Ibid., 29.

19. "Qatari Property Prices Now Stable, Outlook Positive," 11 April 2012, http://www.globalpropertyguide.com/Middle-East/Qatar/Price-History, 11 April 2012.

20. "Dohaland Signs $430 Million Deal with Hyundai, HBK," *Bloomberg Businessweek*, 25 April 2010, http://www.businessweek.com/news/2010-04-25/dohaland-signs-430-million-deal-with-hyundai-hbk-update1-.html.

21. Skocpol, "Bringing the State Back In," 18.

22. Peter B. Evans, Dietrich Rueschemeyer, and Skocpol, "On the Road toward a More Adequate Understanding of the State," in Peter B. Evans, Dietrich Rueschemeyer, and Theda Skocpol, eds. *Bringing the State Back In* (Cambridge, 1985), 351.

23. Francis Fukuyama, "The Imperative of State-Building," *Journal of Democracy* 15, no. 2 (April 2004), 21–22.

24. Linda Weiss, *The Myth of the Powerless State* (Ithaca, 1998), 19.

25. Quoted in Shahar Hameiri, "Failed States or a Failed Paradigm?" *Journal of International Relations and Development* 10, no. 2 (2007), 123.

26. Ibid., 141.

27. Atul Kohli, *State-Directed Development* (Cambridge, 2004), 21.

28. Dan Breznitz, *Innovation and the State* (New Haven, CT, 2007), 3.

29. Meredith Woo-Cumings, "Introduction," in Meredith Woo-Cumings, ed. *The Developmental State* (Ithaca, 1999), 4.

30. Atul Kohli, "Where Do High Growth Political Economics Come From?" in ibid., 133.

31. Weiss, *The Myth of the Powerless State*, 209.

32. T. J. Pempel, "The Developmental Regime in a Changing World Economy," in Meredith Woo-Cumings, ed., *The Developmental State* (Ithaca, 1999), 160.

33. Ziya Öniş, "The Logic of the Developmental State," *Comparative Politics* 24, no. 1 (October 1991), 111.

34. Michael Loriaux, "The French Developmental State as Myth and Moral Ambition," in Meredith Woo-Cumings, ed., *The Developmental State* (Ithaca, 1999), 252. Along similar lines, Sally Cummings and Ole Norgaard introduce the notion of "ideational state capacity," which they take to mean "the degree to which elite members and the population more widely legitimate and accept the state, with the emphasis on elite legitimation." Sally N. Cummings and Ole Norgaard, "Conceptualising State Capacity," *Political Studies* 52 (2004), 687.

35. Öniş, "The Logic of the Developmental State," 114–115.

36. Evans, Rueschemeyer, and Skocpol, "On the Road toward a More Adequate Understanding of the State," 355.

37. Peter Evans, *Embedded Autonomy* (Princeton, NJ, 1995), 12. Embeddedness, Evans argues, "implies a concrete set of connections that link the state intimately and aggressively to particular social groups with whom the state shares a joint project of transformation" (59).

38. Ibid., 72.

39. Woo-Cumings, "Introduction," 10.

40. Ibid., 16.

41. Ibid., 12.

42. Evans, *Embedded Autonomy*, 228.

43. Ibid., 61.

44. Nazih N. Ayubi, *Over-Stating the Arab State* (London, 1999), 228.

45. Barwa, *2010 Annual Report: Building Qatar's Future* (Doha, 2010), 6.

46. UDC, *2011 Annual Report* (Doha, 2011), 6.

47. Ibid., 12.

48. Evans, *Embedded Autonomy*, 248.

49. Weiss, *The Myth of the Powerless State*, 211.

50. Evans, *Embedded Autonomy*, 6.

51. David Waldner, *State Building and Late Development* (Ithaca, 1999), 2.

52. Ibid., 26.

53. Ibid., 3.

54. James C. Scott, *Seeing Like a State* (New Haven, CT, 1998), 89–90.

55. Ibid., 92.

56. Ibid., 93, 95, 346, 95, 104.

57. In a way, this sort of "created" historical depth in Qatar is itself an aspect of the state's social engineering project. Preservation of a very particular state-defined historical path is linked to the present, and used to enhance and add legitimacy to the state-driven project. How else to reconcile the obvious illogic of having an anarchic monarchy leading a modernization project, but to say that this anarchic monarchy is steeped in reified tradition and culture.

58. http://www.lusail.com.

59. Qatari Diar, *The Art of Real Estate* (Doha, n.d.), 1–4.

60. http://www.barwa.com.qa.

61. Mehran Kamrava, "The Political Economy of Rentierism in the Persian Gulf," in Mehran Kamrava, ed. *The Political Economy of the Persian Gulf* (New York, 2012), 39–80.

62. UDC, for example, has recently had to look for investors, as it wants to sell off chunks of its Pearl assets. It has been struggling financially to complete still to be constructed portions of the island, and in early 2012 the company's president is reported to have resigned. Because state authorities consider the failure of the Pearl to be unacceptable, the Qatar National Bank has been brought in to take on an active role in finding the funding for the completion of the Pearl, http://www.gulfbase.com/news/qatar-s-udc-says-investor-still-seeking-stake-in-the-company/200675.

63. Scott, *Seeing Like a State*, 96.

64. Ayubi, *Over-Stating the Arab State*, 235.

65. Ibid., 227.

66. Allen J. Fromherz, *Qatar* (London, 2012), 112.

67. Ayubi, *Over-Stating the Arab State*, 228.

68. Ali al-Tarrah, "Family in the Kinship State," in Alanoud Alsharekh, ed., *The Gulf Family* (London, 2007), 123.

69. Planning Council, *Turning Qatar into a Competitive Knowledge-Based Economy* (Doha, 2007), 26.

70. Ibid., 26, 15, 25.

71. See Louay Constant, et al., *Facing Human Capital Challenges of the 21st Century* (Santa Monica, CA, 2009); Cathleen Stasz, et al., *Post-Secondary Education in Qatar* (Santa Monica, CA, 2008); and Gail L. Zellman, et al., *Education for a New Era* (Santa Monica, CA, 2007).

72. Zamila Bunglawala, "Nurturing a Knowledge Economy in Qatar," Brooking Doha Center, Policy Briefing, September 2011, p. 3.

73. Kristian Coats Ulrichsen, *Insecure Gulf* (New York, 2011), 97.

74. Ibid., 96.

75. "Multiple Positions in the Qatari Federation," *Al Annabi Forum*, 10 March 2010, http://www.al3nabi.com.

76. Faisal Al Marzooqi, "The Rewards of Those Who Read, but Never Understand," *Al Arab* (Doha), 9 October 2011.

77. See, for example, "According to the Constitution, Law, and Religion, Citizens Demand the Banning of Alcohol," *Our Country*, 2 February 2012, http://soso-bldna.blogspot.com.

78. One Twitter post stated: "I never thought the day would come that I have to ask the waiter in a restaurant in Qatar what kind of meat is in their burgers." Quoted in "Qatar, Unveiling Tensions, Suspends Sale of Alcohol," 7 January 2012, http://www.zawya.com.

79. Quoted in ibid.

80. "Qatar Will Break from the Center It Is Plays Too Big of a Role in Libya," *Qatar Shares*, 13 November 2011, http://qatarshares.com.

81. Neil Patrick, "Nationalism in the Gulf States," in David Held and Kristian Ulrichsen, eds., *The Transformation of the Gulf* (London, 2012), 59.

82. Ibid., 61, 59, 62–63.

83. Ibid., 53.

6. Qatar's Moment in History

1. Ziya Önig, "The Logic of the Developmental State," *Comparative Politics* 24, no. 1 (October 1991), 120.

2. See Christopher Davidson, *Abu Dhabi* (New York, 2009).

3. Peter B. Evans, Dietrich Rueschemeyer, and Theda Skocpol, eds., *Bringing the State Back In* (Cambridge, 1985). See also Peter Evans, "The Eclipse of the State?" *World Politics* 59 (October 1997), 62–87.

4. James C. Scott, *Seeing Like a State* (New Haven, CT, 1998), 89.

5. See Rene Richer, "Conservation in Qatar." Occasional Paper, Center for International and Regional Studies Georgetown University School of Foreign Service in Qatar, 2008.

6. Steffen Hertog and Giacomo Luciani, "Energy and Sustainability Policies in the Gulf States," in David Held and Kristian Ulrichsen, eds., *The Transformation of the Gulf* (London, 2012), 237.

7. Sean Foley, *The Arab Gulf States* (Boulder, CO, 2010), 144.

8. Fred Halliday, *The Middle East in International Relations* (Cambridge, 2005), 5.

9. Kristian Coates Ulrichsen, *Insecure Gulf* (New York, 2011), 126.

10. In 2010–2011, for example, when Qatari oil averaged for $84.48 per barrel, the budget was based on calculations of oil at $55 per barrel. Pratap John, "Oil Price Sees Qatar Book Huge Surplus," *Gulf Times* (Doha), 11 May 2011, 33.

11. United States Senate Committee on Foreign Relations, "The Gulf Security Architecture," Majority Staff Report, June 19, 2012, 16.

12. Lindsey Hilsum, *Sandstorm* (New York, 2012), 215; see also Peter Beaumont, "Qatar Accused of Interfering in Libyan Affairs," *Guardian*, 4 October 2011, 22.

13. Hilsum, *Sandstorm*, 215.

14. Giulio M. Gallarotti, *The Power Curse* (Boulder, CO, 2010), 16–22.

15. Giulio M. Gallarotti, *Cosmopolitan Power in International Relations* (Cambridge, 2010), 12.

16. Gallarotti, *The Power Curse*, 153.

BIBLIOGRAPHY

Abboud, Samer N. "Oil and Financialization in the Gulf Cooperation Council." In Bessama Momani and Matteo Legrenzi, eds., *Shifting Geo-Economic Power of the Gulf: Oil, Finance and Institutions.* Burlington, VT: Ashgate, 2011, pp. 91–105.

Aftandilian, Gregory L. *Egypt's Bid for Arab Leadership: Implications for U.S. Policy.* New York: Council on Foreign Relations Press, 1993.

Akarli, Ahmet. "The GCC: Economic Powerhouse between the BRICs and the Developing World." John Nugee and Paola Subacchi, eds. *The Gulf Region: A New Hub of Global Financial Power.* London: Chatham House, 2008, pp. 47–68.

Al-Alkim, Hassan Hamdan. *The GCC States in an Unstable World: Foreign Policy Dilemmas of Small States.* London: Saqi, 1994.

Al-Khalili, Majid. *Oman's Foreign Policy: Foundations and Practice.* Westport, CT: Praeger Security International, 2009.

Alhaj, Abdullah Juma. "The Political Elite and the Introduction of Political Participation in Oman." *Middle East Policy* 7, no. 3 (June 2000): pp. 97–110.

Alissa, Sufyan. "The Challenge of Economic Reform in the Arab World: Toward More Productive Economies." Carnegie Endowment for International Peace Papers, no. 1, Washington, DC, May 2007.

Alsharekh, Alanound. "Introduction." In Alanoud Alsharekh, ed., *The Gulf Family: Kinship Policies and Modernity.* London: Saqi, 2007, pp. 9–20.

al-Tarrah, Ali. "Family in the Kinship State." In Alanound Alsharekh, ed., *The Gulf Family*. London: Saqi, 2007, pp. 119–124.

Anderson, Lisa. "Absolutism and the Resilience of Monarchy in the Middle East." *Political Science Quarterly* 106, no. 1 (Spring 1991): p. 13.

Ansari, Hamied. *Egypt: The Stalled Society*. Albany: State University of New York Press, 1986.

Anscombe, Frederick F. *The Ottoman Gulf: The Creation of Kuwait, Saudi Arabia, and Qatar*. New York: Columbia University Press, 1997.

Appleby, Joyce. *The Relentless Revolution: A History of Capitalism*. New York: W.W. Norton, 2010.

Armitage, Richard L., and Joseph S. Nye, Jr. "How America Can Become a Smarter Power." In Richard Armitage and Joseph Nye, eds., *CSIS Commission on Smart Power: A Smarter, More Secure America*. Washington, DC: Center for Strategic and International Studies, 2007, pp. 5–14.

Augustine, Catherine H., and Cathy Krop. *Aligning Post-Secondary Educational Choices to Societal Needs a New Scholarship System for Qatar*. Santa Monica, CA: Rand, 2008.

Ayubi, Nazih N. *Over-Stating the Arab State: Politics and Society in the Middle East*. London: I.B. Tauris, 1999.

Bahry, Louay Y. "The New Arab Media Phenomenon: Qatar's Al-Jazeera." *Middle East Policy* 3, no. 2 (June 2001): pp. 88–99.

Bahry, Louay Y., and Phebe Marr. "Qatari Women: A New Generation of Leaders?" *Middle East Policy* 12, no. 2 (Summer 2005): pp. 107–108.

Balding, Christopher. "A Portfolio Analysis of Sovereign Wealth Funds." In Renee A. Fry, Warwick J. McKibbin, and Justin O'Brien, eds. *Sovereign Wealth: The Role of State Capital in the New Financial Order*. London: Imperial College Press, 2011, pp. 43–70.

Barkin, J. Samuel. *Realist Constructivism: Rethinking International Relations Theory*. Cambridge: Cambridge University Press, 2010.

Barnett, Michael N. *Dialogues in Arab Politics: Negotiations in Regional Order*. New York: Columbia University Press. 1998.

Barnett, Michael, and Raymond Duvall. "Power in International Politics." *International Organizations* 59, no. 1 (Winter 2005): pp. 39–75.

Barston, R. P. *Modern Diplomacy*. 3rd ed. London: Pearson, 2006.

Barwa. *2010 Annual Report: Building Qatar's Future*. Doha: Barwa, 2010.

Behrendt, Sven. "Gulf Arab SWFs—Managing Wealth in Turbulent Times." Policy Outlook. Washington, DC: Carnegie Endowment for International Peace, 2009.

Berridge, G. R. *Diplomacy: Theory and Practice*. 4th ed. New York: Palgrave Macmillan, 2010.

Bertolotti, Bernardo, Veljko Fotak, William Megginson, and William Miracky. "Sovereign Wealth Fund Investment Patterns and Performance." Unpublished paper, July 2009.

Blanchard, Christopher. "Qatar: Background and U.S. Relations." *Congressional Research Service* (16 May 2011): pp. 1–21.

Blanchard, Christopher, and Paul Kerr. "The United Arab Emirates Nuclear Program and Proposed U.S. Nuclear Cooperation." *Congressional Research Service* (10 March 2009): pp. 1–14.

Brewer, Dominic J. et al. *Education for a New Era: Design and Implementation of K-12 Education Reform in Qatar.* Santa Monica, CA: Rand, 2007.

——. *An Introduction to Qatar's Primary and Secondary Education Reform.* Santa Monica, CA: Rand, 2006.

Breznitz, Dan. *Innovation and the State: Political Choice and Strategies for Growth in Israel, Taiwan, and Ireland.* New Haven, CT: Yale University Press, 2007.

British Petroleum. *BP Statistical Review of World Energy, June 2011.* London: British Petroleum, 2011.

Brodsgaard, Kjeld Erik, and Susan Young. "Introduction: State Capacity in East Asia." In Kjeld Erik Brodsgaard and Susan Young, eds., *State Capacity in East Asia: Japan, Taiwan, China, and Vietnam.* Oxford: Oxford University Press, 2000.

Brumberg, Daniel. "Survival Strategies vs. Democratic Bargains: The Politics of Economic Reform in Contemporary Egypt." In Henri Barkey, ed., *The Politics of Economic Reform in the Middle East.* New York: St. Martin's, 1992, pp. 73–104.

——. "The Trap of Liberalized Autocracy." *Journal of Democracy* 13, no. 4 (October 2002): pp. 57–68.

Bull, Hedley. *The Anarchical Society: A Study of Order in World Politics.* 3rd ed. New York: Columbia University Press, 2002.

Bunglawala, Zamila. "Nurturing a Knowledge Economy in Qatar." Brooking Doha Center, Policy Briefing, September 2011.

Buzan, Barry, and Ana Gonzalez-Pelaz, eds. *International Society and the Middle East: English School Theory at the Regional Level.* New York: Palgrave Macmillan, 2009.

Byman, Daniel L., and Jerrold Green. *Political Violence and Stability in the Northern States of the Persian Gulf.* Santa Monica, CA: Rand, 1999.

Chalcraft, John. "Migration Politics in the Arabian Peninsula." In David Held and Kristian Ulrichsen, eds., *The Transformation of the Gulf: Politics, Economics, and the Global Order.* London: Routledge, 2012, pp. 66–85.

Cheng-Chwee, Kuik. "The Essence of Hedging: Malaysia and Singapore's Response to Rising China." *Contemporary Southeast Asia* 30, no. 2 (2008): pp. 159–185.

Christensen, Svend Aage. "The Danish Experience—Denmark in NATO, 1949–1999." In Erich Reiter and Heinz Gartner, eds. *Small States and Alliances.* New York: Physica-Verlag, 2001, pp. 89–100.

Chomsky, Noam. *World Orders Old and New.* New York: Columbia University Press, 1996.

Chubin, Shahram. "Iran's Power in Context." *Survival* 51, no. 1 (February–March 2009): pp. 165–190.

Constant, Louay, Gabriella Gonzalez, Lynn A. Karoly, Charles A. Goldman, and Hanine Salm. *Facing Human Capital Challenges of the 21st Century: Education and Labor Market Initiatives in Lebanon, Oman, Qatar, and the United Arab Emirates.* Santa Monica, CA: Rand, 2009.

Cooper, Andrew F., and Timothy W. Shaw. "The Diplomacies of Small States at the Start of the Twenty-first Century: How Vulnerable? How Resilient?" In Andrew F. Cooper and Timothy W. Shaw, eds., *The Diplomacies of Small States: Between Vulnerability and Resilience.* New York: Palgrave Macmillan, 2009, pp. 1–18.

Crystal, Jill. *Oil and Politics in the Gulf: Rulers and Merchants in Kuwait and Qatar.* Cambridge: Cambridge University Press, 1990.

Cummings, Sally N., and Ole Norgaard. "Conceptualising State Capacity: Comparing Kazakhstan and Kyrgyzstan." *Political Studies* 52 (2004): pp. 685–708.

Da Lage, Olivier. "The Politics of Al Jazeera or the Diplomacy of Doha." In Mohamed Zayani, ed., *The Al Jazeera Phenomenon: Critical Perspectives on New Arab Media.* London: Pluto Press, 2005, pp. 49–65.

Dahl, Robert A. "The Concept of Power." *Behavioral Science* 2, no. 3 (July 1957): pp. 201–215.

Dargin, Justin. "Qatar's Natural Gas: The Foreign-Policy Driver." *Middle East Policy* 14, no. 3 (Fall 2007): pp. 136–142.

Davidson, Christopher. *Abu Dhabi: Oil and Beyond.* New York: Columbia University Press, 2009.

———. *Dubai: The Vulnerabilities of Success.* New York: Columbia University Press, 2008.

———. *The Persian Gulf and Pacific Asia: From Indifference to Interdependence.* New York: Columbia University Press, 2010.

———. "The United Arab Emirates: Economy First, Politics Second." In Joshua Teitelbaum, ed., *Political Liberalization in the Persian Gulf.* New York: Columbia University Press, 2009, pp. 223–248.

Delving, Julia, ed. *Gulf Economies: Strategies for Growth in the 21st Century.* Washington, DC: Center for Contemporary Arab Studies, Georgetown University, 1997.

Doran, Michael Scott. "The Saudi Paradox." *Foreign Affairs* 83, no. 1 (January–February 2004): pp. 35–51.

Drezner, Daniel W. *Theories of International Politics and Zombies.* Princeton, NJ: Princeton University Press, 2011.

Dutta, Soumitra, ed. *The Global Innovation Index 2012: Stronger Innovation Linkages for Global Growth.* Fontainebleau: INSEAD, 2012.

Easter, Christopher. "Small States Development: A Commonwealth Vulnerability Index." *Round Table* 351 (July 1999): pp. 403–422.

Ehteshami, Anoushiravan. "The Middle East's New Power Dynamics." *Current History* (December 2009): pp. 395–401.

———. "Security and Strategic Trends in the Middle East." In David Held and Kristian Ulrichsen, eds., *The Transformation of the Gulf: Politics, Economics, and the Global Order.* London: Routledge, 2012, pp. 261–277.

Ehteshami, Anoushiravan, and Raymond Hinnebusch. "Conclusion: Patterns of Policy." In Raymond Hinnebusch and Anoushiravan Ehteshami, eds., *The Foreign Policies of Middle East States.* Boulder, CO: Lynne Rienner, 2002, pp. 335–350.

Ehteshami, Anoushiravan, and Steven Wright, eds. *Reform in the Middle East Oil Monarchies.* Reading, Berkshire, UK: Ithaca Press, 2008.

Eickelman, Dale F. *The Middle East and Central Asia: An Anthropological Approach.* Upper Saddle River, NJ: Prentice Hall, 1998.

Eid, Florence. "The New Face of Arab Investment." In John Nugee and Paola Subacchi, eds., *The Gulf Region: A New Hub of Global Financial Power.* London: Chatham House, 2008, pp. 69–80.

Elman, Miriam Fendius. "The Foreign Policies of Small States: Challenging Neorealism in Its Own Backyard." *British Journal of Political Science* 25, no. 2 (April 1995): pp. 171–217.

Emirates Center for Strategic Studies and Research, ed. *Arab Media in the Information Age*. Abu Dhabi: Emirates Center for Strategic Studies and Research, 2006.

———. *Current Transformations and their Potential Role in Realizing Change in the Arab World*. Abu Dhabi: Emirates Center for Strategic Studies and Research, 2007.

———. *France and the Arabian Gulf*. Abu Dhabi: Emirates Center for Strategic Studies and Research, 2007.

———. *The Gulf: Challenges of the Future*. Abu Dhabi: Emirates Center for Strategic Studies and Research, 2005.

———. *The Gulf: Future Security and British Policy*. Abu Dhabi: Emirates Center for Strategic Studies and Research, 2000.

———. *The Gulf Oil and Gas Sector: Potential and Constraints*. Abu Dhabi: Emirates Center for Strategic Studies and Research, 2006.

———. *Gulf Oil in the Aftermath of the Iraq War: Strategies and Policies*. Abu Dhabi: Emirates Center for Strategic Studies and Research, 2005.

———. *International Interests in the Gulf Region*. Abu Dhabi: Emirates Center for Strategic Studies and Research, 2004.

Energy Information Administration. *Country Analysis Briefs, Qatar*. Washington, DC: United States Department of Energy, 2009.

Evans, Peter. "The Eclipse of the State? Reflections on Stateness in an Era of Globalization." *World Politics* 50, no. 1 (October 1997): pp. 62–87.

———. *Embedded Autonomy: States and Industrial Transformation*. Princeton, NJ: Princeton University Press, 1995.

Evans, Peter B., Dietrich Rueschemeyer, and Theda Skocpol. "On the Road toward a More Adequate Understanding of the State." In Peter B. Evans, Dietrich Rueschemeyer, and Theda Skocpol, eds., *Bringing the State Back In*. Cambridge: Cambridge University Press, 1985, pp. 347–366.

Farazmand, Ali, ed. *Administrative Reform in Developing Nations*. Westport, CT: Praeger, 2001.

Farrell, Diana, and Susan Lund. "The World's New Financial Power Brokers." *McKinsey Quarterly* (December 2007). http://www.mckinseyquarterly.com/ Financial_Services/Banking/The_worlds_new_financial_power_brokers_2084.

Fawcett, Lewis. "Alliances, Cooperation, and Regionalism in the Middle East." In Louis Fawcett, ed., *International Relations of the Middle East*. 2nd ed. Oxford: Oxford University Press, 2009, pp. 188–207.

FDI Intelligence. *FDI Global Outlook Report 2011: Manufacturing Makes a Comeback*. London: Financial Times, 2011.

Foley, Sean. *The Arab Gulf States: Beyond Oil and Islam*. Boulder, CO: Lynne Rienner, 2010.

Ford, Neil. "Qatar Punches above its Weight." *Middle East* (March 2004): pp. 49–54.

Fromherz, Allen J. *Qatar: A Modern History*. London: I.B. Tauris, 2012.

Fukuyama, Francis. "The Imperative of State-Building." *Journal of Democracy* 15, no. 2 (April 2004): pp. 17–31.

Fuller, Graham, and Rend Rahim Francke. *The Arab Shi'a: The Forgotten Muslims*. New York: St. Martin's Press, 1999.

Furtiq, Henner. *Iran's Rivalry with Saudi Arabia between the Gulf Wars*. Reading, Berkshire, UK: Ithaca Press, 2006.

Gallarotti, Giulio M. *Cosmopolitan Power in International Relations: A Synthesis of Realism, Neoliberalism, and Constructivism.* Cambridge: Cambridge University Press, 2010.

——. *The Power Curse: Influence and Illusion in World Politics.* Boulder, CO: Lynne Rienner, 2010.

Gartner, Heinz. "Small States and Alliances." In Erich Reiter and Heinz Gartner, eds., *Small States and Alliances.* New York: Physica-Verlag, 2001, pp. 1–9.

Gause, F. Gregory III. "The Foreign Policy of Saudi Arabia." In Raymond Hinnebusch and Anoushiravan Ehteshami, eds., *The Foreign Policies of Middle East States.* Boulder, CO: Lynne Rienner, 2002), pp. 193–211.

——. "The International Politics of the Gulf." In Louis Fawcett, ed., *International Relations of the Middle East.* 2nd ed. Oxford: Oxford University Press, 2009, pp. 272–289.

——. *The International Relations of the Persian Gulf.* Cambridge: Cambridge University Press, 2010.

——. *Oil Monarchies: Domestic and Security Challenges in the Arab Gulf States.* New York: Council on Foreign Relations, 1994.

General Secretariat for Development Planning. *Qatar National Vision 2030.* Doha: GSDP, 2008.

Geurts, Charles-Michel. "The European Commission: A Natural Ally of Small States in the EU Institutional Framework?" In Laurent Goestschel, ed., *Small States Inside and Outside the European Union.* London: Kluwer, 1998, pp. 49–64.

Goestschel, Laurent. "The Foreign and Security Policy Interests of Small States in Today's Europe." In Laurent Goestschel, ed., *Small States Inside and Outside the European Union.* London: Kluwer, 1998, pp. 13–31.

Goh, Evelyn. *Meeting the China Challenge: The US in Southeast Asian Regional Security Challenge.* Policy Studies 16. Washington, DC: East-West Center, 2005.

Goldstein, Andrea, and Fabop Scacciavillani. "Financial Markets under Attack? Gulf Investors and the Rise of Economic Patriotism in the West." In John Nugee and Paola Subacchi, eds., *The Gulf Region: A New Hub of Global Financial Power.* London: Chatham House, 2008, pp. 176–193.

Gräf, Bettina. "Sheikh Yūsuf al-Qaradāwī in Cyberspace." *Die Welt des Islams* 47, nos. 3–4 (2007): pp. 403–442.

Gray, Colin S. *Hard Power and Soft Power: The Utility of Military Force as an Instrument of Policy in the 21st Century.* Carlisle, PA: Strategic Studies Institute, 2011.

Gray, Matthew. "A Theory of 'Late Rentierism': In the Arab States of the Gulf." Center for International and Regional Studies, Georgetown University School of Foreign Service in Qatar Occasional Paper No. 7, 2011.

Guarino, Cassandra M. et al. *Developing a School Finance System for K-12 Reform in Qatar.* Santa Monica, CA: Rand, 2009.

Gulf Cooperation Council. *GCC, A Statistical Glance, Volume II.* Riyadh: GCC Information Center, 2010.

Halliday, Fred. *The Middle East in International Relations: Power, Politics and Ideology.* Cambridge: Cambridge University Press, 2005.

Hameiri, Shahar. "Failed States or a Failed Paradigm? State Capacity and the Limits of Institutionalism." *Journal of International Relations and Development* 10, no. 2 (2007): pp. 122–149.

Han, C. Min. "Country Image: Halo or Summary Construct?" *Journal of Marketing Research* 26 (May 1989): pp. 222–229.

Hanieh, Adam. *Capitalism and Class in the Arab Gulf States.* New York: Palgrave Macmillan, 2011.

Hanna, Daniel. "The Gulf's Changing Financial Landscape: From Capital Source to Destination and Emerging Hub." In John Nugee and Paola Subacchi, eds., *The Gulf Region: A New Hub of Global Financial Power.* London: Chatham House, 2008, pp. 105–117.

Held, David, and Kristian Ulrichsen. "The Transformation of the Gulf." In David Held and Kristian Ulrichsen, eds. *The Transformation of the Gulf: Politics, Economics, and the Global Order.* London: Routledge, 2012, pp. 1–25.

Heradstveit, Daniel, and Helge Hveem, eds. *Oil in the Gulf: Obstacles to Democracy and Development.* Burlington, VT: Ashgate, 2004.

Herb, Michael. *All in the Family: Absolutism, Revolution, and Democracy in the Middle Eastern Monarchies.* Albany: State University of New York Press, 1999.

———. "Princes and Parliaments in the Arab World." *Middle East Journal* 58, no. 3 (Summer 2004): pp. 367–384.

———. "Princes, Parliaments, and the Prospects for Democracy in the Gulf." In Marsha Pripstein Posusney and Michele Penner Angrist, eds., *Authoritarianism in the Middle East: Regimes and Resistance.* Boulder, CO: Lynne Rienner, 2005.

Hertog, Steffen, and Giacomo Luciani. "Energy and Sustainability Policies in the Gulf States." In David Held and Kristian Ulrichsen, eds., *The Transformation of the Gulf: Politics, Economics, and the Global Order.* London: Routledge, 2012, pp. 236–257.

Henrikson, Alan. "Niche Diplomacy in the World Public Arena: The Global 'Corners' of Canada and Norway." In Jan Melissen, ed., *The New Public Diplomacy: Soft Power in International Relations.* New York: Palgrave Macmillan, 2007.

Hey, Jeanne A. K. "Introducing Small State Foreign Policy." In Jeanne A. K. Hey, ed., *Small States in World Politics: Explaining Foreign Policy Behavior.* Boulder, CO: Lynne Rienner, 2003.

Hijjawi, Aref. "The Role of Al-Jazeera (Arabic) in the Arab Revolts of 2011." *Perspectives: Political Analysis and Commentary from the Middle East*, no. 2 (May 2011): pp. 68–72.

Hilsum, Lindsey. *Sandstorm: Libya in the Time of Revolution.* New York: Penguin, 2012.

Hinnebusch, Raymond. "The Foreign Policy of Egypt." In Raymond Hinnebusch and Anoushiravan Ehteshami, eds., *The Foreign Policies of Middle East States.* Boulder, CO: Lynne Rienner, 2002, pp. 91–114.

———. "Introduction: The Analytical Framework." In Raymond Hinnebusch and Anoushiravan Ehteshami, eds., *The Foreign Policies of Middle East States.* Boulder, CO: Lynne Rienner, 2002, pp. 1–27.

———. "The Middle East Regional System." In Raymond Hinnebusch and Anoushiravan Ehteshami, eds., *The Foreign Policies of Middle East States.* Boulder, CO: Lynne Rienner, 2002, pp. 29–53.

———"The Politics of Identity in Middle Eastern International Relations." In Louis Fawcett, ed., *International Relations of the Middle East.* 2nd ed. Oxford: Oxford University Press, 2009, pp. 148–169.

———. "Toward a Historical Sociology of State Formation in the Middle East." *Middle East Critique* 19, no. 3 (Fall 2010): pp. 205–206.

Hollis, Rosemary, ed. *Oil and Regional Development in the Gulf.* London: Royal Institute for International Affairs, 1998.

Hong, Mark. "Small States in the United Nations." *International Social Science Journal* 47, no. 2 (1995): pp. 277–287.

Hopwood, David. "Abu Dhabi's Masdar Plan Takes Shape." *Renewable Energy Focus* 11, no. 1 (January–February 2010): pp. 18–23.

Hubel, Helmut, Lars Berger, and Matthias Heise. *German Foreign Policy in the Gulf.* Emirates Center for Strategic Studies and Research Occasional Paper No. 58, Abu Dhabi, 2005.

Hudson, Michael C. "The United States in the Middle East." In Louis Fawcett, ed. *International Relations of the Middle East.* 2nd ed. Oxford: Oxford University Press, 2009, pp. 308–330.

Hunter, Robert. *Building Security in the Persian Gulf.* Santa Monica, CA: Rand, 2010.

Hvidt, Martin. "Economic Diversification in the Gulf Arab States: Lip Service or Actual Implementation of a New Developmental Model." In Bessama Momani and Matteo Legrenzi, eds., *Shifting Geo-Economic Power of the Gulf: Oil, Finance and Institutions.* Burlington, VT: Ashgate, 2011, pp. 39–54.

International Monetary Fund (IMF). *Qatar: Statistical Appendix.* IMF Country Report No. 10/62, March 2010.

———. *Regional Economic Outlook, Middle East and Central Asia, October 2011.* Washington, DC: IMF, 2011.

Iran Ministry of Commerce. *Bazargani-e Khareji* (Foreign Trade). Tehran: Ministry of Commerce, 1388/2009. http://www.moc.gov.ir/system/upload/doc/r%20.pdf.

Ismael, Tareq Y. *International Relations of the Contemporary Middle East: A Study in World Politics.* Syracuse, NY: Syracuse University Press, 1986.

Jakobsen, Peter Viggo. "Small States, Big Influence: The Overlooked Nordic Influence on the Civilian ESDP." *Journal of Common Market Studies* 47, no. 1 (2009): pp. 81–102.

Janardhan, N. *Boom amid Gloom: The Spirit of Possibility in the 21st Century Gulf.* Reading, Berkshire, UK: Ithaca Press, 2011.

Jones, Jeremy. *Negotiating Change: The New Politics of the Middle East.* London: I.B. Tauris, 2007.

Jreisat, Jamil. "The Predicament of Administrative Reforms in the Arab States." In Ali Farazman, ed., *Administrative Reform in Developing Nations.* Westport, CT: Praeger, 2001, pp. 163–176.

Kamrava, Mehran. "The Arab Spring and the Saudi-Led Counterrevolution." *Orbis* 56, no. 1 (Winter 2012): pp. 96–104.

———. "Conceptualising Third World Politics: The State-Society See-Saw." *Third World Quarterly* 14, no. 4 (November 1993): pp. 703–716.

———. "Iran and Regional Security Dynamics in the Middle East: Trends and Prospects." *International Studies Journal* 9, no.1 (2012): pp. 71–104.

———. "Mediation and Qatari Foreign Policy." *Middle East Journal* 65, no. 4 (Fall 2011): pp. 539–556.

——. "Non-Democratic States and Political Liberalisation in the Middle East: A Structural Analysis." *Third World Quarterly* 19, no. 1 (March 1998): 63–85.

——. "The Political Economy of Rentierism in the Persian Gulf." In Mehran Kamrava, ed., *The Political Economy of the Persian Gulf*. New York: Columbia University Press, 2012, pp. 39–80.

——. "Preserving Non-Democracies: Leaders and Institutions in the Middle East." *Middle Eastern Studies* 46, no. 2 (March 2010): pp. 251–270.

——. "Royal Factionalism and Political Liberalization in Qatar." *Middle East Journal* 63, no. 3 (Summer 2009): pp. 401–420.

Kamrava, Mehran, and Zahra Babar, eds. *Migrant Labor in the Persian Gulf*. New York: Columbia University Press, 2012.

Karoly Lynn A., and Michael Mattock. *Qatar Supreme Council for Family Affairs Database of Social Indicators: Final Report*. Santa Monica, CA: Rand, 2006.

Kassimeris, Christos. "The Foreign Policy of Small Powers." *International Politics* 46, no. 1 (2009): pp. 84–101.

Kassler, Peter, ed. *Environmental issues for the Gulf: Oil, Water, and Sustainable Development*. London: Royal Institute for International Affairs, 1999.

Kechichian, Joseph. "A Vision of Oman: State of the Sultanate Speeches by Qaboos bin Said, 1970–2006." *Middle East Policy* 15, no. 3 (Fall 2008): pp. 112–133.

Kennedy, Paul. *The Rise and Fall of the Great Powers*. New York: Vintage Books, 1989.

Keohane, Robert O. *After Hegemony: Cooperation and Discord in the World Political Economy*. Princeton, NJ: Princeton University Press, 1984.

——. "The Big Influence of Small Allies." *Foreign Policy* 2 (Spring 1971): pp. 161–182.

——. "Lilliputians's Dilemmas: Small States in International Politics." *International Organization* 23, no. 2 (1969): pp. 291–310.

Keohane, Robert O., and Joseph S. Nye. *Power and Interdependence*. 4th ed. Boston: Longman, 2012.

Khalaf, Abdulhadi, and Giacomo Luciani, eds. *Constitutional Reform and Political Participation in the Gulf*. Dubai: Gulf Research Center, 2006.

Kienle, Eberhard, ed. *Politics from Above, Politics from Below: The Middle East in the Age of Economic Reform*. London: Saqi, 2003.

King, Stephen J. *The New Authoritarianism in the Middle East and North Africa*. Bloomington, IN: Indiana University Press, 2009.

Kingdon, John W. *Agendas, Alternatives, and Public Policy*. Boston: Little Brown, 1984.

Kohli, Atul. *State-Directed Development: Political Power and Industrialization in the Global Economy*. Cambridge: Cambridge University Press, 2004.

——. "Where Do High Growth Political Economics Come From? The Japanese Lineage of Korea's 'Developmntal State.'" In Meredith Woo-Cumings, ed. *The Developmental State*. Ithaca, NY: Cornell University Press, 1999, pp. 93–136.

Korany, Bahgat. "The Middle East since the Cold War: Still Insecure." In Louis Fawcett, ed., *International Relations of the Middle East*. 2nd ed. Oxford: Oxford University Press, 2009, pp. 61–78.

Kostiner, Joseph. "GCC Perceptions of Collective Security in the Post-Saddam Era." In Mehran Kamrava, ed., *International Politics of the Persian Gulf*. Syracuse, NY: Syracuse University Press, 2011, pp. 94–119.

Krasner, Stephen D. *Power, the State, and Sovereignty: Essays on International Relations.* London: Routledge, 2009.

Kraus, Volker, and J. David Singer. "Minor Powers, Alliances, and Armed Conflict: Some Preliminary Patterns." In Erich Reiter and Heinz Gartner, eds., *Small States and Alliances.* New York: Physica-Verlag, 2001, pp. 15–23.

Kuosmanen, Antti. "Decision-Making in the Council of the European Union." In Laurent Goestschel, ed., *Small States Inside and Outside the European Union.* London: Kluwer, 1998, pp. 65–78.

Kupchan, Charles A. *The U.S. and Europe in the Middle East and Beyond: Partners or Rivals?* Emirates Lecture Series, 65. Abu Dhabi: Emirates Center for Strategic Studies and Research, 2007.

Lake, David A. *Hierarchy in International Relations.* Ithaca, NY: Cornell University Press, 2009.

Lawson, Fred H. *Constructing International Relations of the Arab World.* Stanford, CA: Stanford University Press, 2006.

———. "Security Dilemmas in the Contemporary Persian Gulf." In Mehran Kamrava, ed., *International Politics of the Persian Gulf.* Syracuse, NY: Syracuse University Press, 2011, pp. 50–71.

Lebow, Richard Ned. *A Cultural Theory of International Relations.* Cambridge: Cambridge University Press, 2008.

Lefebvre, Jeffrey. "Oman's Foreign Policy in the Twenty-First Century." *Middle East Policy* 27, no. 1 (Spring 2010): pp. 99–114.

Lenczowski, George. *The Middle East in World Affairs.* 2nd ed. Ithaca, NY: Cornell University Press, 1956.

Linz, Juan J. *Totalitarian and Authoritarian Regimes.* Boulder, CO: Lynne Rienner, 2000.

Lizza, Ryan. "The Consequentialist: How the Arab Spring Made Obama's Foreign Policy." *New Yorker* (2 May 2011): pp. 44–55.

Long, David, and Christian Koch, eds. *Gulf Security in the Twenty-First Century.* Abu Dhabi: Emirates Center for Strategic Studies and Research, 1997.

Loriaux, Michael. "The French Developmental State as Myth and Moral Ambition." In Meredith Woo-Cumings, ed., *The Developmental State.* Ithaca, NY: Cornell University Press, 1999, pp. 235–275.

Louer, Laurence. *Transnational Shia Politics: Religious and Political Networks in the Gulf.* New York: Columbia University Press, 2008.

Lowi, Miriam R. *Oil Wealth and the Poverty of Politics: Algeria Compared.* Cambridge: Cambridge University Press, 2009.

Luciani, Giacomo. "Oil and Political Economy in the International Relations of the Middle East." In Louis Fawcett, ed., *International Relations of the Middle East.* 2nd ed. Oxford: Oxford University Press, 2009, pp. 81–103.

Maas, Matthias. "The Elusive Definition of the Small States." *International Politics* 46, no. 1 (2009): pp. 65–83.

Mahbubani, Kishore. *The New Asian Hemisphere: The Irresistible Shift of Global Power to the East.* New York: Public Affairs, 2008.

Mann, Michael. *The Sources of Social Power: Volume II, The Rise of Classes and Nation-States, 1760–1914.* Cambridge: Cambridge University Press, 1993.

Mattair, Thomas. *The Three Occupied UAE Islands: The Tunbs and Abu Musa.* Abu Dhabi: Emirates Center for Strategic Studies and Research, 2005.

Mearsheimer, John J. *The Tragedy of Great Power Politics.* New York: W.W. Norton, 2001.

Medeiros, Evan. "Strategic Hedging and the Future of Asia-Pacific Security." *Washington Quarterly* 29, no. 1 (2005–2006): pp. 145–167.

Migdal, Joel. *State in Society: Studying How States and Societies Constitute and Transform One Another.* Cambridge: Cambridge University Press, 2001.

Miles, Hugh. "Al Jazeera." *Foreign Policy*, no. 155 (July–August 2006): pp. 20–24.

———. *Al-Jazeera: The Inside Story of the Arab News Channel that is Challenging the West.* New York: Grove Press, 2005.

Moini, Joy S. et al. *The Reform of Qatar University.* Santa Monica, CA: Rand, 2009.

Momani, Bessma. "Shifting Gulf Arab Investments in the Mashreq: Underlying Political Economy Rationals?" In Bessama Momani and Matteo Legrenzi, eds., *Shifting Geo-Economic Power of the Gulf: Oil, Finance and Institutions.* Burlington, VT: Ashgate, 2011, pp. 163–181.

Momani, Bessama, and Matteo Legrenzi. "Introduction: The Geo-Economic Power of the Gulf." In Bessama Momani and Matteo Legrenzi, eds., *Shifting Geo-Economic Power of the Gulf: Oil, Finance and Institutions.* Burlington, VT: Ashgate, 2011, pp. 1–6.

Moore, Clement M. "The Clash of Globalizations in the Middle East." In Louis Fawcett, ed., *International Relations of the Middle East.* 2nd ed. Oxford: Oxford University Press, 2009, pp. 104–128.

Nasr, Vali. *Meccanomics: The March of the New Muslim Middle Class.* Oxford: Oneworld, 2010.

———. "Regional Implications of Shi'a Revival in Iraq." *Washington Quarterly* 27, no. 3 (Summer 2004), p. 17.

Nau, Henry R. *Perspective on International Relations: Power, Institutions, and Ideas.* Washington, DC: CQ Press, 2007.

Neumann, Iver B., and Sieglinde Gstohl. "Introduction: Liliputians in Gulliver's World?" In Christine Ingebritsen, Iver Neumann, Sieglinde Gstohl, and Jessica Beyer, eds., *Small States in International Relations.* Seattle: University of Washington Press, 2006, pp. 3–36.

Newcombe, Hanna, Michael Ross, and Alan G. Newcombe. "United Nations Voting Patterns." *International Organization* 24, no. 1 (Winter 1970): pp. 100–121.

Niblock, Tim. *Saudi Arabia: Power, Legitimacy and Survival.* London: Routledge, 2006.

Nonneman, Gerd. "Political Reform in the Gulf Monarchies: From Liberalization to Democratization? A Comparative Perspective." In Anoushiravan Ehteshami and Steven Wright, eds., *Reform in the Middle East Oil Monarchies* (Reading, Berkshire, UK: Ithaca Press, 2008), pp. 3–45.

Nye, Joseph. *Bound to Lead: The Changing Nature of American Power.* New York: Basic Books, 1990.

———. *The Future of Power.* New York: Public Affairs, 2011.

———. *Soft Power: The Means to Success in World Politics.* New York: Public Affairs, 2004.

Öniş, Ziya. "The Logic of the Developmental State." *Comparative Politics* 24, no. 1 (October 1991): pp. 109–126.

Onley, James. *The Arabian Frontier of the British Raj: Merchants, Rulers, and the British in the Nineteenth-Century Gulf.* Oxford: Oxford University Press, 2007.

Ottoway, Marina, and Julia Choucair-Vizoso, eds. *Beyond the Façade: Political Reform in the Arab World.* Washington, DC: Carnegie Endowment for International Peace, 2008.

Ottoway, Marina, and Michele Dunne. "Incumbent Regimes and the 'King's Dilemma' in the Arab World: Promise and Threat of Managed Reform." Carnegie Endowment for International Peace Papers, No. 88, Washington, DC, December 2007.

Patrick, Neil. "Nationalism in the Gulf States." In David Held and Kristan Ulrichsen, eds., *The Transformation of the Gulf: Politics, Economics, and the Global Order.* London: Routledge, 2012, pp. 47–65.

Payne, Anthony. "Small States in the Global Politics of Development." *Round Table* 93, no. 376 (2004): pp. 623–635.

——. "Vulnerability as a Condition, Resilience as a Strategy." In Andrew F. Cooper and Timothy W. Shaw, eds., *The Diplomacies of Small States: Between Vulnerability and Resilience.* New York: Palgrave Macmillan, 2009, pp. 279–285.

Pempel, T. J. "The Developmental Regime in a Changing World Economy." In Meredith Woo-Cumings, ed., *The Developmental State.* Ithaca, NY: Cornell University Press, 1999, pp. 137–181.

Peterson, J. E. "Qatar and the World: Branding for a Micro-State." *Middle East Journal* 60, no. 4 (Autumn 2006): pp. 732–748.

——. "Rulers, Merchants and Sheikhs in Gulf Politics: The Function of Family Networks." In Alanound Alsharekh, ed., *The Gulf Family* London: Saqi, 2007.

Planning Council. *Turning Qatar into a Competitive Knowledge-Based Economy: Opportunities and Challenges.* Doha: Planning Council, 2007.

Platt, Gordon. "Sovereign Wealth Funds Prepare to Take More Active Role in M&A." *Global Finance* (October 2009): pp. 107–108.

Polanyi, Karl. *The Great Transformation: The Political and Economic Origins of Our Time.* Boston: Beacon Press, 2001.

Portman, Christopher. "The Economic Significance of Sovereign Wealth Funds." *Economic Outlook* 32, no. 1 (January 2008): pp. 24–33.

Potter, Lawrence G. "Introduction." In Lawrence G. Potter, ed., *The Persian Gulf in History.* New York: Palgrave Macmillan, 2009.

——, ed. *The Persian Gulf in History.* New York: Palgrave Macmillan, 2009.

Pripstein Posusney, Marsha, and Michele Penner Angrist, eds. *Authoritarianism in the Middle East: Regimes and Resistance.* Boulder, CO: Lynne Rienner, 2005.

Qatar Central Bank. *Thirty Second Annual Report 2008.* Doha: QCB, 2009.

Qatar National Bank. *Qatar Economic Review, October 2009.* Doha: Qatar National Bank, 2009.

Qatar Statistics Authority. *Qatar in Figures.* Doha: Qatar Statistics Authority, 2008.

——. *Qatar, Social Trends 1998–2010.* Doha: Qatar Statistics Authority, 2011.

Qatari Diar. *The Art of Real Estate.* Doha: Qatari Diar, n.d.

Rahman, Habibur. *The Emergence of Qatar: The Turbulent Years, 1627–1916.* London: Kegan Paul, 2005.

Richer, Rene. "Conservation in Qatar: Impacts of Increasing Industrialization." Center for International and Regional Studies Georgetown University School of Foreign Service in Qatar Occasional Paper, 2008.

Rossi, Vanessa. "Global Financial Markets: How Emerging-Market Economies Are Enlarging the Playing Field." In John Nugee and Paola Subacchi, eds., *The Gulf Region: A New Hub of Global Financial Power.* London: Chatham House, 2008, pp. 13–33.

Rugh, William. "The Foreign Policy of the United Arab Emirates." *Middle East Journal* 50, no. 1 (Winter 1996): pp. 57–70.

Russell, Richard. *Iran's Nuclear Program: Security Implications for the UAE and the Gulf Region.* Emirates Lecture Series, 70. Abu Dhabi: Emirates Center for Strategic Studies and Research, 2007.

Saif, Ahmed Abdelkareem. "Deconstructing before Building: Perspectives on Democracy in Qatar." In Anoushiravan Ehteshami and Steven Wright, eds., *Reform in the Middle East Oil Monarchies.* Reading, Berkshire, UK: Ithaca Press, 2008, pp. 103–127.

Sangmpan, S. N. *Comparing Apples and Mangoes: The Overpoliticized State in Developing Countries.* Albany: State University of New York Press, 2007.

Schweller, Randall. "Bandwagoning for Profit: Bringing the Revisionist State Back In." *International Security* 19, no. 1 (1994): pp. 72–107.

Scott, James C. *Seeing Like a State: How Certain Schemes to Improve the Human Condition Have Failed.* New Haven, CT: Yale University Press, 1998.

Seznec, Jean-François. "Changing Circumstances: Gulf Trading Families in the Light of Free Trade Agreements, Globalization and the WTO." In Alanound Alsharekh, ed., *The Gulf Family.* London: Saqi, 2007, pp. 80–81.

———. "The Gulf Sovereign Wealth Funds: Myths and Reality." *Middle East Policy* 15, no. 2 (Summer 2008): pp. 97–110.

———. "The Sovereign Wealth Funds of the Persian Gulf." In Mehran Kamrava, ed., *The Political Economy of the Persian Gulf.* New York: Columbia University Press, 2012, pp. 69–93.

Sharabi, Hisham. *Neopatriarchy: A Theory of Distorted Change in Arab Society.* Oxford: Oxford University Press, 1988.

Shepherd, Benjamin. *GCC Land Purchases Abroad: The Case of Cambodia.* Center for International and Regional Studies, Georgetown University School of Foreign Service in Qatar, Summary Report, No. 5, 2012.

Sick, Gary, and Lawrence Potter, eds. *The Persian Gulf at the Millennium: Essays in Politics, Economy, Security, and Religion.* New York: St. Martin's Press, 1997.

Siniver, Asaf. "Power, Impartiality and Timing: Three Hypotheses on Third Party Mediation in the Middle East." *Political Studies* 54, no. 4 (2006): pp. 806–826.

Skocpol, Theda. "Bringing the State Back In: Strategies for Analysis in Current Research." In Peter B. Evans, Dietrich Rueschemeyer, and Theda Skocpol, eds., *Bringing the State Back In.* Cambridge: Cambridge University Press, 1985, pp. 3–37.

Skovgaard-Petersen, Jakob, and Bettina Graf, eds. *The Global Mufti: The Phenomenon of Yusuf al-Qaradawi.* New York: Columbia University Press, 2006.

Snyder, Glenn. "The Security Dilemma in Alliance Politics." *World Politics* 36, no. 4 (1984): pp. 461–495.

Soucek, Svet. *The Persian Gulf: Its Past and Present.* Costa Mesa, CA: Mazda, 2008.

Stasz, Cathleen, Eric R. Eide, and Francisco Martorell. *Post-Secondary Education in Qatar: Employer Demand, Student Choice, and Options for Policy.* Santa Monica, CA: Rand, 2007.

Stein, Janice Gross. "War and Security in the Middle East." In Louis Fawcett, ed., *International Relations of the Middle East.* 2nd ed. Oxford: Oxford University Press, 2009, pp. 208–227.

Sutton, Paul. "What Are the Priorities for Small States in the International System?" *Round Table,* no. 351 (1999): pp. 397–402.

Tammen, Ronald L. et al. *Power Transitions: Strategies for the 21st Century.* New York: Seven Bridges, 2000.

Terrill, W. Andrew. *Kuwaiti National Security and the U.S.-Kuwaiti Strategic Relationship after Saddam.* Carlisle, PA: Strategic Studies Institute, U.S. Army War College, 2007.

Tetreault, Mary Ann. "Gulf Arab States' Investment of Oil Revenues." In Bessama Momani and Matteo Legrenzi, eds., *Shifting Geo-Economic Power of the Gulf: Oil, Finance and Institutions.* Burlington, VT: Ashgate, 2011, pp. 9–21.

Thatcher, Mark. "Governing Markets in the Gulf States." In David Held and Kristian Ulrichsen, eds., *The Transformation of the Gulf: Politics, Economics, and the Global Order.* London: Routledge, 2012, pp. 127–145.

Tilly, Charles. *Democracy.* Cambridge: Cambridge University Press, 2007.

——. "War Making and State Making as Organized Crime." In Peter R. Evans, Dietrich Rueschemeyer, and Theda Skocpol, eds., *Brining the State Back In.* Cambridge: Cambridge University Press, 1985, pp. 169–191.

Toksoz, Mina. "The GCC: Prospects and Risks in the New Oil Boom." In John Nugee and Paola Subacchi, eds., *The Gulf Region: A New Hub of Global Financial Power.* London: Chatham House, 2008, pp. 81–96.

Touval, Saadia. "Mediation and Foreign Policy." *International Studies Review* 5, no. 4 (2003): pp. 91–95.

UDC. *2011 Annual Report: Solid Performance, Steady Growth.* Doha: UDC, 2011.

Ulrichsen, Kristian Coates. "The GCC States and the Shifting Balance of Global Power." Center for International and Regional Studies, Georgetown University School of Foreign Service in Qatar Occasional Paper No. 6, 2010.

——. *Insecure Gulf: The End of Certainty and the Transition to the Post-Oil Era.* New York: Columbia University Press, 2011.

United Nations. *The United Nations E-Government Survey 2010: Leveraging E-Government at a Time of Financial and Economic Crisis.* New York: United Nations, 2010.

United States Senate Committee on Foreign Relations. "The Gulf Security Architecture: Partnership with the Gulf Cooperation Council." Majority Staff Report, 19 June 2012.

Valeri, Marc. "High Visibility, Low Profile: The Shi'a in Oman under Sultan Qaboos." *International Journal of Middle East Studies* 42, no. 2 (May 2010): pp. 251–268.

van Ham, Peter. "The Rise of the Branded State." *Foreign Affairs* 80, no. 5 (September–October 2001): pp. 2–6.

Von Tigerstrom, Barbara. "Small Island Developing States and International Trade: Special Challenges in the Global Partnership for Development." *Melbourne Journal of International Law* 6 (2005): pp. 402–436.

Waldner, David. *State Building and Late Development.* Ithaca, NY: Cornell University Press, 1999.

Walker, Martin. "The Revenge of the Shia." *Wilson Quarterly* 30, no. 4 (Autumn 2006): pp. 16–20.

Walt, Stephen. "Alliance Formation and the Balance of World Power." *International Security* 9, no. 4 (1985): pp. 3–43.

———. *Taming American Power: The Global response to U.S. Primacy.* New York: W.W. Norton, 2005.

Waltz, Kenneth. *Man, the State, and War: A Theoretical Analysis.* New York: Columbia University Press, 2001.

———. *Realism and International Politics.* London: Routledge, 2008.

———. *Theory of International Politics.* Long Grove, IL: Waveland Press, 1979.

Weber, Max. *On Charisma and Institution Building.* Chicago: University of Chicago Press, 1968.

Weiss, Linda. *The Myth of the Powerless State.* Ithaca, NY: Cornell University Press, 1998.

Wignaraja, Ganesh, Marlon Lezama, and David Joiner. *Small States Transition from Vulnerability to Competitiveness.* London: Commonwealth Secretariat, 2004.

Wilkinson, Paul. *International Relations.* London: Sterling, 2010.

Woertz, Eckart, ed. *Gulf Geo-Economics.* Dubai: Gulf Research Center, 2007.

Woo-Cumings, Meredith. "Introduction: Chalmers Johnson and the Politics of Nationalism and Development." In Meredith Woo-Cumings, ed., *The Developmental State.* Ithaca, NY: Cornell University Press, 1999, pp. 1–31.

World Bank. *Small States: Making the Most of Development Assistance.* Washington, DC: World Bank, 2006.

World Wildlife Fund. *Living Planet Report 2012: Biodiversity, Biocapacity and Better Choices.* Gland, Switzerland: WWF International, 2012.

Wright, Steven. "Fixing the Kingdom: Political Evolution and Socio-Economic Challenges in Bahrain." Center for International and Regional Studies, Georgetown University-Qatar, Occasional Paper No. 3, 2008.

———. "Qatar." In Christopher Davidson, ed. *Power and Politics in the Persian Gulf Monarchies.* New York: Columbia University Press, 2011, pp. 113–133.

Yetiv, Steve A. *The Absence of Grand Strategy: The United States in the Persian Gulf, 1972–2005.* Baltimore, MD: Johns Hopkins University Press, 2008.

Zahlan, Rosemarie Said. *The Creation of Qatar.* London: Croom Helm, 1979.

———. *The Making of the Modern Gulf States: Kuwait, Bahrain, Qatar, the United Arab Emirates and Oman.* London: Unwin Hyman, 1989.

Zakaria, Fareed. *The Post-American World.* New York: W.W. Norton, 2008.

Zellman, Gail L., Charles A. Goldman, Dominic J. Brewer, Catherine H. Augustine, and Gery Ryan. *Education for a New Era: Design and Implementation of K-12 Education Reform in Qatar.* Santa Monica, CA: Rand, 2007.

Ziemba, Rachel, and Anton Malkin. "The GCC's International Investment Dynamics: The Role of Sovereign Wealth Funds." In Bessama Momani and Matteo Legrenzi, eds. *Shifting Geo-Economic Power of the Gulf: Oil, Finance and Institutions.* Burlington, VT: Ashgate, 2011, pp. 109–125.

INDEX